THE CULTURAL ECONOMY OF CITIES

Theory, Culture & Society

Theory, Culture & Society caters for the resurgence of interest in culture within contemporary social science and the humanities. Building on the heritage of classical social theory, the book series examines ways in which this tradition has been reshaped by a new generation of theorists. It also publishes theoretically informed analyses of everyday life, popular culture, and new intellectual movements.

EDITOR: Mike Featherstone, *Nottingham Trent University*

SERIES EDITORIAL BOARD
Roy Boyne, *University of Durham*
Mike Hepworth, *University of Aberdeen*
Scott Lash, *Goldsmiths College, University of London*
Roland Robertson, *University of Pittsburgh*
Bryan S. Turner, *University of Cambridge*

THE TCS CENTRE
The Theory, Culture & Society book series, the journals *Theory, Culture & Society* and *Body & Society*, and related conference, seminar and postgraduate programmes operate from the TCS Centre at Nottingham Trent University. For further details of the TCS Centre's activities please contact:

Centre Administrator
The TCS Centre, Room 175
Faculty of Humanities
Nottingham Trent University
Clifton Lane, Nottingham, NG11 8NS, UK
e-mail: tcs@ntu.ac.uk
web: http://tcs@ntu.ac.uk

Recent volumes include:

Spaces of Culture
City, Nation, World
Mike Featherstone and Scott Lash

Love and Eroticism
edited by Mike Featherstone

Polar Inertia
Paul Virilio

Performativity and Belonging
edited by Vikki Bell

Feminist Imagination
Genealogies in Feminist Theory
Vikki Bell

Michel de Certeau
Cultural Theorist
Ian Buchanan

THE CULTURAL ECONOMY OF CITIES

Essays on the Geography of Image-Producing Industries

ALLEN J. SCOTT

SAGE Publications
London • Thousand Oaks • New Delhi

SAGE Publications Ltd
6 Bonhill Street
London EC2A 4PU

SAGE Publications Inc
2455 Teller Road
Thousand Oaks, California 91320

SAGE Publications India Pvt Ltd
32, M-Block Market
Greater Kailash – I
New Delhi 110 048

Published in association with *Theory, Culture & Society*,
Nottingham Trent University

British Library Cataloguing in Publication data

A catalogue record for this book is available
from the British Library

ISBN 0-7619-5454-6
ISBN 0-7619-5455-4 (pbk)

Library of Congress catalog record available

Typeset by Mayhew Typesetting, Rhayader, Powys
Printed in Great Britain by Athenaeum Press, Gateshead

To the memory of
Fred Palacio
Boulevard St Germain/Rue de Buci, Paris
19 August 1944

CONTENTS

PREFACE

This book is about the economic geography of cultural-products industries, and, in particular, about the ways in which these industries tend to materialize on the landscape in the form of dense spatial agglomerations. In parallel with this theme, I also develop an extended argument about how the economic and the cultural interpenetrate one another in modern society and how this relation makes its concrete historic and geographic appearance not only at the local but also at the global level of spatial organization.

It is currently fashionable in some social science circles to claim that the economic is embedded in the cultural. This claim is true enough, but it tells only part of the story. The other part resides in the complementary claim that the cultural is embedded in the economic; and never has this been more the case than in contemporary capitalism. In the present book, I try to take both of these claims seriously. For one thing, I am at pains to show how local (urban and regional) traditions, norms, and sensibilities actively shape the structures and strategies of business operations in the cultural economy and the design of final outputs. For another, I hammer insistently at the theme that the culture we consume, both high and low, is to ever increasing degrees produced under capitalist conditions of economic order and is hence deeply imprinted with the marks of this moment of genesis.

The argument is focused on the cultural economy as represented by a series of manufacturing and service sectors that are involved, in greater or lesser degree, in the production of images, symbols, and messages. This exercise involves three major analytical and descriptive maneuvers. First, I engage in an extended discussion of the spatial logic of the cultural economy, paying special reference to the ways in which locational concentration enhances both its competitive performance and its creative potentials. Second, I offer a series of industry studies focusing on the manner in which this spatial logic is played out in selected cultural-products sectors (jewelry, furniture, films, recorded music, and multimedia). Third, I provide detailed and synthetic accounts of the ways in which the cultural economy is organized in specific places, with an overwhelming focus on two cities which are characterized by exceptionally well-developed but also sharply contrasting cultural economies, namely, Los Angeles and Paris. In addition, I deal throughout the book with many different policy issues as they come into view, especially in so far as they relate to matters of local economic development and growth. The intended contribution of the book to the complex questions raised by all of these matters is to show how geography – in both its local and global dimensions – profoundly shapes the logic and dynamics of the modern cultural economy, and hence also influences the appearances and meanings of the cultural products that now enter world markets in ever rising quantities and varieties.

It is no whim or accident that has induced me to focus here on questions of the cultural economy. Cultural products of all sorts constitute a constantly increasing share of the output of modern capitalism, and cultural-products sectors represent some of the most dynamic growth industries in the world at the present time. These sectors are also coming to constitute the central economic engines of a number of major city-regions across the globe. Moreover, a powerful convergence is occurring between the economic and the cultural spheres in contemporary society, and this is pregnant with consequences for both economic analysis and cultural theory. It is becoming more and more difficult to determine where the cultural economy begins and the rest of the capitalist economic order ends, for just as culture is increasingly subject to commodification, so one of the prevalent features of contemporary capitalism is its tendency to infuse an ever widening range of outputs with aesthetic and semiotic content. For better or worse, then, huge swaths of culture today are coming into the grip of capitalist supply and demand relations just like any other segment of the wider commodity system, and this state of affairs is working profound transformations on the manner in which we approach all issues of aesthetic and semiotic judgment, and on the ways in which we frame our understanding of the social significance of culture generally. In the final chapter of the book I attempt to establish the outlines of a political economy of the cultural commodity as a way of broaching some of the more difficult puzzles raised by these latter remarks.

Much of the material presented in this book has been previously published in specialized academic journals. All of this material, however, has been extensively reworked for the purposes of the present volume, and considerable new analysis and information have been added. Previously published work incorporated into the present volume appeared in: the *Annals of the Association of American Geographers*, *Competition and Change*, *Entrepreneurship and Regional Development*, *Environment and Planning A*, *Geoforum*, the *International Journal of Urban and Regional Research*, *Media, Culture and Society*, the *Monthly Labor Review*, and *Theory, Culture & Society*. Also, much of Chapter 9 was originally published in H.-J. Braczyk, P. Cooke, and M. Heidenreich (eds) *Regional Innovation Systems* (UCL Press, 1998). I wish to express my gratitude to Chase Langford and Roberto Gimeno for drafting the excellent maps and diagrams that accompany this book.

PART 1

PROPAEDEUTICA

The three chapters that constitute the first part of this book are concerned with establishing some basic lines of investigation of the cultural economy generally, and of the cultural economy of cities in particular. Chapter 1 provides a synthetic overview of the entire terrain of inquiry, stressing the importance of cultural-products sectors as foci of economic growth and urban development in modern capitalism. Chapter 2 is a review of general processes of locational agglomeration. Here, an analytical language is developed which is then deployed in later chapters in detailed empirical descriptions of the economic geography of the cultural economy. Chapter 3 builds on this material by showing how creativity and innovation in the cultural economy can at least in part be understood in terms of an under-lying spatial field of economic and social relationships. The discussion in all three chapters reflects *passim* upon the interplay between the local and the global dimensions of the modern cultural economy, and this theme is picked up again repeatedly throughout the remainder of the book.

1

INTRODUCTION TO THE CULTURAL ECONOMY OF CITIES

As Peter Hall (1998) has shown in enormous historic and geographic detail, cities have always played a privileged role as centers of cultural and economic activity. From their earliest origins, cities have exhibited a conspicuous capacity both to generate culture in the form of art, ideas, styles, and ways of life, and to induce high levels of economic innovation and growth, though not always or necessarily simultaneously. At the dawn of the twenty-first century, a very marked convergence between the spheres of cultural and economic development seems to be occurring. This is also one of the distinguishing characteristics of contemporary urbanization processes in general.

These remarks are based on the notion that capitalism itself is moving into a phase in which the cultural forms and meanings of its outputs are becoming critical if not dominating elements of productive strategy, and in which the realm of human culture as a whole is increasingly subject to commodification, by which I mean that the culture we consume is to ever greater degree supplied through profit-making institutions in decentralized markets. In other words, an ever widening range of economic activity is concerned with producing and marketing goods and services that are permeated in one way or another with broadly aesthetic or semiotic attributes (Baudrillard, 1968; Lash and Urry, 1994). There are, to be sure, vast expanses of contemporary culture that remain external to (and even in opposition to) this nexus of relationships, though rarely are they immune from at least some partial form of absorption into the general system of commodity production. Consider, for example, the ways in which aspects of black consciousness, feminism, punk fashion, or gay lifestyles have been incorporated into the design specifications of consumer goods. Rap music and gangsta clothing represent another manifestation of the same phenomenon, and are currently strongly in evidence in much of the cultural economy of contemporary Los Angeles.

Such goods and services (let us henceforth designate them *cultural products*) are extremely heterogeneous in their substance, appearance, and sectoral origins. In some cases they flow from traditional manufacturing sectors engaged in the transformation of physical inputs into final outputs (e.g. clothing, furniture, or jewelry); in other cases, they are more properly thought of as services in the sense that they involve some personalized transaction or the production and transmission of information (e.g. tourist services, live theater, or advertising); and in yet other cases, they may be thought of as a hybrid form (such as music recording, book publishing, or film production). Whatever the physico-economic constitution of such products, the sectors that make them are all engaged in the creation of marketable outputs whose competitive qualities depend on the fact that they function at least in part as personal ornaments, modes of social display, forms of entertainment and distraction, or sources of information and self-awareness, i.e. as artifacts whose symbolic value to the consumer is high relative to their practical purposes (cf. Bourdieu, 1971). Of course, there is considerable overlap between these sorts of cultural products and purely utilitarian objects and there is an enormous range of intermediate products (such as kitchen utensils, luxury cars, downtown office buildings, and so on) that are complex composites of the symbolic and the utilitarian. This phenomenon is a reflection of the tendency in modern capitalism for cultural production to become increasingly commodified while commodities themselves become increasingly invested with symbolic value.

As this two-pronged movement occurs, the cultural economy is coming to the fore as one of the most dynamic frontiers of capitalism at the dawn of the twenty-first century. Further, with the growth of disposable consumer income and the expansion of discretionary time in modern society, the consumption of cultural products of all kinds is expanding at an accelerating pace. In this book, I argue that the specifically geographic meaning and impacts of this vigorously evolving situation are proving to be extremely complex, and they are especially evident in a number of giant cities representing the flagships of a new global capitalist cultural economy (Knox, 1995).

Place, Culture, Economy

Place and culture

Place and culture are persistently intertwined with one another, for any given place – as it is understood here – is always a locus of dense human interrelationships (out of which culture in part grows), and culture is a phenomenon that tends to have intensely local characteristics thereby helping to differentiate places from one another. The point is sharply underlined by the work of cultural critics, urbanists, and historians like Clark (1984), Davis (1990), Schorske (1980), and Zukin (1991; 1995) among many others, who have described the extraordinarily rich cultures that are to be found in a variety of urban settings.

As we begin the twenty-first century, however, a deepening tension is evident between culture as something that is narrowly place-bound, and culture as a pattern of non-place globalized events and experiences (Appadurai, 1990; Morley and Robins, 1995; Peet, 1986; Webber, 1964). Thus, on the one hand, and even in a world where the ease and rapidity of communication have become watchwords, place is still uncontestably a repository of distinctive cultural conventions and traditions. On the other hand, certain privileged places represent points from which cultural artifacts and images are broadcast across the world and this same process has deeply erosive or at least transformative effects on many local cultures. The geography of culture, like the geography of economic activity, is stretched across a tense force-field of local and global relationships (Featherstone, 1995; Robertson, 1992), with the production of culture tending to become more and more concentrated in a privileged set of localized clusters of firms and workers, while final outputs are channeled into ever more spatially extended networks of consumption. Accordingly, if the cultural traditions and norms of some parts of the world are under serious threat at the present time, others are finding widening and receptive audiences. In fact some places, and nowhere more so than in the heartlands of modern world capitalism – places like New York, Los Angeles, London, Paris, and Tokyo, to mention only a few of the most obvious examples – continue to be unique and highly creative generators of culture, and above all, to function as the bulwarks of a new cultural economy of capitalism. Whatever the political consequences of this predicament-laden situation may be, it does not so much herald a trend to absolute cultural uniformity across the world as it does an alternative and subtle kind of regional cultural differentiation articulated with an expanding structure of national and international cultural niches (e.g. adolescents, environmentalists, art collectors, and so on).

One of the reasons – though not the only reason – for this claim about the reassertion of place as a privileged locus of culture is the continued and intensifying importance of massive urban communities characterized by many different specialized economic functions and dense internal social relationships. Large cities in modern capitalism are typically the sites of leading-edge economic activity in the form of substantial agglomerations of industrial and business activity. These cities also represent nodes of location-specific interactions and emergent effects in which the stimulus to cultural experimentation and renewal tends to be high. In this context, many complex interactions between the cultural and the economic are set in motion. Local cultures help to shape the character of intra-urban economic activity; equally, economic activity becomes a dynamic element of the culture-generating and innovative capacities of given places. This comment applies, of course, to forms of economic activity that are concerned with non-cultural as well as cultural products (Salais and Storper, 1993; Thrift, 1994). However, in cultural-products industries, the connection has special significance because of the intensity and idiosyncrasy of the relations between the cultural attributes of place and the qualitative aspects of final outputs. The contrasting cases of Los Angeles and Paris – two places that figure prominently in this book – sharply exemplify this point (see below).

In these senses, then, place, culture, and economy are symbiotic on one another, and in modern capitalism this symbiosis is reemerging in powerful new forms as expressed in the cultural economies of certain key cities. At the same time, the more the specific cultural identities and economic order of these cities condense out on the landscape, the more they come to enjoy monopoly powers of place (expressed in place-specific process and product configurations) that enhance their competitive advantages and provide their cultural-products industries with an edge in wider national and international markets. As Molotch has written:

> The positive connection of product image to place yields a kind of monopoly rent that adheres to places, their insignia, and the brand names that may attach to them. Their industries grow as a result, and the local economic base takes shape. Favorable images create entry barriers for products from competing places. (1996: 229)

It should be clear already from these preliminary remarks that the present account seeks to go beyond – though not to abandon entirely – the notion of the cultural economy of cities as either (a) the commercialization of historical heritage, or (b) large-scale public investment in artifacts of collective cultural consumption in the interests of urban renovation (Bassett, 1993; Bianchini, 1993; Frith, 1991; Kearns and Philo, 1993; Landry and Bianchini, 1995; Moulinier, 1996; Wynne, 1992). What is of primary concern here is an exploration of the intertwined effects of capitalist production processes and the ever increasing cultural content of outputs, and the ways in which these effects make themselves felt in the growth and development of particular places.

Fordist and post-Fordist places

Notwithstanding these emphatic remarks about the importance of place as a crucible of cultural and economic interactions, they require serious qualification depending on what moment in the historical geography of capitalism we have in mind.

In particular, in the era when Fordist mass production held sway in the cities of the US Manufacturing Belt, a very different set of relationships between place, culture, and economy prevailed from those that seem to be observable today in so-called post-Fordist cities (Dear, 1995; Scott, 1995). This is not to say that large Fordist industrial cities were not at this moment in time stamped by distinctive cultural formations (the variegated social landscapes of Chicago, Detroit, and Pittsburgh provide obvious and persuasive evidence to the contrary), or that their economies were bereft of cultural-products industries. However, the production apparatus of Fordist industry was focused above all on reaping the advantages of economies of scale through the standardization of products and the cultivation of mass markets. As a result, the cultural content of much of the consumer output of Fordist industry tended to become subservient to the more functional design imperatives imposed by the need for manufacturing efficiency and competitive cost-cutting (Sack, 1992). Production for specialized niche markets was relatively restricted, and even elite consumption at this time was much influenced by the functionalist, minimalist aesthetic of high

modernism (cf. Banham, 1960; Giedion, 1948). In the 1930s, the Hollywood film industry itself had ambitions – only in part ever realized – to
turn out films on the same technological and economic principles as auto-
mobiles in Detroit (Storper and Christopherson, 1987). Frankfurt School
critics among others were deeply troubled by the 'eternal sameness' of mass
society and its alleged incompatibility with serious cultural values (Adorno,
1991; Horkheimer and Adorno, 1972); and even as late as the 1970s,
cultural geographers like Relph (1976) were lamenting the 'placelessness'
that they tracked down to prevailing forms of large-scale urbanization and
industrial development. What few of the prevailing critics of mass society
envisioned – though whether or not they would have applauded its development is altogether another matter – was the major restructuring of
capitalist social and economic relations that began some time in the early
1970s and the emergence of new cultural-products sectors together with
increasingly differentiated and fragmented consumer cultures. This restructuring was manifest above all in a strong shift away from Fordist forms of
production and by the remarkable proliferation of new post-Fordist or
flexible industries. The reasons underlying this historical change and the
precise modalities of its occurrence are the subject of much debate at the
present moment (see, for example, Boyer and Durand, 1993; Leborgne and
Lipietz, 1992; Jessop, 1992) and need not detain us here. What is of interest
is its expression in a new kind of cultural economy and in the rise of new
patterns of urbanization.

We are, in short, currently observing the appearance of a distinctly post-
Fordist cultural economy in the advanced capitalist societies (Crane, 1992;
Lash and Urry, 1994). This remark does not signify that mass production
has no place in today's cultural economy, but it does reaffirm the idea that
a vast extension is taking place in an assortment of craft, fashion, and
cultural-products industries throughout the advanced capitalist economies,
along with a great surge in niche markets for design- and information-
intensive outputs. A provocative but revealing manner of designating this
trend might be to label it as a postmodern expression of changing consumer tastes and demands involving a general aestheticization and semi-
oticization of marketable products (cf. Albertson, 1988; Baudrillard, 1968;
Harvey, 1989; Soja, 1989; 1996). Not that these products – for the most
part – possess what Benjamin (1973) alluded to as auratic quality. They
range over the gamut from, say, masterworks of cinematic art or designer
jewelry to, say, tourist souvenirs or throwaway shopping bags, with the
vast majority representing goods and services that trade on the basis of
short- or medium-term fashion, information, and entertainment value, and
on their merits as social markers (Ryan, 1992).

On the supply side, these characteristics of cultural products encourage
firms to engage in highly competitive marketing strategies based on insistent
differentiation of outputs. On the demand side, consumer demands are
apt to be unstable and unpredictable if not outright faddish (Crewe and
Forster, 1993; Hirsch, 1972; Peterson and Berger, 1975). The net effect is

that the technology and organization of production tend strongly to flexible specialization, meaning that firms concentrate on making small and specialized batches of output for tightly defined but constantly changing market segments (Piore and Sabel, 1984; Shapiro et al., 1992; Storper and Christopherson, 1987). In locational terms, firms subject to this sort of productive-cum-competitive regime typically converge together into transactions-intensive agglomerations. Examples can be found in (a) traditional centers of craft production that have experienced a renascence in the post-Fordist era (as in the cases of the Third Italy and other areas in Western Europe), or (b) resort centers like Las Vegas, Rio de Janeiro, or the cities of the French Riviera, or (c) most importantly for present purposes, those large metropolitan areas as mentioned earlier that are rapidly becoming the principal hubs of cultural production in a post-Fordist global economic order.

Empirical Observations on the Cultural Economy of Cities

Not only are there many different centers of cultural production in the modern world, but each also tends to be quite idiosyncratic in its character as a place. This idiosyncrasy resides in part in the (necessary) uniqueness of the history of any given place, and in part in the very functioning of the local cultural economy which in numerous instances, through round after round of production, becomes ever more specialized and place-specific. As capitalism globalizes, moreover, the cultural economies of cities become, if anything, yet more pronounced. In light of the observation of Adam Smith that 'the division of labour is limited by the extent of the market' (1970: 121), globalization enhances the likelihood of vertical disintegration and agglomeration within the cultural economies of individual cities and provides new possibilities for inter-city differentiation (cf. Scott, 1988a). Our task now is to assess the empirical meaning and theoretical logic of these phenomena.

Employment in the cultural economy of American cities

Let us begin with a scrutiny of some simple statistical measures of employment in cultural-products sectors in American cities. Unfortunately, we are severely hampered in this task by the deficiencies of official sources of data and above all by the limitations imposed by the US Standard Industrial Classification (SIC). The main problem in this regard is that the categories of the standard classification are rarely fully informative, and this is especially true in the case of the cultural economy. Many sectors, even at the four-digit level of definition, are made up of collections of establishments whose outputs are quite disparate in terms of their cultural attributes. For example, SIC 232 (men's and boys' furnishings) includes establishments that make high-fashion items such as ties and fancy shirts as well as establishments that produce cheap, standardized, utilitarian outputs such as work clothes. Furthermore, the standard classification frequently provides no direct or explicit information whatever about certain noteworthy segments of the cultural economy (such as recording studios, multimedia industries, or tourist services). The data for different SIC categories that we now consider, therefore, have a purely symptomatic and indicative value and should be taken as pointing to no more than some gross tendencies subject to correction by more careful empirical research.

With these reservations in mind, we now examine employment patterns in selected sectors of the cultural economy of American cities for the year 1992, as shown in Table 1.1. The table identifies a series of SIC categories selected after scrutiny of the lists of their constituent subsectors as reported in the official US *Standard Industrial Classification Manual*; these categories seem to provide a reasonable compromise between descriptive parsimony on the one hand and detailed characterization of the cultural economy on the other. The statistical information is broken down under two main headings, i.e. (a) aggregate employment in cultural-products industries for all 40 metropolitan areas (CMSAs and MSAs) in the United States that had populations of one million or more in 1990, and (b) aggregate employment in cultural-products industries for the US as a whole.

Three main points now need to be made. First, the cultural economy is represented by an extremely wide variety of both manufacturing and service activities. Second, with total employment exceeding three million, the sheer magnitude of the cultural economy of the United States is surprising (even admitting the makeshift definition of the cultural economy as given in Table 1.1); and examination of the record suggests that it has been growing rapidly of late. Third, a very significant proportion of employment in the country's cultural economy is concentrated in large metropolitan areas, and the proportion seems to increase as the cultural content of final products increases. Hence, only 11.6% of total employment in SIC 314 (footwear, except rubber) – a sector that comprises many standardized producers – is found in large metropolitan areas, in contrast to 96.8% of employment in SIC 781/2 (motion picture production and distribution). By way of comparison, 53.2% of the country's total population is concentrated in the 40 designated metropolitan areas. At the same time, employment in these sectors is unevenly distributed over the 40 metropolitan areas, and is for the most part concentrated in one or both of two main metropolitan areas, namely New York and Los Angeles. Exceptions to this observation are the furniture industry and the costume jewelry industry whose principal foci, respectively, are the Greensboro–Winston Salem–High Point MSA, and the Providence–Fall River–Warwick MSA. A few cultural-products sectors tend to avoid major metropolitan areas, though they still have a proclivity to agglomeration. Perhaps the clearest example of this phenomenon is the musical instruments industry whose main center in the country is Elkhart, Indiana.

Table 1.1 *Employment in selected cultural-products industries in US metropolitan areas (CMSAs and MSAs) with populations of more than one million, 1992*

SIC	Industry	Employment in metropolitan areas (000)	Employment in United States (000)	Metropolitan areas as % of US
225	Knitting mills	51.0	194.0	26.3
231	Men's and boys' suits and coats	16.3	43.8	37.2
232	Men's and boys' furnishings	46.5	263.5	17.6
233	Women's and misses' outerwear	187.6	303.9	61.7
234	Women's and children's undergarments	12.2	53.6	22.8
235	Hats, caps, and millinery	6.5	18.8	34.3
236	Girls' and children's outerwear	14.9	53.7	27.7
237	Fur goods	0.6	1.0	60.0
238	Miscellaneous apparel and accessories	13.4	35.7	37.4
2511	Wood household furniture	28.6	121.1	23.6
2512	Upholstered household furniture	18.6	79.2	23.5
2514	Metal household furniture	8.9	25.8	34.3
271	Newspapers	190.6	417.0	45.7
272	Periodicals	85.2	116.2	73.3
2731	Book publishing	53.2	79.6	66.9
277	Greeting cards	11.4	22.8	49.9
314	Footwear, except rubber	5.7	49.0	11.6
316	Luggage	5.1	9.7	52.1
317	Handbags and personal leather goods	4.8	11.2	42.9
391	Jewelry, silverware and plated ware	29.2	46.0	63.5
393	Musical instruments	3.2	12.0	26.3
394	Toys and sporting goods	31.8	96.0	33.1
396	Costume jewelry and notions	16.7	28.0	59.6
483	Radio and television broadcasting	102.8	221.8	46.4
484	Cable and other pay-TV services	58.4	129.0	45.3
731	Advertising	146.8	195.8	75.0
781/2	Motion picture production/ distribution	241.2	249.2	96.8
792	Producers, orchestras, entertainers	58.5	69.0	84.8
8712	Architectural services	93.7	121.7	77.0
	Totals	1,543.2	3,068.0	

Sources: US Department of Commerce, Bureau of the Census, (a) *Census of Manufactures*, 1992, (b) *Census of Transportation, Communications, and Utilities*, 1992, (c) *Census of Service Industries*, 1992

Cultural synergies and semiotic fields

I suggested above that post-Fordist places and their cultural economies are inclined to exhibit well-developed individual identities, as a consequence of the play of history, agglomeration, and locational specialization. This same feature is also doubtless rooted in the fact that cultural-products industries compete increasingly on crowded global markets, and that success in this competition is aided where the monopoly powers of place are mobilized to the maximum in implicit and explicit branding of products. It is fostered, too, by the positive spillover effects that almost always tie different cultural sectors within a single city together into an industrial community with its characteristic styles, sensibilities, and thematic associations. This synergistic relation is due both to the circumstance that these sectors often transact intensively with one another and participate in shared labor markets, and to their exploitation of design cultures and images drawn from the local urban context, representing a generalized externality or competitive advantage for all.

The significance and potency of these relationships can be exemplified in many different ways. The traditional craft industries in the towns of the Third Italy represent one dramatic illustration. Since the early 1970s, industrial employment in these towns has grown by leaps and bounds, and the cultural products of the region have successfully penetrated international markets thanks to their superior quality and style based on a legacy of skilled craftsmanship dedicated to serving a traditionally discerning clientele (Becattini, 1987; Pyke et al., 1990; Scott, 1988a). Woollen textiles from Prato, knitwear from Carpi, ceramics from Sassuolo, high-fashion shoes from Porto Sant'Elpidio, furniture from Pesaro, lace from Como, and leather goods from Florence, are just a few of the products that have driven much of the remarkable recent economic growth of the Third Italy. Another set of examples might be adduced by reference to tourist resorts, each with its complex of interlocking production and service functions, and each luring consumers on the basis of some unique collective asset (physical or social) that is then made accessible and continually reimaged as the local production system does its work of commercialization (Urry, 1990; 1995). In addition, a number of major metropolitan regions (New York, London, Tokyo, Los Angeles, Paris, etc.) possess multiple clusters of cultural-products industries such as book and magazine publishing, art and design endeavors of all varieties, theatrical and musical production, radio and television broadcasting, and advertising, together with craft industries like clothing and jewelry, that thrive on the urbane climate of the great international metropolis.

Of all the individual examples of large-scale localized cultural-economic systems that might be cited in evidence of these notions, two of the most compelling are represented by the cases of Los Angeles and Paris, both of which project strong and sharp-edged cultural images, and both of which have effective global reach in terms of their ability to connect with consumers. In the former case, the cultural economy is for the most part focused on products that cater to demotic, informal, post-bourgeois tastes, and it exploits an abundant multifaceted imagery drawn from a mixture of natural local color (sunshine, surf, palm trees) and a relaxed texture of social life combined with purely fictional associations that are themselves the residues of previous rounds of cultural production (Molotch, 1996; Soja and Scott, 1996). The cultural economy of Paris, by contrast, is very much more focused on the production of luxury articles for a more select clientele. It draws on a long tradition of superior craftsmanship and artistry, extending from the seventeenth and eighteenth centuries through the *belle époque* to the present day (Bourdieu, 1977; Castarède, 1992; Claval, 1993; Salais and Storper, 1993), and, unlike the case of Los Angeles, the concessions that it occasionally makes to everyday commercial values tend to be signs of enervation rather than success.

If the cultural products of Los Angeles share a set of characteristics that can for the most part be variously described as casual, colorful, occasionally fantastic, and accessible to mass sensibilities, those of Paris by contrast – or at least those that are most distinctively Parisian – appeal to more discriminating consumers who put a premium on traditional craftsmanship, refinement, and luxury. At the same time, the cultural economies of Los Angeles and Paris face pressing internal problems, not the least of which is the propensity in both cases for some sectors (such as clothing and furniture) to breed sweatshop forms of production relying on cheap, unskilled, immigrant labor, with the result that the quality of their final outputs is often dubious and the reputation of local producers as a whole becomes compromised (Montagné-Villette, 1990; Scott and Rigby, 1996). Problems like this pose difficult questions about the kinds of local policies and modes of collective action needed to sustain cultural production in modern cities, and such questions will be broached in some detail in later chapters.

Production and Distribution

Production relations

The concept of a cultural economy (like the concept of high-technology industry) is incoherent in some respects, for it refers to a diverse collection of sectors displaying many different kinds of technologies, transactional arrangements, employment profiles, products, and so on. What provides special meaning to the concept in the present context is that the outputs of cultural-products industries are almost always susceptible – actually or potentially – to a sort of convergence on place-specific product design contours and cultural content. They are subject, in other words, to the influence of peculiar imageries and sensibilities rooted in place and appropriatable by individual firms as competitive advantages. There are, too, some prominent points of correspondence among at least important segments of these industries in so far as they participate in general structures of flexible specialization and vertically disintegrated production processes. In fact, the cultural-products industries as a whole can be roughly epitomized in terms of five main technological-organizational elements:

1 The technologies and labor processes utilized in cultural-products industries usually entail considerable amounts of direct human involvement

(as in the clothing industry), often and to an increasing degree complemented by advanced flexible computer technologies (as in the multimedia industry).

2   Production is almost always organized in dense networks of small- and medium-sized establishments strongly dependent on one another for specialized inputs and services. However, it is also common to find large and relatively integrated firms participating in these same networks, as for example in the case of the major Hollywood film studios or the leading New York publishers (cf. Cosner et al., 1982; Maltby, 1981; see also Driver and Gillespie, 1993).

3   These networks form multifaceted industrial complexes that in aggregate tend to exert huge demands on local labor markets and to require an enormous variety of worker skills/attributes. The employment relation in the cultural-products industries is typically intermittent, leading to frequently recurrent job search and recruitment activities (cf. Menger, 1991; 1994). In this regard, risks for both workers and employers are reduced as the size of the local production complex increases.

4   As a result of these different features, complexes of cultural-products industries are invariably replete with external economies, many of which can only be effectively appropriated via locational agglomeration (Becattini, 1987; Scott, 1988a; 1988b). Agglomeration gives rise to yet further external economies through a system of emergent effects, and in the cultural-products industries these concern above all the mutual learning, cultural synergies, and creativity effects made possible by the presence of many interrelated firms and industries in one place. In particular, creativity is not just an expression of the lonely ruminations of the individual cultural worker, but more importantly an outgrowth of multiple stimuli situated at points of interaction between many different participants in the local economy (cf. Jacobs, 1969; Powell et al., 1996; Russo, 1985). This in turn suggests the hypothesis that innovation, all else being equal, is likely to be a geometric function of the size of the relevant reference group.

5   Agglomeration also facilitates the emergence of different kinds of institutional infrastructures that can ease the functioning of the local economy by providing critical overhead services, facilitating flows of information, promoting trust and cooperation among interlinked producers, ensuring that effective strategic planning is accomplished, and so on (cf. Crewe, 1996; Lorenz, 1992).

These five main points underline once again the collective character of localized cultural-economic systems and their special interest as image-producing complexes. As we have seen, such systems represent considerably more than the simple sum of their parts, for they are invariably shot through with multiple interdependencies, some of them traded, some of them untraded. For the same reason, firms caught up in these systems often face a shared competitive fate irrespective of their individual competencies and capacities. This composite order of things means that appropriately attuned local economic development policies are not only in order but also imperative. If we take a cue from the above five points, these policies presumably need to focus heavily on such agglomeration-specific tasks as the provision of technological research services, the training of labor, the social governance of inter-industrial networks, and institution-building generally in the interests of coordinated and synergistic regional development (Scott, 1993b).

Distribution relations and multinationalization

While the cultural economies of many cities today consist of dense, complex, and locationally convergent groups of producers, they are also typically embedded in far-flung global networks of transactions (Amin and Thrift, 1992; Scott, 1996). Their success, then, depends not only upon their ability to tap deeply into local sources of value-adding externalities and innovative energies, but also to distribute their outputs on national and international markets and to ensure that they can negotiate their way through a variety of cultural barriers in different parts of the world.

The process of distribution is not infrequently undertaken by phalanxes of specialized firms that straddle the critical interface between any given agglomeration and global markets. These firms are the inter-local equivalent of the intra-local agents, contractors, *impannatore*, dealers, representatives, jobbers, and others that are almost always to be found within individual agglomerations. All of these peculiar types of firm represent a response to the existence of chronic information gaps in regard to specialized trading opportunities. The essential feature of inter-local distributors is their technological and organizational capacity to funnel information and outputs from many different producers in one geographic context to many different consumers in others, and because this feature is apt to be marked by internal economies of scale, they are sometimes anomalously large in size when compared to the average size of the producers that they serve. Oftentimes, they are also engaged in different aspects of production or financing. This is the way the major film studios in Hollywood operate, though even here actual film production is being increasingly relegated to clusters of smaller production companies and their subcontractors (Christopherson and Storper, 1986; Storper, 1993). Other illustrative cases of the same phenomenon are Benetton, IKEA, and the large American radio and television networks.

The intricate tissue of the cultural economy of cities is further complicated by the fact that multinational corporations, and in particular large media conglomerates, are now making determined moves into different cultural-products sectors. These corporations ceaselessly scavenge the world for production sites, synergistic takeover and merger opportunities, and market outlets (Aksoy and Robins, 1992; Barnett and Cavanagh, 1994; Flichy, 1991; Garnham, 1987; 1990; MacDonald, 1990; Morley and Robins,

1995; Robins, 1995). As they make ever more insistent incursions into different cultural-products agglomerations, they bring about many significant changes by speeding up flows of information, by helping to streamline the financing and commercialization of new products, and by intensifying competition. But they are also a critical ingredient of success for they are essential mediating organizations, distributing products world-wide and pumping money back into localized agglomerations. Time-Warner, Turner Broadcasting, Viacom, and Walt Disney (each of which is a member of the *Fortune* 500 group of companies) are typical examples of this phenomenon. So are European firms like Bertelsmann, Philips, and Thorn-EMI, and Japanese firms like Matsushita and Sony, all of which are firmly implanted in US cultural-products agglomerations.

Many of these corporations are also engaged in developing electronic platforms for the dissemination and consumption of cultural products on a global basis. Numerous analysts and commentators have suggested that the appearance of these new distribution technologies (especially when they are harnessed to the sales strategies of multinational media corporations) will have the effect of severely eroding existing levels of cultural-geographic diversity. This, however, does not seem to be occurring in quite the way that some critics have suggested. Granted that we are likely to see the further emergence of world-wide non-place cultural communities with specific kinds of tastes and preferences, it nevertheless seems improbable that commercial cultural production will shift in the direction of entropy whether in terms of locational patterns or substantive content. On the contrary, the production of goods and services for sale on world-wide cultural markets is still almost certainly going to be tied to individual specialized agglomerations, if the arguments deployed in this book have any validity. Even with the prospective development of fully globalized electronic media spaces, geographically differentiated cultural production nodes are liable to be the rule rather than the exception (Storper and Scott, 1995). As I shall argue later, the emergence of global media spaces, by contributing to the extension of markets and thus to the deepening of the social division of labor, is likely to be associated with heightened forms of local economic development and corresponding redifferentiation of the cultural specificities of place.

A Preliminary Assessment

I have tried to demonstrate in this introductory chapter how the cultural geography of place and the economic geography of production are intertwined, and how this relationship is played out above all in selected urban centers. Above all, the argument describes how, in contemporary capitalism, the culture-generating capabilities of cities are being harnessed to productive purposes, creating new kinds of localized competitive advantages with major employment and income enhancing effects.

Every output of the cultural economy represents a text of greater or lesser complexity to be read (Ryan, 1992), and few aspects of contemporary social experience remain untouched by this connection between the cultural product and the consumer. Since culture is also always about identity and power, the pervasive influence of the cultural economy raises serious political questions. A familiar expression of what is at stake here is the invasion and dilution of traditional cultures in one place or in one segment of society by commodified cultures produced in other places/ segments. Another expression – perhaps even more important than the former – involves the social recuperation that flows from certain types of popular commercial culture. Neither of these predicaments, however, is unconditional. Alongside the grim analyses of the Frankfurt School about the leveling and stupefying effects of capitalist culture we must set not only the resilient and creative reception that it encounters in many sorts of traditional cultures, but also the enlightening and progressive cultural forces constantly unleashed by capitalism (Garnham, 1987), e.g. from the novel and the newspaper in the eighteenth century, to such twentieth century cultural phenomena as Bauhaus design, the films of Hollywood directors like Frank Capra, John Ford, Howard Hawks, and Billy Wilder, and those modern forms of music from jazz to rock 'n' roll that habitually challenge any notion of cultural consumption as a process of docile osmosis. There are also strong potentialities for heightened forms of cultural differentiation from place to place as the cultural economy moves into high gear, for if capitalism dissolves away certain sites of cultural expression, it actively recreates other sites elsewhere. I shall contend more elaborately below – and contrary to a number of alarmist visions about increasing cultural uniformity in the modern world – that as the trend to economic and cultural globalization deepens, these processes of differentiation are more likely than not to become more sharply inscribed in the economic geography of cultural production.

2
THE MAINSPRINGS OF URBAN ECONOMIC PERFORMANCE

Before we proceed further into specific details of the geographic bases of development and growth in image-producing industries, we need to pause briefly to take stock of some basic issues in the theory of spatial organization. In this chapter, then, I lay out the groundwork for an understanding of the main processes linking economic and regional development together, and how these combine to generate dynamic growth centers with specialized but internally variegated production systems. These general remarks will be deployed in succeeding chapters in diverse conceptual and empirical investigations of the cultural economy of cities.

Here, I seek to build a view of the geography of capitalist production activities as having a special proclivity (under specified conditions) to form dense localized production complexes that function as the essential economic backbone of thriving cities and regions. I argue that this proclivity is strongly developed because it is the source of potent increasing returns effects with major impacts on local economic performance and competitive advantage. I argue further that with the passage of time, these increasing returns effects tend to become self-reinforcing, thereby boosting the competitive lead of leading regions and amplifying patterns of regional specialization.

The Space Economy of City-Regions

Industrial organization and economic space

There is a long tradition in economic analysis, ranging from von Böhm-Bawerck (1891) through Young (1928) and Leontief (1941) to Perroux (1961) and Isard (1960), in which the structure of production is described in terms of a social division of labor held functionally together by roundabout networks of input–output linkages. One of the conditions of existence for any structure of this kind is that it function as a repository of external economies in that individual producers must always be able to obtain at least some of their needed materials or equipment more cheaply by purchasing them from other producers in the (socially divided) system of production than they can by manufacturing them themselves.

Any such system can in the first instance be thought of as existing in a purely *economic space* defined as a matrix of transactional interrelationships between firms or sectors (Perroux, 1961). Thus, for the present, all reference to *geographic space*, in the sense of an ensemble of definite locations and places, is held in abeyance. Economic space itself can assume many different forms, though two archetypes are of great relevance in the present context. One of these is represented by pyramid-like industrial complexes where large lead plants sit at the top of transactional hierarchies of smaller direct and indirect input suppliers. This organizational form, of course, typifies the car industry or the aerospace industry. The other involves finely grained transactional networks linking together many small producers without any strongly evident lead plant effects, as exemplified by industries such as clothing, jewelry, or furniture. Various hybrids of these two contrasting models are both conceivable and observable in practice. No matter what their specific form, however, industrial systems in economic space are sites of intense exchange, not just of simple physical inputs and outputs, but also of business information, know-how, technological expertise, and so on. This exchange occurs in both traded form (mediated by relations of sale and purchase) and untraded form (where producers obtain useful inputs in the guise of non-commercial transactions), and it occurs in sundry institutional environments ranging from simple spot markets to tightly knit collaborative organizations, as in the case of Japanese *keiretsu*. Analysts like Patchell (1993), Russo (1985), and von Hippel (1988) have argued that economic spaces characterized by intense transactional exchange are often important loci of learning effects and of informal but active innovation. These spaces are also apt to function as the physical foundations of specialized cultures and conventions that partially evolve in response to the peculiar tasks and problems that interrelated groups of producers face at every turn (Salais and Storper, 1993). Thus, such specific sectoral settings as the clothing industry, the film industry, or the financial services industry constitute the social milieux of identifiable business cultures. We might say that the idea of industrial atmosphere as proposed long ago by Marshall (1920) – i.e. a set of sociocultural norms and practices revolving around the production system – relates in the first instance to an underlying, placeless structure of production, and only in the second instance to a place-specific economic geography. Even in a placeless world, if such a thing were possible, differentiated cultural expressions of particular articulations of economic activity are perfectly imaginable, though they would now presumably have only a sectoral as opposed to a spatial expression.

That said, the fact that a place-specific economic geography is a persistent if not dominating feature of the world we live in now calls urgently for attention.

From external economies to locational agglomeration

The classical theory of regional economic development and specialization was based on the proposition that natural endowments differ from place to place, and that inter-regional trade would then encourage producers to concentrate on their (given) comparative advantages. This theory is still a valuable item in the toolkit of the economic geographer and the regional economist, though as is now widely recognized it also suffers from fatal weaknesses, and it never came fully to grips with the real complexities of development and trade in capitalism, even in the nineteenth century when natural endowments unquestionably shaped the pattern of world economic geography more forcefully than they do today. This theoretical deficiency derives in part from the condition that production and exchange are shot through with increasing returns effects that undermine the conventional approach to this issue – as the new trade and growth theorists such as Krugman (1990; 1991) and Romer (1986) have argued. More importantly for present purposes, it also derives from the circumstance that regional development is – and to an ever increasing degree – based on competitive advantages that are socially and politically created, and not simply given by nature (Scott, 1988b; 1993a). In contradistinction to the conventional approach, I propose to show that we can only start fully to decipher the locational logic of the economic landscape when we approach it in terms of its origins as a pure social construct, and more specifically as a question about external economies and locational agglomeration. The argument is made in two stages. In a first stage, I deal largely with static spatial issues; and in a second stage, I broach a series of more complex dynamic and historical considerations.

We may begin with the rather simple notion that since the core elements of capitalist industrial systems are invariably organized as networks of producers bound together in dense criss-crossing relationships, there will always be a tendency for at least some of the individual producers tied together in this manner to converge locationally toward a common geographic center of gravity (Scott, 1988a; 1988b). Another way of expressing the same idea is to say that in the absence of magic carpets (i.e. cost-free, instantaneous transportation and communication over any distance), transacting is often more efficiently and effectively accomplished where mutual proximity is assured – even in today's world where electronic communications technologies have become so pervasive a part of the business environment. In the present instance, I intend the notion of transacting not to be restricted only to the case of commercial linkages but, equally importantly, to apply to all of those additional kinds of social interaction that underpin business cultures and whose operation is often much enhanced when they are embedded in place-specific communities of interest. At the outset, then, industrial agglomeration gives rise to three primary kinds of benefits, namely, (a) reductions in the costs of inter-industrial exchange, (b) an acceleration of the rate at which circulating capital and information flow through the industrial system, and (c) reinforcement of transactionally based modes of social solidarity that in many subtle ways help to underpin the functioning of industrial complexes (e.g. by intensifying Marshallian atmosphere or by promoting cooperative relationships between producers).

Accordingly, there is in many industrial sectors an important analytical and empirical relation between generalized external economies on the one hand, and geographically determinate agglomeration effects on the other. The former, as we have seen, reside in the organizational/transactional characteristics of production systems at large. The latter come into existence because producers, in their efforts to avail themselves of external economies, frequently engage in locational strategies that lead to spatial clustering. At the same time, the tendency to agglomeration is further magnified by a variety of other forces and beneficial emergent effects. Thus, locational agglomeration with its attendant reduction of transactions costs makes it possible for a widening of the social division of labor to occur (i.e. vertical disintegration), leading to yet more pronounced external economies. Multifaceted labor markets, with workers' skills and habits attuned to local needs, also take shape in and around each specific agglomeration. Job search and recruitment become more efficient than would be the case if producers were located at widely dispersed locations. Educational and training programs responsive to local needs can be provided at relatively low unit cost, and these help to upgrade the quality of the labor force. Equally, where geographic concentration prevails, and thus where the bases of local social solidarity are strengthened, distinctive business cultures and industrial communities are prone to emerge. Hence, agglomeration frequently facilitates (though it does not inevitably result in) the social construction of localized politico-cultural assets such as mutual trust, tacit understandings, learning effects, specialized vocabularies, transactions-specific forms of knowledge, and performance-boosting governance structures such as the Japanese *kanban* system (Harrison, 1994). Lastly, the concentrated assemblage of numerous production activities and workers' residences in one place means that significant efficiencies can be achieved in the local provision of essential infrastructural artifacts and services.

Even in this simple static world, however, the pressures to locational convergence are not limitless. In principle and practice, there are always counter-forces that threaten the increasing returns effects alluded to above and that impose heavy costs on producers. Such counter-forces are associated, for example, with congestion, pollution, or high land prices, and at certain levels of agglomeration they may seriously disrupt the functioning of the industrial system. Nor are the pressures to locational convergence constant over all industries. They will be very intense in those cases where inter-industrial linkages are small in scale, unstable, and unpredictable (hence subject to high unit costs), where speed of interaction is critical to competitive advantage, and where the successful operation of the production system is especially dependent on Marshallian atmosphere and transactions-intensive forms of inter-industrial cooperation; and a converse tendency to the deterritorialization of industrial complexes may prevail where the opposite kinds of characteristics are dominant (for producers will now be relatively free to search for locational advantages other than those that come from agglomeration). Even when industrial agglomerations do materialize on the economic landscape, they are not hermetically sealed off from the outside world, for we will almost always find many of the producers that they harbor engaged in extra-regional trading activities. In point of fact, the ability of these producers to compete on wider national and international markets is often possible only because they draw major benefits from their participation in a strong and multifaceted regional economic system (Porter, 1990).

In these ways, the logic of the production system and its social append-ages, irrespective of the distribution of natural endowments, will tend to give rise to locational agglomeration and specialization. Notwithstanding the exceedingly schematic outlines of the discussion so far, it adduces the main synchronic elements, as it were, of the theory of urban and regional economic development. But industrial cities and regions are also subject to peculiar diachronic tendencies that greatly modify the operation of these synchronic elements and that further transform the outlines of the econ-omic landscape. The next section provides a brief exposition of these issues.

The Dynamics of City-Region Development

The first and most obvious point to be made with regard to urban and regional dynamics is that the heavy fixed costs of agglomerated industrial development are reflected in the pervasive inertia of the economic land-scape over time. The second is that urban and regional clusters of industrial activity are invariably the source of increasing returns to scale and scope (i.e. productivity increases due to increments in absolute size and in the number of different but mutually supportive types of economic functions, respectively, in any given cluster), so that their competitive advantages tend to intensify over time (cf. Kaldor, 1970). As Romer (1986) has suggested, situations like this are characterized by a temporal logic in which growth leads constantly onward to yet more growth. Consequently, in any given locational system at any given moment of time, we are unlikely to observe anything even approaching static equilibrium. What we are much more liable to observe is a cross-section through a developmental trajectory that can only be understood in terms of a path-dependent pro-cess of evolution and adjustment structured by the phenomenon of local-ized increasing returns (Arthur, 1990; David, 1985; Nelson and Winter, 1982).

Each city-region, of course, has its own unique history. The total set of (observed and imaginable) histories of regional development in capitalism, however, can be partially characterized in a sort of archetypical story. I shall try to capture what appear to me to be the more significant elements of this story by means of a schematized description of the agglomerated growth of an industry from infancy to full-blown development. For the sake of argument, I shall suppose that as it begins to make its appearance on the economic landscape, this industry is locationally indifferent to the existing spatial distribution of natural endowments, and that it can effectively be carried on – intially at least – at a wide variety of locations.

At the outset, then, the locational structure of the industry will be largely indeterminate in economic terms; it can be seen simply as an 'accident' – an effect, for instance, of where its founding figure(s) happened to be living, or a result of a peculiar constellation of political forces in certain places at certain times. Let us suppose that this structure comprises several different locales, no one of which has any particular pre-given competitive advantage over the others. Even so, small chance events alone are likely to push one locale into a leading position, if only in the sense that it begins fortuitously to expand more rapidly than the others (Arthur, 1990). In other cases, a particular locale may experience in the post-infant industry stage what we might refer to as a 'breakthrough moment', namely, a decisive technological or commercial incident that pushes it to the leading edge of development (examples are Henry Ford's managerial and organizational experiments in Detroit, Donald Douglas' development of the DC-3 aircraft in Los Angeles, and, arguably, the mushrooming of an enterprising film industry in Hollywood far from the New York patent trust in the early 1900s). Once this occurs, there is a good chance that the locale will start to consolidate and extend its lead, especially where increasing returns and dynamic learning effects come into play.

Provided that markets continue to grow, the leading locale is now likely to be subject to a many-sided process of developmental self-transformation in which the agglomeration effects described in the previous section will be greatly amplified. Thus, there is apt to be a deepening and widening of the social division of labor leading to economic diversification and increased industrial synergies in the local area. Concomitantly, new labor skills are likely to emerge, and the general rounding out of local labor markets will occur. The industrial atmosphere of the locale will tend to consolidate, and the business community may well begin to take on identifiable cultural attributes marked by distinctive conventions and routines. Information exchanges and learning effects are liable to become increasingly densely textured, with a corresponding sharpening of the stimuli to technological and commercial innovation. The ramifying social division of labor will in turn offer more and more real opportunities for such innovation. And as these processes move forward, a complex regional economic system will start to materialize and – at least for a time – to evolve forward on the basis of a deepening stock of external economies of scale and scope.

There are always, of course, numerous hazards (including the onset of agglomeration diseconomies) scattered along this pathway of regional development, and things do not always work out in practice quite so unproblematically. But in the simple world of this imaginary example, our region's small head start will steadily be extended into massive competitive superiority, and it will progressively follow a recursive developmental trajectory characterized by what David (1985) has called 'lock-in'. In other words, many indurated and mutually reinforcing relationships within the regional economy will ensure that this trajectory acquires a marked dependence on its own past. This does not mean that the regional economic system will now be set inevitably on a course to one final historical destination. The notion of path dependence also implies the possibility that critical branching points exist, representing conjunctures where the regional economy may move in any one of a number of different possible directions (though once it has moved, its future is then to that degree committed). It may thus occasionally be important for regional policy-makers to nudge the system toward certain auspicious horizons and away from others that seem to be less promising over the long run, even though the latter may be quite rewarding in the short run.

Unless there are bounds to the appropriation of increasing returns by producers in the region, development will continue in this manner, and the region will eventually tend to become a leading-edge center of production in its specialized domain of economic activity. Thus, our infant industry, which began as a set of essentially footloose ventures, will now have attained a stage of historical and geographical development where it can only be effectively carried on in an extremely limited number of locational contexts. This, in part, is how it comes to pass that at certain historical moments, places like Lancashire, Detroit, Silicon Valley, the City of London, or Hollywood become virtually synonymous with a particular type of product. By the same token, regions that fail to make an early start in fostering the development of a particular industry, or that fall behind in some way, are susceptible to 'lock-out' in the sense that they are liable to find it increasingly difficult to catch up to – much less overtake – the leading contenders.

Nevertheless, the onward march of development in economically successful regions is always in practice subject to eventual cessation or reversal, not only because there *are* often limits to the continued generation of external economies, but also because radical shifts in markets, technologies, skills, and so on, can undermine any given regional configuration of production. Indeed, the very existence of lock-in effects means that regions, as they develop and grow, will eventually find it difficult to adapt to certain kinds of external shocks. At times like these we are apt to observe dramatic shifts in the geographic bases of production, involving the demise of formerly growing industrial regions, and the rise of alternative growth centers unhampered by the weight of antecedent production routines, cultures, and norms, and more able to take advantage of the changing economic climate. The recent study by Saxenian (1994) of the relocation of the dominant spatial nexus of the US computer industry over the 1980s, from the rather rigid production complex that had developed along Route 128 to the more open and flexible Silicon Valley, provides a vivid illustration of this point. On a grander scale, the decline of the US Manufacturing Belt and the rise of the Sunbelt after the late 1960s can in significant degree be interpreted as a locational response to the crisis of Fordist mass production and the rapid growth of new kinds of flexible production systems that right from the outset were indifferent to (if not averse to) the specific kinds of agglomeration effects available in the large industrial cities of the Northeast (Scott, 1988b).

A Historical-Geographic Perspective

From the very historical beginnings of capitalism, city-regions have functioned in important ways as sites of agglomerated and specialized production activities. The conceptual generalizations of the previous two sections represent important stepping stones toward an understanding of this phenomenon, but we also need to pay close attention to substantive problems of historical geography. This is an especially significant issue because the complex relationships discussed above do not play themselves out in stable configurations of forces at all times and in all places. Quite apart from the specific effects of variables like scale, sector, or nation on the way these relationships operate, they are subject to massive restructuring as a function of periodic temporal shifts in the organization and modalities of accumulation in capitalism. Moreover, as the Manufacturing Belt/Sunbelt example cited above suggests, such restructuring often has the effect of freeing production from dependence on the pre-existing geographic pattern of agglomeration economies, thereby opening up windows of locational opportunity and making it possible for new industrial spaces and regions to come into being. Three specific examples are apposite here.

In the first place, then, the *workshop and factory system* that emerged so strongly in parts of England in the late eighteenth and early nineteeenth centuries gave rise to a veritable revolution in patterns of urban and regional development at that time. Considerable segments of the production apparatus were made up of small and vertically disintegrated firms forming dense transactional networks. The geography of production was accordingly and to a significant degree arranged in classical Marshallian industrial districts forming the basis of much of the peculiar pattern of urbanization that characterized the period. Familiar examples of this phenomenon are cottons in Lancashire, woolens in Yorkshire, cutlery in Sheffield, and the metal trades of Birmingham.

In the second place, the system of *Fordist mass production* that flourished in the Northeast of the United States from the 1920s to the 1960s also brought about significant reorganization of the economic landscape. In this instance, the leading edges of production were to a great degree embodied in large lead plants in growth pole industries, around which multitiered complexes of direct and indirect input suppliers congregated in both functional and spatial terms. Such complexes typically constituted the economic foundations of the overgrown industrial metropolitan regions of the twentieth century (Detroit, Chicago, Pittsburgh, and so on). This was a moment in the historical geography of capitalism when distinctive relations of polarization and trickledown were established between the principal industrial core regions and a dependent set of peripheral areas, culminating in the so-called 'new international division of labor' of the 1970s and 1980s (Fröbel et al., 1980; Hirschman, 1958; Myrdal, 1957). The polarization/ trickledown relationship was epitomized above all by a tendency for core regions to evolve as agglomerations of high-wage economic activities and for peripheral regions (now increasingly identified with the Third World) to become depots for dispersed low-wage, blue-collar branch plants.

In the third and final place, a contemporary process of *flexible industrialization* is helping to create a series of new industrial spaces in selected regions of world capitalism (cf. Scott, 1988b). This third case is distinguished by a proliferation of flexible production networks in industries as diverse as biotechnology and multimedia games production, and by a resurgence of industrial districts and agglomerations in many different parts of the world. In their turn, the cities and regions that have most actively participated in this type of industrialization now also find themselves bound tightly together in world-wide webs of interdependence, with multinational firms playing a major role in mediating between the local and the global. The principal locations of this current model of industrialization and regional development are places like Silicon Valley, the Third Italy, the rapidly growing industrial regions of East and South East Asia, or the many cultural-products agglomerations that are now developing in many different parts of the world.

This latest espisode in the historical geography of capitalism is based on industrial systems with a high degree of functional decentralization and open-endedness, and yet which are also capable of efficient and diversified production at many different levels of scale (Coriat, 1990; Piore and Sabel, 1984). We might say – very schematically – that whereas nineteenth century workshop and factory systems were able to produce variety of output but were limited in the total scale that they could achieve, and whereas Fordist mass production freed industry from quantitative restraint but at the expense of product variety, modern flexible production systems (with the aid of new electronic and information technologies) are able to achieve considerable variety of output while they also often generate significant economies of scale. Further, because flexible production systems tend to be strongly externalized (hence transactions-intensive), spatial agglomeration seems once more to be resurgent, in contrast to the steady break-up of many industrial regions that was occurring as Fordism approached its climacteric. Regions are once again emerging as important foci of production and as repositories of specialized know-how and technological capability, even as the globalization of economic relationships proceeds apace.

Despite the claims one sometimes hears to the effect that this trend to globalization represents a sort of universal deterritorialization/liquefaction of world capitalism, modern flexible production activities remain firmly anchored in durable regional clusters of capital and labor. As Storper (1992) has very aptly pointed out, there are limits to globalization in the sense that agglomerated production systems remain critical foundations of value-adding activity in production and of competitive advantages in trade.

Policy Issues

I have contended that regional clusters of industrial activity are generally endowed with latent productivity effects, though these are not always fully realized in practice, and, furthermore, not all regional clusters perform equally well. Thus, I now propose to look at some of the ways in which urban and regional economic performance can falter and at how policy can help to ameliorate this state of affairs. More generally, I describe the beneficial effects of certain kinds of non-market coordination on regional economic development, and the role of public action in the construction of localized competitive advantages. The search for effective policy of this sort in regard to cultural-products sectors will no doubt grow more intense in the future as these sectors become ever more important vehicles of local employment growth.

I argued earlier that one of the essential characteristics of industrial regions is their status as *collectivities* of producers, i.e. as clusters of inter-dependent activities whose mutual proximity to one another creates complex, dynamic flows of agglomeration economies. Because many of these agglomeration economies take the form of externalities that fall outside of any market system of allocation they are likely to be significantly misallocated in the absence of some ameliorative social institutions. Variation in these kinds of institutions from region to region can have important implications for differences in industrial performance, and because they are inherently in the domain of collective (as opposed to individual) decision-making and behavior, they represent important opportunities for political mobilization in the interests of local economic competitiveness. Here, I am concerned not so much with the conventional problem of policy as viewed by many neoclassical economists where the issues boil down to a trade-off between (lower levels of) market-driven economic efficiency on the one hand and social goals on the other, but with the actual enhancement of efficiency itself by means of collective action.

In its simplest form, the imperative of regional economic policy grows directly out of the general need to patch up manifest market failures in the external milieu of regional production systems. Indeed, regional authorities commonly deal in practice with this need by engaging in activities such as the provision of urban equipment, the planning of industrial land use, or the mitigation of pollution problems. But the imperative goes far beyond this initial point of departure. It also grows out of the circumstance that economic competitiveness and growth can often be much improved by policies that take direct aim at the regional production system as such, and that seek to promote many-sided spatial and temporal externalities as described above. It goes without saying that this is a tactic that is fraught with heavy risks, and conventional economic ideology suggests that market-clearing mechanisms can always do the job more effectively than policy-makers. But quite apart from the possibility of market failures and dysfunctional competitive contests at the very heart of the regional production system itself, markets in any case can never (except in libertarian fantasies) occur in a pure form in capitalism. The very existence of markets is contingent on a framework of social norms and institutions – legal conventions, managerial ideologies and practices, structures of inter-firm cooperation and collaboration, forms of worker socialization, traditions of craftsmanship, reputation effects, etc. – that at the same time profoundly shape the manner of their operation (North, 1990). I want to argue that in the case of localized industrial complexes, significant augmentation of market capability by means of collective adjustment of the social bases of production can be achieved on at least three main fronts, as follows.

First, *critical inputs and services* supplied as public goods to producers can be decisive factors in stimulating urban and regional growth. They are of special significance in cases (a) where private firms have a propensity to underinvest in the provision of essential needs, and (b) where these needs also have an agglomeration-specific character. Two notable cases of this phenomenon are technological research and labor training activities relevant to specialized regional requirements. However, many additional examples might be offered, ranging from the gathering of information about export opportunities to the advertising and marketing of regional products. The municipalities of the Third Italy have been in the vanguard of this sort of policy-making and planning (Bianchi, 1992).

Second, *cooperation* among firms in the tasks of production makes it possible to achieve more efficient transactional interactions, though its attainment is dependent on the willingness of firms to sacrifice some of their autonomy for the sake of higher aggregate levels of productivity. To achieve this goal, some sort of (formal or informal) governance relation is needed to maintain order and continuity over time, and to minimize disruptive defections from the regional cohort of producers. Organized collaboration between firms also makes it more feasible for them to learn from one another and to pool critical technologies and labor skills in the interests of superior combinations of productive resources. Regional industrial consortia and private–public partnerships are one way of stimulating this sort of collaboration.

Third, *forums for strategic choice and action* are essential for regional economic success in the modern world. In some cases, they may have quite limited scope and aims, as exemplified by agencies concerned with tasks like securing trademarks for regional products, or producers' associations that seek to head off short-term forms of wage or price gouging that might undermine the long-term viability of the regional production system as a whole. But they are also on occasions much more ambitious in their objectives, as in the case of regional economic councils (in Germany, for example) that regularly bring together major local constituencies (e.g.

employers, banks, workers' organizations, and municipal government) to debate questions of long-term industrial order and that seek to forge viable strategies of regional management. Steering mechanisms like this are exceptionally significant given the tendency of regional economic systems to evolve through time on the basis of branching processes whose structure is such that there can be no assurances that the market will always select out the best long-run developmental options (David, 1985; Lipsey, 1994).

Observe that I refrain from intrusive pronouncement on the appropriate form of the agencies and organizations that might undertake the tasks enumerated above. Depending on local traditions, culture, and political dispositions, such tasks might be performed by local government bodies, associations of relevant civil parties such as employers and workers, or any number of different kinds of private–public consortia or partnerships. The point here is simply to aver that there is an important and positive role for agents of collective order to play in local industrial development. Quite apart from its significance in promoting agglomeration economies and regional competitive advantage, this role is critical to the maintenance of commitments by all major parties in the region to continued and creative participation (i.e. voice as opposed to exit), and thus to the reinforcement of the social cohesion of the entire regional economy (cf. Friedmann, 1993).

This is a view of local economic development that diverges greatly from the standard approach based on direct and indirect fiscal incentives. In this standard approach, an arsenal of subsidies and tax relief measures is typically deployed by state and municipal authorities in an effort to attract new industrial investments, often without proper scrutiny of the total social costs involved. By contrast, the kinds of development strategies suggested in the present chapter involve system-wide (bottom-up) approaches and institutional reorganization – rather than large-scale financial commitments to narrowly defined objectives – and because of this, they are presumably quite cost-effective. They also have the desirable feature that they allow markets to eliminate firms that fail. The catch, of course, is that the approach outlined here is not a guaranteed passport to unhindered further development. In particular, it does not seem to offer a great deal of hope to regions that have not already moved some distance down the pathway of development and that have not yet managed to acquire at least some sort of internal industrial synergy. To make matters even more difficult for the left-behinds (and in view of the existence of first-mover advantages and dynamic lock-out effects, as argued earlier), any region that seeks to initiate a process of local economic development within its borders needs to pay very close attention indeed to the task of identifying feasible production niches, i.e. forms of economic activity that have not yet been irreversibly dominated by more highly developed regions. As the experience of many actual local economic development efforts over the 1980s demonstrates, it is in general not advisable to attempt to become a Silicon Valley when Silicon Valley already exists elsewhere (that is, unless there are grounds for supposing that some decisive and hitherto unexploited local advantage can be brought into play).

* * *

If correct, this overall analysis suggests that we are likely to witness an efflorescence of region-based modes of economic regulation as modern flexible production begins to run its course and the imperative of localized coordination and cooperation becomes more pressing. The gales of intensified competition unleashed by economic globalization make this imperative all the more urgent, especially as much of the most intense competition comes precisely from regions (e.g. in Germany, Italy, Japan, Singapore, and Taiwan) that have made substantial progress toward addressing problems of regional economic coordination and planning. Should the world's major industrial regions begin systematically to build strong collective political identities in this fashion, the result will almost surely be sharply intensified conflicts and collisions between them over the ways in which they seek individually to promote their economic interests.

The latter observation leads in turn to the prediction that in the new global mosaic of regional economies, we are also going to see novel forms of institution-building precisely for the purpose of regulating such friction, not just at the national level, but at the international level as well. This sort of institution-building is already well under way in the European Economic Community, and I believe that it is likely to become significantly evident in North America and Mexico as NAFTA begins to run its course. Inter-regional coordination will be necessary, too, to eliminate predatory poaching of any one region's industrial assets by others, to head off wasteful developmental races between different regions, and to promote beneficial inter-regional joint ventures. Such coordination will be even more essential if disputes between the world's succesful regions and the left-behinds should begin to escalate, and if there should be concomitant political pressures to achieve some form of inter-regional income redistribution. As we shift increasingly into the new global framework of regional production systems described here, many further tasks of political integration will predictably appear on the horizon, and many new and unforeseen challenges to democratic rules of order will no doubt need to be dealt with.

Geography and Economics

In all of the above, I have attempted to provide a broad understanding of the ways in which economic geography and industrial performance are intertwined with one another. I have argued that the endemic tendency in capitalism for dense localized clusters of productive activity to appear at different locations on the landscape has major implications for economic growth and productivity. These clusters are constituted as transactions-intensive regional economies which are in turn caught up in structures of interdependency stretching across the entire globe. As such, they also represent important foundations of much contemporary international trade. I have shown that these clusters can be effectively scrutinized in terms of three main analytical maneuvers involving the study of (a) the synchronic formation of external economies in transactions-intensive production systems, and (in a world that is still without benefit of magic carpets) the associated tendency to agglomeration, (b) the dynamics of path-dependent development within complex localized economic systems, and (c) the periodic restructuring of these relationships, and their differential regional manifestation (including the cultures and habits that help to sustain them) in varying historical-geographical contexts.

In the light of these basic axes of analysis, I have also tentatively proposed a generic policy agenda for dealing with those tasks of regional development that will in all probability become urgent as we move more decisively into an era of international flexible capitalism. No doubt, if and when these tasks are more clearly formalized in practice, various kinds of intra-regional as well as inter-regional political cleavages will start to take shape around them.

In sum, I have set forth a story about processes and patterns of regional development that is an amalgam of various theoretical influences, ranging from modern economic geography on the one side to institutionalist/evolutionary economics on the other, with gestures to the new trade and growth theory along the way. It is a story that breaks decisively with neoclassical regional science, and that sees structural relations, discontinuities, and increasing returns where the neoclassical approach remains fixated on the assumptions of perfect competition and the quest for static equilibrium descriptions of the space economy. Perhaps even more strikingly, this story also goes resolutely against the grain of those recent and numerous commentaries that describe the modern world as a sort of placeless expanse caught up in a universal structure of flows. It is true, of course, that the extraordinary efficiency of modern transportation and communication technologies makes possible many new and far-flung spatial configurations of the world economy. This possibility is realized, however, not through the elimination of the effects of geography, but in the concrete appearance of ever more finely grained patterns of locational differentiation and specialization and inter-regional trade. In the world we inhabit today, space has not become less important as a factor in the structuring of economic processes; on the contrary, it has become considerably more important.

3
THE CREATIVE FIELD AND THE LOGIC OF INNOVATION IN IMAGE-PRODUCING COMPLEXES

In the previous chapter, I argued that production systems in modern capitalism are often geographically configured as dense and many-sided agglomerations of firms and workers. Such agglomerations typically function as fields of creative effects promoting high rates of innovation in products and processes. In cultural-products industries the manner in which these effects are played out in practice is especially perplexing because they are manifest above all in subtle shifts in the form and meaning of final outputs. The special challenge posed by focusing on creativity and innovation in the cultural economy is that the problem has a peculiar purity due to its relative (but not absolute) freedom from underlying technological constraints and its dominantly cognitive character.

In its most compactly stated formulation, the question of creativity and innovation is concerned with how new ways of acting or doing come to be envisioned (roughly, *creativity*) and how they are implemented in practice (roughly, *innovation*), though the meanings of the two italicized terms can never in practice be sharply differentiated from one another. In addition, the question is centrally concerned with whether or not creativity and innovation are themselves engendered or bounded by wider social processes, and if so how. If this question has relevance to all forms of social life, it takes on special meaning in relation to the cultural economy because this is a domain of production whose outputs consist of artifacts imbued with imaginative aesthetic and semiotic content – sometimes even at high levels of artistic accomplishment – while at the same time they are subject to the discipline of profitability criteria and market signals (i.e. they are produced in commodity form).

The Production of Culture

There is an extended literature in the social sciences which argues that culture – even, let us say, in Williams' (1982) rather general sense of the 'informing spirit' of a whole way of life – can best be understood as a social phenomenon rather than as the expression of some transcendent personalized impulse. Culture, in short, is an immanent construct whose form and substance are comprehensible only in terms of the wider systems of human relationships with which it is bound up (see, for example, Bordwell et al., 1985; Crane, 1992; Negus, 1998; Wolff, 1981). Furthermore, this argument can be advanced not just for the case of culture as embodied in the tangible artifacts that constitute the materiality of everyday life, but also as it is expressed in such apparently rarified domains of human activity as art or science. To be sure, there are powerful versions of aesthetic and epistemological theory that arrogate to themselves special authority to issue warrants for artistic and scientific activity, respectively (cf. Hennion, 1989), but this view is increasingly in retreat in the light of recent scholarly work showing how aesthetic and scientific practices connect even at their most intimate moments of genesis with concrete social conditions.

Writers on the sociology of art and culture, such as Becker (1974; 1976; 1982), Bourdieu (1983), Crane (1992), or White and White (1965), and on the sociology of knowledge, such as Barnes (1974), Barnes et al. (1996), Latour and Woolgar (1979), Mannheim (1952), or Mulkay (1972), have very effectively dealt a blow to any attempt to consign creativity and innovation to that special and mysterious primal moment signaled by a flash of light in the brain of the lonely prodigy. The arguments that may be advanced in support of this sociological approach are representable crudely in four broad (overlapping) remarks, all of which emphasize the intensely socialized nature of all artistic or scientific (more generally, cultural) labor:

1 What can be identified as viable (i.e. intersubjectively meaningful) topics for art works or scientific projects are socially given out of conditions of practical and political life.

2 Practical artistic or scientific work is always actively molded by the contextual conditions in which it occurs. For present purposes, one of the more significant aspects of this issue is represented by the division of labor in cultural production, even in such apparently elusive cases as a music recording studio or a modern scientific laboratory.

3 Art and science are forms of expression that rely on interpersonal norms, theories, methods, and so on, in order for them to achieve communicability. This means that both practitioners and audiences will have had to undergo some degree of socialization and habituation in regard to these common points of reference if they are to participate in the process of communication. Even while these points of reference are being transformed by ongoing artistic and scientific work, they provide a necessary social infrastructure of understandings and expectations.

4 The social profile of consumers of art and science, and the conscious or unselfconscious uses to which they put the outputs that they consume, invariably plays a role in how producers conceive and present their finished work. This is all the more the case where intermediaries (such as agents, editors, owners of art galleries, and so on) play an active role

in linking producers to consumers, and vice versa, so that these inter-mediaries themselves often come to have an important influence on the molding of the final product (Hennion, 1989; White and White, 1965).

The significance of these propositions to the issue of creativity and innovation in the cultural economy can be summarized in two simple remarks. In the first place, they help us to demystify the notion of cultural production in general, and to see the cultural economy as just another way of producing human culture. In the second place, they help to drive home the important point that while the cultural economy may be just another way of producing culture, it does not produce just any kind of culture. On the contrary, the outputs of the modern cultural economy bear a determinate relationship to their social conditions of production.

In none of this is there any necessary denial of the talents, imagination, dispositions (*à la* Bourdieu), or even genius of the individual cultural worker. The point is not that these qualities do not exist or are always submerged in the anonymous machinery of commodified production, but that on the contrary, they are mobilized and channeled by the broad functional characteristics of that machinery, including the specific ways in which many different specialized but complementary workers come together in the tasks of cultural production (cf. DiMaggio, 1977; DiMaggio and Hirsch, 1976). This statement applies no matter whether we are dealing with sectors like furniture or clothing where workers' identities tend to be relatively hidden from the consumer, or sectors like film or music where (some) workers' identities are more overtly inscribed on the final product. It applies in particular because modern cultural-economic systems almost always take the form of complex inter- and intra-firm networks in which many different hands and interests are brought to bear on products as they go through the process of conception, elabora-tion, and final embellishment. The functional attributes of these networks are deeply marked by economic pressures, which in cultural-products sectors are often contradictorily expressed – depending on wider circum-stances – in efforts either (a) to economize on costs by standardizing outputs, or (b) to ward off competitive threats by means of constant product differentiation.

The cultural element in the cultural economy, then, needs to be treated as both an endogenous construct and an authentic vehicle of aesthetic and semiotic expression (no matter how well or badly achieved in any given instance).

Place and Community

An initial and rather obvious way of proceeding is to point to the circum-stance that many types of cultural production, whether in the commodity form or not, are rooted in unique communities of workers anchored to particular places. Examples range over the gamut from traditional craft communities, such as the brahmin painters of Nathdwara in northwest India as described by Maduro (1975), through the numerous artistic and intellectual circles in nineteenth and twentieth century European cities (cf. Bourdieu, 1977; Hall, 1998; Menger, 1993), to the groups of writers, actors, directors, special effects personnel, and so on that make up the film colonies of contemporary Paris or Hollywood. Place-based communities such as these are not just foci of cultural labor in the narrow sense, but also active hubs of social reproduction in which crucial cultural competencies are maintained and circulated. They are, too, magnets for talented individuals from other places who migrate to these centers in search of professional fulfillment and who in turn help to maintain local cultural energies (Denisoff and Bridges, 1982; Menger, 1983; 1993).

The examples cited above already hint at one of the representative features of such communities, namely, that they are less constituted as miscellaneous jumbles of individuals following many different and disconnected pursuits, than they are comparatively homogeneous collectivities whose members are caught up in mutually complementary and socially coordinated careers (cf. Montgomery and Robinson, 1993). A major factor binding such collectivities together is the traditions and conventions that invariably come into being in any localized social group that has subsisted over some period of time. As such, they are the repositories of an accumulated interpersonal cultural capital connecting generations of workers to one another through time and serving to orchestrate each collectivity's internal and external relations. This capital is maintained and renewed in daily contact both in the workplace and out of it.

Cultural capital is further sustained by the distinctive institutional infrastructures with which most agglomerations of image-producing industries are endowed. The core of these infrastructures is typically made up of the specialized apprenticeship programs, schools, training establishments, and so on that are a recurrent feature of well-established communities of specialized workers and that provide for a ready supply of appropriately prepared neophytes. Workers' organizations, such as unions, guilds, or professional associations, aid in securing the material interests of those engaged in the tasks of production, and in various ways contribute further to the maintenance of local standards of cultural and economic performance. Other, more idiosyncratic institutions, too, will occasionally be found in these communities, ranging from specialized museums or associations devoted to keeping alive memories of past accomplishments, to annual festivities focused on celebrating the achievements of the immediate present.

This kind of ideational and relational collective order is very much what is meant by Marshallian industrial atmosphere, i.e. an externality or public good providing a stock of resources that facilitate the adaptation of workers into relevant skills, habits, and sensitivities, that help to keep a due sense of craftsmanship alive, and that simultaneously provide a platform for creative and innovative activity. Atmosphere, too, eases the tasks of intra-community communication, and can be the essential common ground on which groups of firms or workers come together in the solution of workaday problems.

Each given community represents a unique and complex case in which inventiveness on the one hand and conventional or institutional constraint on the other create a tension-filled developmental dynamic. In the traditional brahmin painter community described by Maduro (1975) a highly restrictive tradition keeps creativity and innovation within tight bounds. In the case of the country music performers who congregate in large numbers in and around Nashville, Tennessee, common adherence to a strongly demarcated musical genre is tempered by occasional bravura demonstrations of originality that periodically stretch its boundaries (cf. Peterson and DiMaggio, 1975; Ryan and Peterson, 1982). In contemporary Hollywood, a new wave of creativity and innovation has been unleashed by the digital effects revolution which has prompted a wholesale reevaluation of the art and practice of making feature films.

Production System and Milieu: The Logic of Creativity and Innovation

Communities of skilled and socialized cultural workers are one thing; mobilizing them into efficacious patterns of productive employment is another. It is only when we introduce the much more expansive notion of the production system and its milieu that we really start to grapple with the mainsprings of creativity and innovation in the cultural economy. We need, however, to go well beyond conventional 'gatekeeping' models of the cultural economy (Hirsch, 1969; 1972). In these models, the production system is described simply as a filtering device through which some kinds of (exogenously-given) novelties are allowed to pass while others are rejected along the way. Gatekeeping in this sense is no doubt an epiphenomenon of commercialized forms of cultural production, but it does not take us very far in understanding the actual origins of cultural products. The objective in the discussion below is to focus more intently on creativity and innovation as endogenous properties of the production system itself.

We may begin with a brief allusion to the work of Hennion (1981; 1983; 1989) and Kealy (1979) on the internal operations of recording studios in the popular music industry, though we might equally as well have started off with such analogous sites of cultural labor as the fashion designer's workshop, magazine editing and paste-up operations, the role of teamwork in the production of a multimedia game, or film shooting and editing procedures.

In his 1989 paper, Hennion likens the production of recorded music to the execution of scientific experiments in that the recording studio and the laboratory both represent organized social milieux where groups of workers seek by trial and error to obtain results that can then be made public. What is never made public, however (except by the inquisitive social anthropologist), is how these results are influenced by the purely human and often quite messy internal order of the laboratory or studio. In the recording studio, the interactions between the composer/arranger, the individual performers (including studio musicians), the producer, the sound engineer, and other critical individuals, constitute an inherently collective sphere of artistic experimentation and invention, and even the efforts of the performers themselves do not necessarily always comprise the most decisive ingredient of what is actually realized on the final recording (Kealy, 1979).

This is a perspective on cultural production that resolutely eschews any attempt to ascribe the commercial and artistic success of a given recording uniquely to some irreducible primary property of the original musical text. And where, as in much popular music recording today, there is no original text outside of the nexus of commercial interests that defines the industry, the argument holds with all the more emphasis. The finished products that emerge out of the cultural economy are the results of a collaborative labor process that involves many different specialized operations by many different individuals (cf. Frith, 1992; Negus, 1996; Ryan and Peterson, 1982). Even the stars who occupy the pinnacle positions on the work ladder of the cultural economy are in a certain sense an intrinsic expression of its logic.

In view of these remarks, there is no special reason why we should call a halt to our investigations at the outer walls of the recording studio. The studio is only one element, a sort of microcosm, of a much more extensive field of production activities in the cultural economy, and hence of creative and innovative energies. This field includes not just the production system *sensu stricto* but also the entire geographic milieu within which production occurs. Indeed, the production system and the geographic milieu are just two faces of a single economic and cultural reality represented by dense agglomerated structures of employment and social life.

Regional systems of creativity and innovation

One of the central claims of the ample literature on learning and technical change in industrial systems generally is that many improvements in product and process configurations flow steadily from the multiple, small, unrecorded, day-by-day encounters that occur between the different participants in production networks as they go about their business (Lundvall and Johnson, 1994; von Hippel, 1988). Encounters like these are particularly common in industrial agglomerations with deeply disintegrated production systems. Those that involve negotiations over the design specifications of products and services as they pass along the input–output chain appear to be a remarkably rich source of ameliorative action. In a study of ceramic tile production in Sassuolo, Italy, Russo (1985) showed that a constant flow of small-scale but cumulatively important adjustments in production practices could be traced back to detailed interactions between firms at different levels in the social division of labor as they learned how to deal with each other's strengths and weaknesses in regard to specific projects.

In cultural-products agglomerations, these types of interactions are usually well developed given the many different specialized functions that make them up. Moreover, in the cultural economy, they are apt to be characterized by close collaboration between the different parties involved, no matter whether it be in the design and fabrication of a piece of jewelry or in the planning and execution of a media event, so that the conse-quences in terms of learning will tend to be all the more sharply in evidence. The gains in know-how and the beneficial on-the-job adjustments that occur in this manner refer not only to concrete practices and tech-niques, but also to the emotive content of products. Workers caught up in this sort of transformative activity are likely to emerge with a deepened and heightened awareness of the imaginative and emotive possibilities to be discovered within and around their domains of expertise.

The frequent shifts and turns of markets for cultural products mean that these interactions are typically subject to rapid rotation, thus heightening the learning effects described. In fact, with sufficiently large pools of appropriately specialized firms and workers, the number of different com-binatorial variations in the structure of production networks is effectively unlimited, and in industries where there is an incessant search for just the right kind of fashion or novelty effect in final products, this degree of system flexibility carries great weight. Perhaps the most dramatic instance of this phenomenon can be found in the popular music industry where recording companies maintain a profuse but ever changing flow of short single releases in the effort to win a place on the lottery of the hit parade (see Chapter 8).

These remarks pick up on and extend the notion of the learning region as it has been described, for example, by theorists such as Cooke and Morgan (1998) or Storper (1996). However, the concept of regional systems of creativity and innovation as developed in preliminary form in the preceding pages goes well beyond the domain of technology-intensive production – the usual focus of learning-region studies – and incorporates the even more enigmatic phenomenon of the cultural economy generally. This concept refers not only to agglomerations of technologically dynamic firms, but also to places where qualities such as cultural insight, imagina-tion, and originality are actively generated from within the local system of production, and put into service in the shaping of final outputs. At the level of the regional collectivity, these qualities can be theorized not so much as the outward expression of inscrutable psychological processes as the determinate effects of a many-sided economic and geographic system of production (cf. Csikszentmihalyi, 1990).

This last proposition is well illustrated by modern film industry agglo-merations, as in Hollywood or Paris, where scores if not hundreds of different specialized firms come regularly but always variously together on particular projects. In these circumstances, any film – even a *film d'auteur* – is actually a huge collective venture. Nor can we meaningfully describe the final film in Manicheistic terms as the reflection of an initial and unadulterated artistic concept distorted and coopted (depending on the balance of power between the director and the producer) by business interests. The final product is always, from the first, a cultural and an economic artifact at one and the same time. It is no doubt from this perspective that we can finally make sense of the celebrated but otherwise cryptic afterthought that Malraux (1946) appended to his study of the psychology of cinema to the effect that film-making is not only an art but also, intrinsically, an industry.

Temporality of the Creative-Innovative Field

Thus far in the analysis, I have treated creativity and innovation in the cultural economy as largely synchronic processes. How, we might ask, are these activities realized and shaped through time, and, again, what are the spatial correlates of any dynamics that we might uncover?

A pioneering attack on the question of temporal shifts of creativity and innovation in the cultural economy was mounted by Peterson and Berger (1975; 1996) in their study of the recorded music industry in the United States. Peterson and Berger defined diversity as simply the number of different recording companies, or labels, with titles listed on *Billboard's* Hot 100 music charts. Their study of data from these charts over the 1950s and 1960s concluded that the diversity of hit records is subject to cyclical oscillations over time.

These oscillations appear to depend on an intricate competitive interplay between major recording companies and small independents in final product markets. Peterson and Berger observed that at times when the majors dominate the market, product diversity as defined diminishes; when independents are in the ascendant, diversity increases. These phases succeed one another in a revolving sequence in accordance with the following logic:

1 When the diversity of hit records is at a low level due to the majors' control of the market, new niches nevertheless begin to appear beyond the margins of the current mainstream.
2 Many of these niches are explored by risk-taking independents, and as some of them find popular favor the diversity of entries on the hit parade will increase.
3 Some of these niches accordingly become commercially lucrative, and the majors will proceed to take them over, thus creating a new mainstream with eventually diminished diversity of products.
4 But then new margins and exploratory possibilities for risk-taking independents appear; and so on.

This general approach has been extended and corroborated by analysts such as Alexander (1996), Christianen (1995), and Gronow (1983). In addition, Burnett (1990; 1992; 1993) and Lopes (1992) have pointed out that since the end of the 1970s an independent time trend toward increasing diversity in Hot 100 hits appears to have become intertwined with – and is now possibly beginning to override – this cyclical process (see Chapter 8). In all likelihood, this circumstance is due to the increasing tendency for majors to absorb (in the form of affiliates) independent recording companies so as to diversify their portfolios of market offerings.

A more extended analysis of the temporal field of creativity and innovation in the cultural economy can be developed by examining the evolutionary dynamics of the cultural economy *qua* interlocking networks of production. Complexes of producers in the cultural economy are by definition made up out of arrays of closely interdependent firms and individuals, and the intensity of their interactions tends to be especially great in large agglomerations. In these circumstances, any given complex will be apt to trace out a developmental trajectory that is governed in some degree by the interdependent logic of all of its different component elements. This usually means that the complex as a whole is subject to the system-wide branching and lock-in processes, as described in the previous chapter.

Obviously, levels of creativity and innovation are very much at stake as this sort of evolutionary process works its course. One of the most pervasive forms of lock-in in the types of systems under scrutiny here is the situation exemplified by Maduro's brahmin painters where the codes and styles of cultural performance become so highly conventionalized that further structural change is negligible. In the immediate postwar years, the film industry of Hollywood was relatively locked in to a studio system of production, and this state of affairs greatly impeded it at first from responding to the competitive pressures that were increasingly coming from the burgeoning television industry (Maltby, 1981). Under the stimulus of this external threat, the industry gradually and painfully restructured over the 1950s and 1960s, above all by pursuing strategies of horizontal and vertical disintegration, and by this means its range of developmental alternatives began greatly to expand again. New rounds of creativity and innovation were thus unleashed in the industry, both in business practices and in the cultural content of films, culminating in the Hollywood of today with its myriad small adaptable firms moving rapidly from project to project, its wholesale embrace of digital production techniques, and its advanced distribution capabilities giving it a fully global reach.

Conclusion

Creativity and innovation in the modern cultural economy are thus in significant ways social phenomena that emerge directly out of the logic of the production system and its geographic milieu. As we have seen, these phenomena can be understood specifically in relation to four main levels of analysis: the formation of cultural communities, the organization of economic activity, the dynamics of agglomerated production systems, and the nature of competition. Once again, this claim about the immanence of creativity and innovation does not in any way depreciate the role of the individual as a repository of specific kinds of skills, aptitudes, and imaginative capacities. Indeed, the individual as the bearer of these endowments is indispensable to the whole process. Yet creativity and innovation are also imbricated in definite spatial and temporal fields of social activity in the specific sense that in the modern cultural economy they come actively into being in organized work situations where the talents and abilities of different individuals assume a collective order directed to economically determinate ends.

When the Frankfurt School theorists wrote their pessimistic prognostications about the looming eternal sameness and alienating effects of popular culture, they were making inductions from then current trends which they no doubt correctly apprehended. These trends were evident above all in the deepening corporate control of culture, and its expression in Fordist or proto-Fordist production methods, especially in film, commercial music, and the popular press. However, the world has not quite evolved as the members of the Frankfurt School anticipated. For one thing, there has been a shift to increasing diversity in many different sectors of the cultural economy, if only in the minimal sense of a widening of consumer choice in the range of products on offer. For another, one can plausibly argue, along with contemporary theorists like Featherstone (1995), Frith (1996), Garnham (1987), or Rowe (1995), that there are many segments of the cultural economy that can be said to be at the leading edges of cultural advancement and experimentation in modern society, and further that there is no necessary internal contradiction in this latter state of affairs. That said, large segments of the cultural economy will always no doubt produce dross of one sort or another, and the political critique of capitalist culture remains as urgent as ever, a point on which I shall elaborate at greater length in the final chapter of this book.

PART 2

TWO CRAFT INDUSTRIES: COLLECTIVE ORDER AND REGIONAL DESTINY

We turn now to an investigation of two craft sectors and their changing collective fortunes in selected regional clusters. The two sectors under scrutiny here are the gem and jewelry industry on one side, and the furniture industry on the other. These are sectors that are perhaps more commonly thought of as being traditional artisanal industries rather than cultural industries in the narrow sense of the term. However, they are assuredly elements of the cultural economy at large given that their outputs frequently exhibit strong design-intensive characteristics and function as both ornaments and social identifiers. These industries typically occur geographically in the form of specialized industrial districts located in large city-regions in various parts of the world. The firms in any one of these districts are almost always marked to an extraordinary degree by a common fate reflecting their intense local interdependencies.

Chapter 4 is a comparative study of gem and jewelry production in Los Angeles and Bangkok, with special emphasis on the contrasting competitive experiences of the industry in these two places. Chapter 5 deals with the household furniture industry of Los Angeles, showing how it has steadily dissipated its regional advantages by focusing on short-run cost-cutting business strategies as opposed to more long-term issues of product innovation and quality. The analytical emphasis in both of these chapters is on the relations between industrial organization, location, and institutional structure, and their effects on economic performance. Detailed examination of these issues provides an important bridge between the theoretical discussions of Part 1 and the studies of the various media industries that are at the core of Part 3.

4

THE GEM AND JEWELRY INDUSTRY IN LOS ANGELES AND BANGKOK

The gem and jewelry industry is for the most part a small craft-based and labor-intensive industry producing luxury goods for limited markets, and it has little of the imposing economic amplitude or dynamism of major cultural-products industries such as, for example, film production or music recording. It turns out on closer examination, however, that the gem and jewelry industry is of considerable interest and importance, both in its own right and as an instance of certain of the key conceptual issues that are at stake in this book; it is an especially noteworthy exemplar of the complex relations between spatial agglomeration and economic performance in the contemporary cultural economy. This remark rests on three main observations about the industry. First, gem and jewelry production tends to crystallize out in geographic space in the form of localized industrial districts, and these same districts also typically function as the focal points of world-wide networks of linkages. Second, in both its local and global dimensions, the industry is underpinned by peculiar cultural and social institutions governing inter-firm relations and the employment of labor. Third, notwithstanding its craft-based and labor-intensive character, the industry is potentially a significant motor of regional development (and in the specific case of Thailand over the 1980s and 1990s it has actually been a major source of economic growth and foreign exchange earnings).

The investigation here proceeds by means of a comparative empirical analysis of the gem and jewelry industry in Los Angeles and Bangkok, both of which cases are of a sufficient size to offer grist to the analyst's mill, while they also bear a number of striking contrasts to one another in terms of national context, patterns of growth, and the institutional bases of production. A major objective of the present account is to describe and account for the different economic fortunes of the two cases. After a brief description of the gem and jewelry industry in general, an overview of the specific features of the industry in both Los Angeles and Bangkok is offered on the basis of detailed questionnaire and interview data. The relations of production and exchange in both instances are shown to depend strongly on institutional arrangements that ensure security and trust. However, security and trust alone do not necessarily guarantee economic success. Unlike producers in Los Angeles, producers in Bangkok have been extremely effective in securing forceful political and quasi-political expression of their collective needs and goals, and this helps in part to explain the vastly more dynamic character of the industry in the latter area. The juxtaposition of these two cases provides the basis for a series of rather sharply defined and analytically revealing comparisons and contrasts.

The Organization of the Gem and Jewelry Industry

In the present study we are concerned only with *precious* (as opposed to artificial) gem and jewelry production.

The industry comprises a great many different specialized tasks and trades, though basic production processes can be broken down into three broad stages (cf. USITC, 1987). First, the rough gemstones (diamonds, emeralds, rubies, sapphires, etc.) are cut and polished. Second, precious and semi-precious metals are wrought into metallic settings by cutting, stamping, or casting; these settings may then be plated or treated in some way. Third, the cut and polished gemstones are set into place in the metallic settings and the final pieces of jewelry prepared for display. In practice, each stage may be broken down into yet more finely grained sets of production tasks.

These three main stages of production are concatenated with one another in varying degrees of vertical integration and disintegration; and much subcontracting of detailed tasks occurs in the industry. In addition, the industry is generally supported by phalanxes of service providers offering a wide range of inputs including machinery repair, security systems, courier services, bill factoring, jewelers' findings, and so on. The complexity of the industry is yet further augmented by the circumstance that it is usual to find widely variable degrees of overlap between the functions of manufacturing and wholesaling, and even retailing is rarely in practice clearly demarcated from either of these functions.

The industry is composed for the most part of small firms employing only a handful of workers, though large producers can also be found. Workers in the industry range from the highly skilled (in trades such as gem cutting, jewelry design, model-making, and so on) to the unskilled, with the latter being found especially in firms that operate toward the lower end of the market where craftsmanship and quality tend to give way before strong pressures to cut costs. The industry as a whole is markedly labor-intensive and technologically unsophisticated, in spite of recent attempts to introduce computer-integrated manufacturing systems into a number of factories. Like other industries (such as clothing or furniture) that are subject to rapid changes in fashion and taste, the gem and jewelry industry is highly competitive and unstable, and markets are typically fragmented into many different niches.

An important outcome of these structural characteristics is that the industry tends to be very transactions-intensive, and individual producers are almost always caught up in dense networks of inter-establishment linkages. In response to this state of affairs, producers are inclined to locate in close proximity to one another so as to reduce their overall transactions costs, and hence they form dense agglomerations – i.e. industrial districts – giving rise to potent externalities. Gem and jewlery industrial districts of this sort are to be found close to the cores of major cities throughout the world (e.g. New York, Amsterdam, Paris, Hong Kong, Tokyo, as well as Los Angeles and Bangkok), very often in association with a more dispersed pattern of larger factories at other locations. However, while the industry typically assumes this geographically concentrated form, jewelry industry products and services circulate with great ease on global markets so that the individual districts are bound together in intricate networks of business relations spanning the whole world. Each particular district is a focus of employment for many workers, and the intricate local labor market dynamics that ensue (e.g. the constant shifting of workers in and out of jobs, and the daily routine of homeplace–workplace commuting) serve to reinforce the spatial concentration of producers.

One final point must be made here. Because of the high value of the raw materials and outputs of the gem and jewelry industry, producers must take special care to ensure that security and confidence are established in both transactional relations and the employment of labor. This objective can be achieved by means of diverse controls, ranging from intensive direct policing to unselfconscious forms of socialization that inculcate requisite norms of behavior in inter-firm dealings and labor-force activities (cf. Coleman, 1988; Granovetter, 1985; Hanson, 1992; Herrigel, 1993; Lorenz, 1992).

The Jewelry Industry in Los Angeles

An overview

There is a significant jewelry manufacturing industry in Los Angeles, though (unlike the case of Bangkok) only negligible employment in gem cutting and polishing as such. In terms of the Standard Industrial Classification (SIC), the industry in Los Angeles can best be described in terms of SIC 3911 (jewelry and precious metal manufacturing) and SIC 5094 (jewelry and precious stones – wholesale). Recall that jewelry firms often combine both of these functions (in varying proportions) under one roof.

The jewelry industry of Los Angeles is actually a distant but significant outlier of the US jewelry industry as a whole, most of which is concentrated in the northeast of the country, and above all in New York City and Providence, RI. Table 4.1 lays out data on employment trends in the industry for Los Angeles County from 1974 to 1996. The table reveals that the industry is rather small in terms of employment (though it is characterized by large numbers of individual establishments), and that it has on the whole expanded only moderately over the 1980s and 1990s, with the manufacturing function showing a particular tendency to stagnation or at best slow growth. Los Angeles County accounted for 4.4% of all US employment in SICs 3911 and 5094 in 1974, and it accounted for as much

Table 4.1 *Employment in the jewelry industry of Los Angeles County, 1974–96*

	SIC 3911 (jewelry and precious metal manufacturing)	SIC 5094 (jewelry and precious stones – wholesale)
1974	938	1,681
1975	907	1,633
1976	1,073	1,938
1977	1,383	2,258
1978	1,543	2,152
1979	2,227	2,972
1980	1,832	3,107
1981	1,746	3,244
1982	1,861	3,070
1983	1,811	3,115
1984	1,886	3,294
1985	1,891	3,235
1986	2,075	3,487
1987	2,303	4,389
1988	2,352	4,117
1989	2,602	4,262
1990	2,381	4,336
1991	2,279	4,444
1992	1,994	4,877
1993	2,351	5,118
1994	2,012	4,995
1995	2,619	4,886
1996	2,990	4,916

Source: United States Department of Commerce, Bureau of the Census, *County Business Patterns*

as 9.2% in 1996. In 1996, the 7,906 employees in the county in SICs 3911 and 5094 were employed in 1,065 individual establishments. Average establishment size for the case of SIC 3911 in Los Angeles County was 11.9 workers, and for the case of SIC 5094 it was 6.0.

Within Los Angeles, the jewelry industry is predominantly located in a small area covering a few blocks at the core of the city, and located just to the north of the garment district (see Figure 4.1). This area lies between 5th Street in the north and 8th Street in the south, and between Olive Street in the west and Spring Street in the east. In this small but densely developed area are concentrated the vast majority of jewelry industry establishments in Los Angeles. This is the scene of an intense daily round of work activities and business transactions, and it is also the central axis of an elaborate network of formal and especially informal social institutions.

Many of the firms in the Los Angeles jewelry district belong to two major associations (whose headquarters, however, are in the northeast of the United States), namely, the Jewelers Board of Trade (JBT) and the Manufacturing Jewelers and Silversmiths of America (MJSA). The former organization maintains an office in Los Angeles. There is also a West

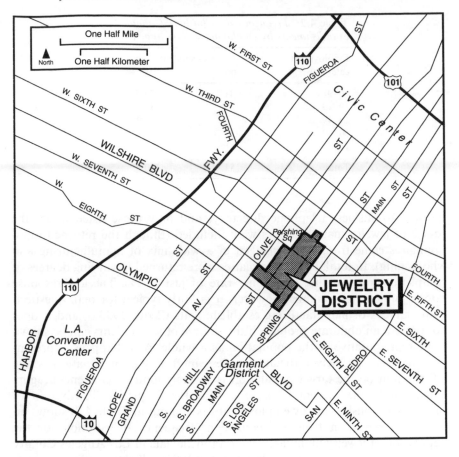

Figure 4.1   *The jewelry district of Los Angeles*

Coast Diamond Club which, unlike the JBT and MJSA, is directly focused on local issues, though the membership of the Club is confined to a select group of highly specialized firms. The purpose of the Club is to maintain business and ethical standards in the diamond trade and to serve as a forum of adjudication in the event of business disputes. It is associated with the World Federation of Diamond Bourses which seeks to promote these same standards on a global basis. In addition to these formal associations, the Gemological Institute of America, which provides specialized labor training services, maintains an establishment in Santa Monica; however, the Institute is far from the central jewelry district, and it serves a national – indeed global – clientele as much as it does a purely local one.

A questionnaire survey of the Los Angeles jewelry industry

Early in 1992, a mail questionnaire was sent to 593 jewelry producers in Los Angeles. The addresses of these producers were taken from the Los Angeles

Table 4.2   *Frequency distribution of sampled establishments by employment, Los Angeles*

Employment	Respondents	
category	no.	%
0–9	41	74.5
10–19	7	12.7
20–49	4	7.3
50–99	2	3.6
100+	1	1.8
Total	55	100.0

business-to-business telephone directory, and only those listed under the rubric of jewelry manufacturers were included (though the returned questionnaires came from firms engaged in a wide mix of manufacturing and wholesaling). In total, 60 questionnaires were returned in varying degrees of completion, representing a response rate of just 10.1%. The low response rate is, of course, troubling; however, it is fairly typical for mail questionnaire surveys of manufacturing establishments (Scott, 1993a), and it does not present an obdurate problem if the sample of respondents can be shown to be representative of the population as a whole. As it happens, representativeness is extremely difficult to assess in this type of situation where information on the target population is severely limited. One encouraging indication in the present instance is that the frequency distribution of surveyed establishments by employment (as laid out in Table 4.2) shows no significant deviation from the equivalent frequency distribution for the population of jewelry manufacturing establishments in Los Angeles County as reported in *County Business Patterns* for 1992; a Kolmogorov–Smirnoff test reveals that the sample distribution conforms to the underlying population distribution at well over the 99% level of confidence. Even so, there are likely to be hidden biases elsewhere in the survey data, and we must thus proceed with due caution. Much supplementary information was collected in interviews conducted by the author with 29 different jewelry producers in Los Angeles, and this information is also invoked in the overall discussion. The following is a brief statistical profile of establishments participating in the questionnaire survey.

By far the majority (i.e. 67.8%) of producers that responded to the questionnaire were located in downtown Los Angeles. Few respondents specialized exclusively in either manufacturing or wholesaling; on average they claimed to derive 48.9% of their business from manufacturing and 29.8% from wholesale activity, with the residue being made up by retail sales, repair work, and other activities. As many as 30.5% of the establishments surveyed were founded before 1970, with a small number actually pre-dating World War II. However, 28.8% were founded over the decade from 1970 to 1980, and 40.7% over 1980 to 1990. As Table 4.2 indicates, the vast majority of surveyed establishments were extremely small in size.

Table 4.3   *Methods used by employers to find new workers, Los Angeles jewelry industry*

	% respondents
Ask a current employee to recommend someone	53.3
Call another employer for a recommendation	46.7
Advertise in paper or trade magazine	31.7
Accept a random job applicant with references	13.3
Accept a random job applicant without references	6.7
Other	15.0

Up to 32.0% of establishments that responded to the questionnaire survey were run as partnerships, with two-thirds of all partnerships being composed of individuals related to one another through family. Owners of jewelry firms in Los Angeles come from an extraordinarily varied background in terms of ethnicity and place of birth. Out of 55 respondents, 15 indicated that they were Armenian, 12 Jewish, 10 Asian, 6 Hispanic, and 5 from Arab backgrounds. Fully 69.5% of the same respondents were born outside of the United States.

Among workers in these establishments, 24.6% were Hispanic and 17.2% were Asian. Females comprised 29.6% of the labor force. However, Hispanics, Asians, and women are evidently somewhat less well represented in the jewelry industry labor force than they are in the case of the adjacent garment industry (cf. Scott, 1988a), and many employers prefer to hire individuals who share their own ethnic or religious background (see below). As the interviews with jewelry firms revealed, much of the labor force is made up of unskilled, low-wage workers. There appears to be active circulation of workers through the job system of the jewelry industry, for 20.3% of the workers in surveyed establishments had been employed for less than one year. But the questionnaire also revealed the existence of a remarkably large stable core of employees in the industry, with 52.8% of all workers having been employed at the same workplace for three years or more. When employers search for new workers, they use a variety of different methods (see Table 4.3), though two in particular are clearly dominant. These involve either (a) asking their own employees to recommend prospective job applicants, or (b) asking other employers to suggest possible applicants. Both of these approaches ensure some degree of prior screening of prospective employees.

The questionnaire results indicate that on average respondents purchased 66.4% of all their inputs from other firms in the Los Angeles area; and they sold 53.9% of their output in the local area. Thus, while the industry in Los Angeles most certainly has wider national and international links, it is strongly turned in upon itself. Respondents also indicated that as much as 23.6% of all their business consisted of work subcontracted to them by other firms, which underlines the transactions-intensive nature of the Los Angeles complex.

From the above, we gain a provisional picture of the jewelry industry of Los Angeles as long-standing, transactions-intensive, marked by an extreme diversity of human resources, and both functionally and geographically convergent upon its own center of gravity. The industry is not, however, especially noted for the quality or cachet of its final products, and as the data presented in Table 4.1 suggest, its pattern of growth exhibits a marked absence of dynamism. By contrast, as we shall see, the gem and jewelry industry of Bangkok has expanded with exceptional rapidity over the 1980s and 1990s.

The Gem and Jewelry Industry in Bangkok

The national context

Thailand is today a major producer and exporter of both gems and jewelry. Rubies and sapphires have traditionally been mined in the country, especially in the provinces of Chantaburi and Kanchanburi. There is now a large industry in cutting and polishing these and other gems, much of it in the countryside where it exists as a cottage industry and provides a major supplement to farming income. The jewelry industry proper in Thailand grew in part out of this tradition of gem production.

By and large the gem and jewelry industry in Thailand operates at the cheaper end of the market where its advantage in labor costs is most conspicuous. Thus, it tends to specialize in the production of smaller stones and in large-batch jewelry manufacture. The industry, however, has recently been shifting into a mode of operation that entails increasingly higher labor skills, leading to improved product quality. There is no official count of the numbers of workers employed in the Thai gem and jewelry industry, either in Bangkok or in the country as a whole. The national total is commonly estimated by industry representatives as being close to 100,000 workers, though much of this is probably accounted for by part-time employment in rural areas. Still, this estimate compares dramatically with the few thousands of workers claimed to have been employed throughout Thailand in the industry in the 1950s (cf. Department of Export Promotion, 1991; *Thailand Gems and Jewellery Directory, 1991–1992*).

The magnitude and growth of the gem and jewelry industry in Thailand can be gauged by the changing value of its exports (see Table 4.4). These export figures are divided between gems and jewelry roughly in the ratio of three to two, respectively. According to a spokesperson for the Thai Gem and Jewelry Traders Association, perhaps 10% of the gems and almost all of the jewelry exported originate from firms in Bangkok. After the late 1970s, there was an explosion of growth in the industry, and its outputs became one of Thailand's major exports. Gems and jewelry indeed, along with clothing, have been among the most important sectors in Thailand's recent program of low-technology, labor-intensive industrialization

Table 4.4   *Thailand's exports of gems and jewelry, 1980–96*

	Gem and jewelry exports		Exports of all commodities		Gem and jewelry exports as % of all exports
	Current baht (millions)	1996 baht (millions)	Current baht (millions)	1996 baht (millions)	
1980	3,857	6,652	133,197	229,710	2.9
1981	5,148	8,795	153,000	261,393	3.4
1982	5,361	8,975	159,728	267,402	3.4
1983	7,352	12,078	146,471	240,624	5.0
1984	7,523	12,788	175,237	297,881	4.3
1985	8,727	14,506	193,365	321,415	4.5
1986	13,766	22,523	233,382	381,839	5.9
1987	29,825	46,335	299,853	465,845	9.9
1988	25,981	38,390	403,569	596,319	6.4
1989	39,225	55,212	516,315	726,745	7.6
1990	36,929	49,626	589,812	792,600	6.3
1991	38,393	48,607	725,777	918,856	5.3
1992	39,854	48,477	833,413	1,013,733	4.8
1993	44,215	52,031	949,608	1,117,480	4.7
1994	48,163	53,926	1,149,923	1,287,529	4.2
1995	54,272	57,449	1,405,633	1,487,925	3.9
1996	54,159	54,159	1,409,520	1,409,520	3.8

Source: National Statistical Office, Office of the Prime Mininster, *Statistical Yearbook of Thailand*

(Dollar, 1991), though by the early 1990s exports of electronic equipment and components were beginning to outstrip gems and jewelry.

This program of industrialization is based in the first instance upon the large reserves of cheap labor available in Thailand, and it has been propelled forward by government policies that have aggressively fostered the export orientation of the Thai economy. At the same time, the massive growth of the gem and jewelry industry over the 1980s and 1990s has been achieved in the context of active and constant collaboration between representatives of the industry and various governmental agencies. In particular, the Thai Gem and Jewelry Traders Association (the main industry association in Thailand), the Board of Investment (which is under the direction of the Prime Minister's Office), and the Department of Export Promotion (a branch of the Ministry of Commerce) have jointly promoted a series of important initiatives bolstering the industry's expansion. Before the late 1970s, gem and precious metal imports into Thailand were severely restricted by customs regulations, thus impeding the development and diversification of the jewelry industry. In a series of moves over the late 1970s and early 1980s, the Board of Investment progressively eliminated import duty on all the inputs (including machinery) used to make any jewelry that was subsequently exported from Thailand. These measures directly sparked off the gem and jewelry industry boom in Thailand in the 1980s. As just one example of the striking effect of these measures, a diamond cutting and polishing industry based on imported rough stones began to emerge in Bangkok after about the mid 1980s, and the industry is now widely estimated to employ upward of 10,000 workers. By 1988, the Board of Investment was also providing five-year tax holidays for some 103 approved gem and jewelry firms in Thailand, and had cleared the way for the recruitment of skilled foreign personnel to come to Thailand to train local workers. The Department of Export Promotion, for its part, has supported the annual Bangkok Gems and Jewelry Fair since 1983. The Department also provides extensive services facilitating interactions between local gem and jewelry manufacturers and overseas buyers. One consequence of these developments has been a large incursion of foreign capital and foreign entrepreneurs into the Thai gem and jewelry industry.

The Bangkok gem and jewelry district

Bangkok has been a center of gem and jewelry production over much of the present century. Until recent years, however, the industry was small in size and its outputs were sold mainly on local markets. In geographic terms, the industry was originally concentrated in and around Bangkok's traditional Chinatown, where it was dominated above all by ethnic Chinese and a much smaller number of Indians. Here, goldsmiths used to be an important element of the local industrial fabric, but these have now largely disappeared. As output and employment in the industry began to surge in the 1970s, it broke beyond the bounds of Chinatown, and shifted decisively toward the modern commercial center of Bangkok in the Surawong–Silom Road area (Figure 4.2).

Bangkok today thus has essentially two adjacent jewelry districts, i.e. an older traditional district made up of small workshops and retail outlets selling primarily to local markets, and a newer, very much more dynamic one producing precious gems and fashion jewelry on a large scale for international markets. Small workshop owners and traders are represented collectively by the Thai Jewelry Association, which has some 500 members (in both Bangkok and the rest of Thailand), and is concerned exclusively with a narrow range of local business issues. Larger firms selling on international markets are represented by the Thai Gem and Jewelry Traders Association with some 360 members, all of whom are located in Bangkok; this association engages aggressively in efforts to create political advantages for the industry and to promote international markets. Even today, a significant proportion of the firms belonging to the Thai Gem and Jewelry Traders Association are owned by ethnic Chinese who are the sons and daughters of producers who were originally in business in the older traditional industry.

As in the case of Los Angeles, Bangkok thus has a highly developed gem and jewelry district close to the urban core (though in Bangkok there are also many large factories located in special industrial zones toward the edge of the city). Similarly, Bangkok's gem and jewelry district is the site of much inter-firm transacting, and it is the focus of a large local labor market. The industry is also served by a dense fabric of social institutions

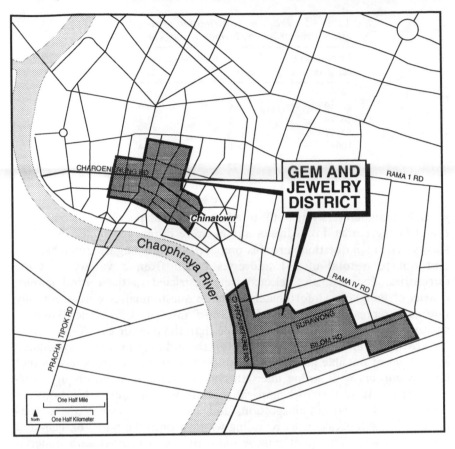

Figure 4.2 *The gem and jewelry district of Bangkok*

that help to sustain its economic momentum. These include the afore-mentioned trade associations and governmental agencies, to which we must add the recently founded Thai Diamond Manufacturers Association. The industry also benefits from a number of major trade magazines published locally, and from various educational establishments offering specialized courses and training for the gem and jewelry industry (e.g. the Asian Institute of Gemological Sciences, the Bangkok Design Institute, and Srinakharinwirot University).

A questionnaire survey of the Bangkok gem and jewelry industry

In the summer of 1992, extensive field work and interviews with gem and jewelry industry representatives were carried out in Bangkok. In total, 15 different manufacturers and 8 other individuals (in jewelry industry associations or in relevant governmental agencies) were interviewed by the author. At the same time, a mail questionnaire survey of Bangkok gem and

Table 4.5   *Frequency distribution of sampled establishments by employment, Bangkok*

Employment	Respondents	
category	no.	%
0–9	2	9.1
10–19	0	0.0
20–49	6	27.3
50–99	6	27.3
100+	8	36.4
Total	22	100.0

jewelry manufacturers was put into effect. As far as possible, the questions posed in the earlier Los Angeles survey were duplicated in the Bangkok survey. The mail questionnaire was prepared in both English and Thai and sent out to a total of 631 addresses culled from a variety of trade directories. The addresses selected were restricted to the central jewelry district of Bangkok. Unfortunately, only 26 questionnaires were eventually returned, representing a meager response rate of 4.1%. The Bangkok survey is thus probably even less reliable than the one for Los Angeles, and the absence of any aggregate statistics on the industry precludes systematic assessment of possible biases. Casual inspection of the results suggests that large producers with strong international connections are probably over-represented. It is therefore imperative that we approach this body of evidence with great circumspection, and to see it as essentially a non-random but still occasionally revealing window onto the Bangkok gem and jewelry industry. The questionnaire data are supplemented with material from secondary sources (including trade journals) as well as the field interviews and site visits mentioned above, and the information thus garnered helps to provide an occasional cross-check on the proceedings. For ease of comparison, description of the questionnaire results runs parallel to the presentation made for the case of Los Angeles.

The gem and jewelry producers in Bangkok who returned questionnaires had a very similar pattern of business activities to respondents in Los Angeles: on average, 50.0% of their business stemmed from manufacturing activities, and 33.8% from wholesaling. However, surveyed establishments in Bangkok tended to be of more recent foundation than those of Los Angeles, with 57.8% of businesses created in 1980 or later. These establishments were also much bigger than their Los Angeles counterparts, with the average employment being 186.8 workers and the median 75.0 (see Table 4.5). The latter comparison must be treated cautiously, of course, given the likelihood of some overrepresentation of large producers in the Bangkok survey, though it undoubtedly is valid in a broad sense. Thus, out of the 26 establishments in Bangkok that returned a questionnaire, no fewer than eight employed more than 100 workers, whereas in the whole of Los Angeles County in 1996 according to *County Business Patterns*, there were

Table 4.6   *Methods used by employers to find new*
workers, Bangkok gem and jewelry industry

	% respondents
Ask a current employee to recommend someone	38.5
Call another employer for a recommendation	46.2
Advertise in paper or trade magazine	61.5
Accept a random job applicant with references	53.9
Accept a random job applicant without references	23.1
Other	3.8

just seven jewelry manufacturing establishments (in SIC 3911) employing more than 100 workers.

A total of 73.9% of respondents indicated that they were in business with a partner or partners. Also, the chances are virtually even that any pair of partners will have some family relationship to one another. The majority of the owners of surveyed gem and jewelry firms were Thai citizens of Chinese descent, though the survey also uncovered 12 foreign owners (i.e. two Europeans, two Americans, three individuals from the Middle East, and five from other parts of Asia), which is consistent with the known trend in the Thai industry to increasing levels of internationalization.

Both the questionnaire data and information gleaned in site visits indicated that workers in the Bangkok gem and jewelry industry are overwhelmingly of ethnic Thai origin, and often they are recruited directly from the countryside. Among surveyed establishments, 54.9% of the labor force was female. Wages are of course low, with US$125 per month (in 1992) being frequently cited by employers and other industry representatives as the 'typical' wage. Working conditions are frequently exceptionally bad, and are exacerbated by the dust and fumes generated by the manufacturing process. Nevertheless, respondents indicated that they have a sizable core labor force, with 53.7% of their workers having been employed for three years or more, and only 15.5% for less than one year. Methods of recruiting new workers show some arresting contrasts with the Los Angeles case, as suggested by both the questionnaire data and field interviews. While Bangkok employers used social networks to a considerable degree for recruitment purposes, they were more prone than their Los Angeles counterparts to advertise for workers and to accept random job applicants (see Table 4.6). This comparatively casual approach to recruitment is perhaps accounted for by the much larger average size of establishments in the Bangkok survey compared to Los Angeles, and it is further reflected in the circumstance that Bangkok gem and jewelry establishments tend to impose high levels of internal control and discipline in the form of numerous security personnel and extensive and systematic checks on work-in-progress.

Establishments that responded to the survey indicated that on average they purchased 61.9% of their inputs from within the local metropolitan area, a very similar percentage value to that which was observed in the case

of Los Angeles producers. However, only 37.6% of the output of the
Bangkok producers was sold locally. Most of it is in fact exported to major
markets in Hong Kong, Japan, the United States, Germany, Switzerland,
and other parts of the world. Only 11.6% of the business of surveyed
establishments was generated by subcontract orders, a rather low figure
that presumably reflects the bias of the sample toward large and relatively
integrated producers.

Security, Trust, and Politics: The Social Bases of Industrial Agglomeration and Performance

Neither in the Los Angeles nor in the Bangkok jewelry districts do we find
anything even approaching the standard textbook account of market
relations in which the various participants encounter one another through
depersonalized short-term transactions, like buyers and sellers haggling
over a counter. On the contrary, both questionnaire and interview data
suggest that production and exchange within the industry in both places
are supported by complex relationships of family, ethnicity, and religion.
In addition, various institutions of collective order and regulation play a
role in the way the industry functions, strongly so in the case of the
Bangkok industry, much less so in the case of Los Angeles. The divergences between the two cases in this regard seem to account for at least
some of the observable differences in their economic performance. In
addition, both individual and collective security measures are critical to the
industry, for without them, the omnipresent temptations of fraud and
theft, and the high cost that the latter practices impose on the unwary,
would undoubtedly paralyze the industry.

Let us deal with the last point first. Gem and jewelry producers are very
security-conscious, especially in Bangkok where close supervision of
workers, tight internal methods of stock control, and exceptionally heavy
in-house surveillance commonly prevail. The fact that many employers in
Los Angeles and Bangkok tend to recruit labor by a system of direct
recommendation (see Tables 4.3 and 4.6) is also no doubt in part a means
of trying to keep a screen over their operations. Customers too are subject
to considerable surveillance. In Los Angeles, 81.0% of questionnaire
respondents *always* seek to verify their customers' bona fides by means of a
credit check, a letter of reference, a word of recommendation from a
trusted colleague, and so on; in Bangkok, the equivalent figure is 96.2%.
Prospective subcontractors are typically subject to similar forms of prior
evaluation.

Formalized checks and controls of these kinds, however, are likely to be
imperfect. They are subject to failure, they are often expensive to implement, and they interfere with the free flow of business. Informal relations
of trust are an essential adjunct to blunt security measures if smooth
business and employment relations are to be achieved. Trust also fosters

creative collaboration between different producers by facilitating their ability to pool resources and to work on common problems. In both Los Angeles and Bangkok, highly developed mechanisms of trust creation are observable within the gem and jewelry industry, operating both within and between establishments.

Within establishments, family relations play an important role, as revealed by questionnaire data and as confirmed by interviews. In all, 56.7% of surveyed establishments in Los Angeles employ at least one relative, and 57.7% do so in Bangkok. Partners in the industry, as noted, are commonly related. Businesses, too, are regularly passed down through families. In Los Angeles, 16.7% of respondents took over their business from a relative, and 34.6% expect eventually to hand it on to a relative. In Bangkok the equivalent figures are 43.6% and 50.0%, respectively. Moreover, in Los Angeles, 53.9% of the labor force in the average establishment belongs to the same ethnic/religious group as the owner. In Bangkok, by contrast, there is a pervasive split between the ethnic Chinese who tend to occupy positions of control, and the dominantly Thai labor force. However, in both cases, the fact that there is a sizable stable core of workers who have been continuously employed for three years or more is presumably a guarantee of at least some degree of workers' socialization and habituation to employers' standards of trust.

External business relations in the industry are also in part regulated by family ties and it is not unusual to find that inter-firm transactions involve siblings, cousins, and other relatives. In Bangkok, this tendency has been carried very far indeed. Here, the ethnic Chinese traditionally organize their businesses into networks of different firms each run by a family member who holds shares in every other firm in the network. These firms often extend over a number of different subsectors, such as manufacturing, wholesale trade, retailing, commercial real estate, and so on. Several of the largest and most powerful gem and jewelry industrial groups in Bangkok are organized in precisely this way. At the same time, buyer–seller relations in the gem and jewelry industry tend to be quite steady. In Los Angeles, surveyed establishments claim that 60.0% of their customers on average have been regularly purchasing from them for three years or more, while in Bangkok the equivalent figure is an almost identical 59.7%. Again, the broad magnitude of these figures is confirmed by field interviews. In both places, a customer may, after a period of time, be assigned the status of preferred buyer, in which case, merchandise worth large sums of money is apt to change hands with minimal formality (cf. Coleman, 1988). Within any given jewelry district, the spatial proximity of producers to one another further helps to create trust by facilitating personal acquaintanceship, just as it intensifies and broadens the general flow of information about the reputations of different individuals. The various trade associations also underpin levels of trust between their members by promulgating fiduciary standards and regulating business practices. These diverse mechanisms of trust creation seem to be modestly effective in the Los Angeles industry where 49.1% of questionnaire respondents signified that they believe the majority of their colleagues in the local area to be trustworthy; and they are evidently rather more effective in the Bangkok industry (with its much greater social cohesion) where the equivalent figure is 58.3%.

It is apparent that the Los Angeles and Bangkok jewelry districts share much in common in the matter of security and trust, give or take a number of detailed differences. Just the opposite is the case in the matter of political representation and organization of the industry. In this respect, the industry in Los Angeles, and indeed in the United States at large, has to its cost remained underdeveloped. By contrast, in Thailand since the 1970s, the industry and its representatives have displayed a remarkable spirit of political activism. In the first place, the government has been lobbied hard and with much success for gem and jewelry trade liberalization, tax concessions, industry support programs, and so on. In the second place, significant resources have been mobilized to create an infrastructure of supporting services, ranging from training and educational programs to international marketing and information-providing agencies. Perhaps most importantly of all, the Thai Gem and Jewelry Traders Association has now openly recognized that Thailand's competitive advantage in cheap labor gives it only a temporary edge on world markets, and that countries with even cheaper labor (e.g. Cambodia, China, India, Sri Lanka, Vietnam) are likely to move decisively onto international gem and jewelry markets in the future. Within the Association and in several governmental agencies, much thought and effort are now therefore being devoted to devising strategies for the transformation of the Thai gem and jewelry industry so that it can begin to move up the curve of skill requirements and product quality, and to compete not with the world's cheapest but with the world's most prestigious producers. One manifestation of this concern is the recent importation of skilled workers from countries with strong traditions of jewelry manufacturing to train local workers. Another is the effort to create a local network of training and educational facilities. Yet another is the strong assertion of Thailand's competitive ambitions via the government-sponsored Bangkok Gems and Jewelry Fair. Already, indeed, the Thai gem and jewelry industry's reputation for mass production of low-end products is giving way before a new-found sophistication in production and design (Holmes, 1992).

In Los Angeles, the jewelry industry persists as a modestly growing but not especially vibrant industry, focused on local markets, and largely represented by national associations with a rather limited outlook and scope. With the exception of a handful of dynamic and high-quality manufacturers and international gem dealers, much of the industry in Los Angeles seems to be prone to sluggishness, and is notably passive with regard to collective means of facing up to and overcoming barriers to enhanced competitive advantage. Moreover, like many of the other craft industries of Los Angeles, the jewelry industry seems to have become locked into a vicious circle of cost squeezing and dependence on cheap and unskilled labor, and it has not managed to establish for itself any sort of reputation for product quality or style. The net effect is that the industry has grown, largely in response to the growth of local demand in Southern California over the 1980s and 1990s, but remains something of a backwater in comparison with the industry world-wide. Nor can this state of affairs simply be attributed to an assumed shadow cast by producers in the northeast of the United States. In fact, the statistics quoted earlier on the relative growth of the jewelry industry in Los Angeles indicate that the industry has fared even worse in the United states as a whole than it has in Southern California over the last couple of decades.

The extraordinary momentum of the gem and jewelry industry in Bangkok is finally and most dramatically expressed in the Gemopolis project, essentially a planned industrial district which when fully completed will offer as full a range of agglomeration economies as any that can be found in spontaneously developed industrial districts. It is not unusual in both Los Angeles and Bangkok to come across large real estate projects aimed specifically at accommodating firms engaged in different facets of the jewelry industry (e.g. the International Jewelry Center in Los Angeles or the Jewelry Trade Center in Bangkok), but Gemopolis goes far beyond any of these precursors. The project was initiated in 1990 by the Shiangheng Group, a Thai organization with many connections to the gem and jewelry industry at large, in concert with various government agencies and industry associations. It covers 258 acres located to the east of Bangkok. Phase I is already complete, and it is projected to accommodate 46 gem and jewelry factories employing 22,000 workers. Much of the housing for the workers will also be contained within Gemopolis. Additionally, a wide range of services to the industry will be provided; these include banks, hotels, showrooms, shopping centers, recreational facilities, and a trading center that will function as a bourse for gemstones, diamonds, and jewelry. The Gemopolis project seeks, through planning and cooperative interaction between many different parties, to bring into existence a locus of massive and many-sided agglomeration economies, and to internalize the resulting benefits within a unified land development venture.

Gemopolis has already been designated by the Thai government as a special industrial zone with free trade privileges. It is a notably daring and imaginative industrial real estate undertaking, which, if ultimately success-ful, will become one of the world's largest centers of the gem and jewelry industry. Even if the project fails to achieve all of its stated goals, its very conception stands as dramatic testimony to the collective dynamism and capacities for forethought of the Bangkok gem and jewelry industry as a whole.

* * *

Much of the recent literature on industrial districts has emphatically invoked the notion of trust as one of the principal keys to any under-standing of the inner dynamics of local economic systems (e.g. Becattini,

1992a; Gertler, 1992; Harrison, 1992; Lorenz, 1992). And yet, essential as trust may be for the effective day-to-day functioning of industrial districts, it is not in and of itself a guarantee of high levels of competitive performance, as the example of the Los Angeles jewelry industry makes clear. In the case of Bangkok, political mobilization and collective self-consciousness have been essential additional ingredients of the industry's ascent to global prominence (see Saxenian, 1992, for a somewhat similar argument directed to the example of Silicon Valley). To be sure, the political element in the Bangkok gem and jewelry industry is not the sole growth-creating factor, but it has been a crucial moment in the remarkable expansion of the last decade.

In summary, the failure in Los Angeles to build beyond trust to more dynamic forms of collective action has resulted in relative lethargy; but in Bangkok, the concerted private–public efforts, in the first instance to promote the industry internationally on the basis of cheap labor, and then in the second instance to leverage the industry into a developmental pathway characterized by rising skills and product quality, have created notably high rates of growth. The data presented in Table 4.4 indicate how extraordinarily successful this latter effort has been.

Conclusion

I have tried in this chapter to draw out a series of critical comparisons and contrasts between the gem and jewelry industries of Los Angeles and Bangkok. I have shown in particular how these industries are constituted as both geographical and functional systems, and the critical role that cultural, social, and political relations play (in both their presence and their absence) in shaping patterns of growth and competitiveness.

Two apparent paradoxes emerge strongly from this analysis. The first is that the gem and jewelry industry in Bangkok has developed in the context of a much less advanced economy than is the case for the industry in Los Angeles, and yet it has achieved a degree of success and assertiveness that Los Angeles producers cannot even begin to match. I have argued that the Bangkok industry has in part attained this enviable condition by means of the political and quasi-political institutions that underpin its high levels of market performance, and that have helped it to build continually and with remarkable discipline toward ever improving conditions of production and rising agglomeration economies; the Los Angeles industry on the other hand displays a deficit of these kinds of institutions, and its market performance remains notably inferior. The second apparent paradox is that the gem and jewelry industry in Bangkok, despite its dominantly labor-intensive and low-technology configuration, has been a major source of foreign exchange earnings and a motor of economic development. This observation runs counter to the theoretical and normative claim that is sometimes (though decreasingly) made to the effect that economic progress in developing countries can only proceed on the basis of large-scale modern industries and technologies. In fact, as contended more fully elsewhere (Scott and Storper, 1992; Storper 1991), significant rounds of growth in developing countries *can* be secured through traditional craft-based industries, providing that the right sorts of locational and functional synergies have been successfully put into place. The Bangkok gem and jewelry industry illustrates the point with some force.

More generally, the argument presented above underlines the ways in which existing industrial districts can sometimes lie fallow through collective inaction, and at other times take off on a sustained developmental trajectory as they cultivate an enveloping structure of cooperative interaction and political participation. In this regard, the Bangkok gem and jewelry industry offers a number of object lessons that participants in the Los Angeles industry might study to their advantage.

5

THE HOUSEHOLD FURNITURE INDUSTRY OF LOS ANGELES: DECLINE AND REGENERATION

The household furniture industry is one of those economic sectors in which the tension between localization and globalization is particularly acute at the present time. On the one hand, virtually every country in the world, and most large population centers, possess at least some household furniture manufacturing activities serving local markets. On the other hand, the products of the industry have entered world trade with increasing insistence of late years (facilitated by the emergence of international mass marketing firms like BIF, IKEA and STOR), and many localized production complexes have come under strong competitive pressure because of this state of affairs.

As a consequence, the industry is in the throes of major locational adjustments across the globe. Household furniture manufacturers in certain cheap labor countries such as Taiwan or Mexico have had notable success because they are able to sell furniture to low- and medium-income consumers in the United States, Europe, and Japan at extremely competitive prices; equally, manufacturers in countries like Italy or Denmark that export high-priced but also high-quality furniture have been successful because their products have gained a reputation for their design cachet, and because they are able to cater to niche markets and exigent tastes. Caught between these two competitive pincers, many localized furniture manufacturing complexes in different parts of the world have suffered severe economic stress. One of the more dramatic examples of this syndrome is represented by the once vibrant London furniture industry which more or less collapsed over the 1960s and 1970s (Best, 1989; GLC, 1985; Hall, 1962; Oliver, 1966). Another is the Los Angeles furniture industry which in recent years has been struggling to make headway against intensifying foreign competition while also contending with a number of purely local circumstances that have exacerbated the industry's problems.

In the present chapter, I attempt to elucidate the current condition of the household furniture industry in the greater Los Angeles region, and to offer a few diagnoses as to its possible future prospects. I seek above all to show how the industry operates as a regional system or agglomeration of producers tied to low- or middle-income markets in the local area, and how it could potentially operate much more effectively by focusing on design-intensive forms of production and wider market reach. An effort is then made to pinpoint some of the important predicaments that the industry faces at the present time, and to show how many of its difficulties can be traced to its pursuit of a self-defeating and unidimensional strategy of cost-cutting. On the basis of these analyses, I offer several suggestions as to how policy-makers can begin to deal with the industry's recent decline and how they might attempt to foster more skills-intensive and quality-conscious forms of manufacturing. Some ideas are then proposed as to how certain segments of the industry might not only be retrieved from continued deterioration, but also be actively promoted in a world of sharply escalating competition.

The study is based on a multiplicity of data sources, none of which is entirely satisfactory or fully informative in isolation from the others, but all of which, in combination, point in a number of convergent directions. These sources comprise (a) publicly available statistical reports, (b) a telephone survey of all household furniture manufacturers in Southern California, (c) a detailed mail questionnaire survey in which data were provided by a total of 58 manufacturers, and (d) 22 individual interviews with and site visits to household furniture manufacturers in Southern California.

The Household Furniture Industry in Southern California

In 1996, total employment in SIC 251 (household furniture) in the United States as a whole stood at 264,000. The industry is widely scattered over the entire country, but two main states stand out as dominant centers of employment. The first is North Carolina, with 25.1% of all employment in SIC 251, and the second is California with 10.3%. In fact, the vast majority of the jobs in California are concentrated in the southern part of the state. Here is to be found a major agglomeration of household (as well as office) furniture manufacturers concentrated mainly in Los Angeles County but spilling over into the adjacent counties of Orange, Riverside, San Bernardino, and Ventura (Herman, 1994; Hise, 1992).

Southern California's household furniture manufacturers are typically artisanal in character. Manufacturing processes are simple and quite labor-intensive, and can be broken down into four basic sets of tasks, namely, (a) cutting and shaping wooden or metal parts, (b) assembling these parts into frames for upholstered furniture or into products like cabinets or tables, (c) finishing exposed wooden or metal parts by varnishing, lacquering, painting, etc., and (d) upholstering. Only a few wood household furniture manufacturers have installed advanced factory automation systems, and the upholstered segment of the industry has effectively resisted mechanization (Seldon and Bullard, 1992). As a consequence, most establishments in the household furniture industry are not able to achieve significant internal economies of scale, and they remain for the most part quite small

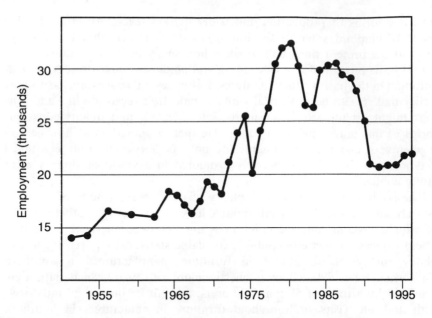

Figure 5.1   *Employment in SIC 251 (household furniture) in Southern California, 1951–96 (source of data: US Department of Commerce, Bureau of the Census,* County Business Patterns)

in size and focused on short production runs. These attributes of the industry are compounded by the circumstance that it is subject to strong cyclical fluctuations in demand and to the vagaries of fashion, and hence the markets that it serves are usually quite unstable and intensely competitive.

Employment trends in Southern California's household furniture industry

Annual employment in SIC 251 in the five counties of Southern California over the period from 1951 to 1996 is traced out in Figure 5.1. Figure 5.2 shows employment broken down by the two main four-digit sectors that make up SIC 251; these are SIC 2511 (wood household furniture) and SIC 2512 (upholstered household furniture) which together accounted for 71.2% of all employment in SIC 251 in Southern California in 1996.[1] Figures 5.1 and 5.2 reveal a pattern of rather consistent growth until the late 1970s, followed by a sharp decline in subsequent years and stagnation over much of the first half of the 1990s. This pattern runs more or less parallel to employment trends in the household furniture industry in the entire United States over the same period, except that the decline set in earlier (i.e. in the mid 1970s) in the case of the US industry as a whole. Also, the aggregate decline was, if anything, steeper in the US than in Southern California, until about 1987 when the Southern Californian

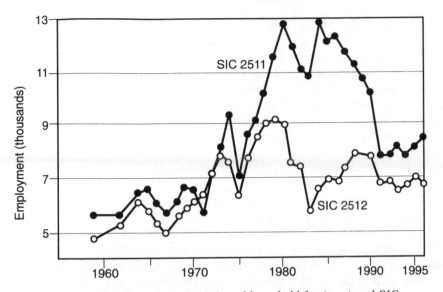

Figure 5.2   *Employment in SIC 2511 (wood household furniture) and SIC 2512 (upholstered household furniture) in Southern California, 1959–96 (source of data: US Department of Commerce, Bureau of the Census, County Business Patterns)*

industry (and especially SIC 2511) began to contract at an especially alarming rate.

The locational pattern of the household furniture industry in Southern California

Southern California commands a simple but critical locational advantage as a center of household furniture manufacturing. Because transportation costs still constitute an important element of the final price of furniture (especially of upholstered furniture which is difficult to ship in knocked-down form), the enormous local market of the metropolitan area is a major locational attraction for producers, and it offers, in addition, a strategic site from which to serve markets for household furniture throughout the West of the United States. But the existence of the industry in Southern California is not just a reflection of simple market-oriented locational processes. The region has also developed as a disproportionately concentrated locus of specialized furniture production in response to the external economies of scale and scope (both static and dynamic) that are typically engendered as industries agglomerate together in one place.

Agglomeration in this sense is a pervasive characteristic of the furniture industry, not only in Southern California, but also in such diverse places as Britain, Denmark, Germany, northeast and central Italy, and many less developed countries such as Brazil, Egypt, Indonesia, Thailand, or Mexico (Acheson, 1982; Amorim, 1994; Dowds, 1989; Guenzi and Marelli, 1965;

Kristensen, 1992; Mead, 1982; Nadvi and Schmitz, 1994; Oliver, 1966; Silvestrelli, 1985). Producers in the industry commonly derive cost advantages from participation in dense agglomerated networks of inter-industrial exchange and by sharing in specialized local labor markets. The industry in some agglomerations is also permeated by dynamic learning and innovation effects that come into being as large numbers of individual producers do business with one another and thereby generate continual flows of useful know-how. As we shall see, however, household furniture manufacturers in Southern California have actually failed to capitalize as fully as they might have done on the advantages of agglomeration and mutual association, and, as I shall indicate, many of the current problems that the industry faces can evidently be traced in part to this deficiency of regional collective order.

Figure 5.3 shows the geographical distribution of the household furniture industry in Southern California as it was in 1994. The employment and address data on which this figure is based were gathered in an exhaustive telephone survey of all furniture manufacturers in the region. The survey uncovered a total of 435 individual establishments or production units employing 17,346 workers in the five counties (note that these figures are somewhat lower than the 588 establishments and 20,722 workers officially recorded by *County Business Patterns* in 1994). The locational pattern revealed by Figure 5.3 can be described in terms of two spatial elements, i.e. (a) a main cluster of producers in and around a well-developed central industrial district (focused on Huntington Park and the adjacent communities of Vernon, Maywood, Bell, Cudahy, Walnut Park, and Florence) a few miles to the south and just slightly to the east of downtown Los Angeles, and (b) a wide scattering of establishments throughout the rest of the region. Interwoven with this latter pattern are several subsidiary furniture industry clusters in places like El Monte to the east of downtown, Gardena and Compton to the south of the City of Los Angeles, and Orange County in the southeast of the study area.

These different elements of the overall locational pattern actually combine into a single system of geographical organization and land use marked by a steadily declining incidence of establishments per unit area as a function of distance from their aggregate center of gravity. The latter proposition can be illustrated with data made available on compact disk from the 1987 *Census of Manufactures*. These data represent a complete enumeration of all manufacturing establishments in every zip code area in the United States by detailed SIC category. Table 5.1 records information from this source on the distribution of household furniture manufacturing establishments in Southern California by a series of concentric rings radiating out from the industry's geometric center of gravity. The table presents statistics on the number and density of establishments per ring for SIC 251 as well as for the two four-digit sectors, SIC 2511 and SIC 2512. For each sector, the spatial arrangement of establishments is characterized by relatively high densities per unit area in the innermost ring, with generally decreasing densities as we move further and further outward.

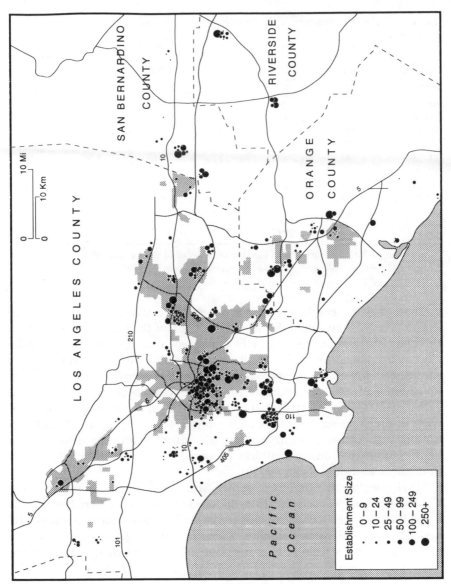

Figure 5.3   The geographical
distribution of household
furniture manufacturing
establishments in the greater
Los Angeles region, 1994: areas
where Hispanics represent more
than 50% of the total population
are shaded

Table 5.1   *Annular structure of the household furniture industry in Southern California*

Miles from center of gravity	Number of establishments			Density per square mile		
	SIC 251	SIC 2511	SIC 2512	SIC 251	SIC 2511	SIC 2512
0–5	134	46	25	1.71	0.59	0.32
5–10	142	61	60	0.60	0.26	0.25
10–15	118	63	42	0.30	0.16	0.11
15–20	87	37	17	0.16	0.07	0.03
20–25	54	49	12	0.08	0.07	0.02
25–30	63	22	3	0.07	0.03	0.00
30–35	18	10	4	0.02	0.01	0.00
35–40	8	4	2	0.01	0.00	0.00
40+	11	8	3	–	–	–
Totals	635	299	168			

Source: United States Department of Commerce, Bureau of the Census, *1987 Economic Censuses CD-ROM, Volume 2: Zip Code Statistics*, Release 2B, 1992

These static geographic patterns are in reality inscribed within a long-run dynamic process involving the decentralization of the industry from central to suburban locations, especially in the recent past. In 1962, Los Angeles County accounted for 96.1% of all employment in SIC 251 within the five counties; in 1979 the percentage remained little changed at 87.6%; by 1996, however, it had fallen noticeably to 65.4%. As a corollary, there is some evidence of the incipient formation of new furniture manufacturing districts in the outer reaches of the metropolitan area (see Figure 5.3), though nothing that comes close to the sort of massive spatial reconstitution of high-technology industry that has occurred at suburban technopoles in Southern California (Scott, 1993a).

Much shifting of furniture plants and employment from Southern California to *maquiladora* locations in Mexico has also occurred, mainly as a result of the onerous state and local regulations governing environmental and labor conditions in Southern California. Among the more severe of these regulations is Rule 1136 of the South Coast Air Quality Management District (covering the entire region of Southern California), which since 1983 has imposed costly restrictions on furniture manufacturers by seeking to control volatile organic compound emissions from the use of paints and solvents (GAO, 1991). Health and safety laws, minimum wage legislation, and workers' compensation (the latter recently reformed but still widely resented by manufacturers) have also helped to drive producers to Mexico. In the telephone survey mentioned above a special question was asked about firms' investments in production facilities in Mexico, with the results showing that as many as 23 producers in Southern California (i.e. 5.3% of the total) maintained at least one plant south of the border. As we might expect given the specific objectives of Rule 1136, all but two of these plants were owned by manufacturers in the wood segment of the household

Table 5.2   *Frequency distributions of establishments by size category in SIC 251 (household furniture), SIC 2511 (wood household furniture) and SIC 2512 (upholstered household furniture) for the five counties of Southern California, 1996*

Employment size category	% of establishments		
	SIC 251	SIC 2511	SIC 2512
1–20	64.8	68.0	62.4
20–49	16.9	16.3	15.2
50–99	9.0	7.4	10.3
100–249	6.9	6.0	7.3
250–499	2.1	1.8	4.2
500–999	0.3	0.4	0.6
1000+	0.0	0.0	0.0
Total establishments	611	282	165

Source: US Department of Commerce, Bureau of the Census, *County Business Patterns*

furniture industry. The latter point is underlined by the observation that from 1984 (immediately after the passage of Rule 1136) to 1991, employment in the wood household furniture sector in Southern California declined by 39.3%, whereas employment in the upholstered household furniture sector grew by 4.1% (see Figure 5.2).

Performance and Strategic Posture of Southern California's Household Furniture Industry

The structure of the industry

As indicated above, Southern California's household furniture industry is composed almost entirely of small- and medium-sized establishments. The frequency distributions of establishments by size class for SIC 251, SIC 2511, and SIC 2512 in the five counties are laid out in Table 5.2. In all three of these sectors, more than 60% of total establishments have fewer than 20 employees, and more than 75% have fewer than 50 employees. Only a handful of establishments employ more than 250 workers, and there are no establishments in Southern California with more than 1,000 workers.

In order to gain further information on the structural characteristics of the industry, a mail questionnaire was sent to all 435 manufacturers of wood and upholstered household furniture in the region in 1994. In total, 58 returns were received, though not all returns were fully completed. The self-selected sample of respondents was compared statistically against the target population in terms of (a) the proportion of establishments engaged in producing wood as opposed to upholstered furniture, (b) average size of plant, and (c) the distribution of establishments by geographical area (i.e. Los Angeles County versus the rest of the region). The sample was found to be comparable to the population at the 0.05 level of significance in regard to the proportion of establishments engaged in wood or upholstered furniture manufacture, and in regard to distribution by geographic area, but it was also found to be significantly biased in favor of larger employers (average plant size for the population being 39.9, and for the sample 53.0). Hence, although the sample exhibits some desirable features, it is also problematical because it is small and in certain respects non-representative. Circumspection must therefore be exercised in interpreting the statistical results reported on the basis of the sample data.

With these provisos in mind, the data collected in the mail questionnaire survey more or less confirm the picture of the household furniture industry that has already been presented, i.e. an industry that is overwhelmingly composed of small, labor-intensive producers facing highly unstable and competitive markets. Most importantly for present purposes, the questionnaire survey allows us to explore some of the subtle but revealing contrasts between the wood and upholstered segments of the household furniture industry. Probably the most dramatic difference between the two is revealed in their capital–labor ratios, where capital is defined here as the current value of all installed machinery and equipment, and labor is measured as total employment. In the wood furniture segment, the average capital–labor ratio per establishment was $10,387, whereas in the upholstered segment it was $3,250. The latter figure reflects the particularly artisanal nature of upholstered furniture production. Average batch size in the case of manufacturers of wood household furniture was 118, and in the case of manufacturers of upholstered furniture it was just 27. The two groups of manufacturers claimed to make furniture that is on average slightly above medium quality and price range, but this self-assessment is almost certainly inflated (particularly for wood furniture manufacturers), a conclusion that is borne out by observations made during the many site visits that were conducted while the mail questionnaire survey was proceeding.

In addition, both wood and upholstered furniture manufacturers engage in varied subcontracting activities, though at a rather modest level in quantitative terms. The mail questionnaire survey brought to light a number of tasks that are typically subcontracted out by manufacturers, such as frame-making, metal parts fabrication, wood turning and carving, laminating, painting and varnishing, fabric cutting, sewing, and upholstering. For both subsectors, about 8% to 10% on average of all production costs were accounted for by work subcontracted out, and while there is much variance around these figures, this seems by the standards of many other industries in Southern California (such as clothing, electronic components, or advanced medical instruments) to be fairly restrained. Information gathered in interviews with industry representatives suggests that a significant part of the work subcontracted out is performed under conditions that are actually beyond the pale of the law, thereby allowing manufacturers to circumvent the onerous environmental and labor regulations that govern production activities in the industry.

These simple statistical descriptions based on the mail questionnaire data were supplemented by a factor analytic study, the detailed specifications of which need not be reported here. The factor analysis brought to light three principal dimensions of variation in the questionnaire data. First (and as already noted above) there is a basic split in the household furniture industry of Southern California between makers of wood furniture (who evince a tendency to use relatively capital-intensive production methods and to occupy peripheral locations), and makers of upholstered furniture (who are much more labor-intensive and are inclined to more central locations). Second, we can distinguish an effect that varies mainly according to establishment size and output quality. Thus, small establishments (no matter whether focused on wood or upholstered products) are more likely than large to make high-priced furniture. Third, there is a concentration of labor-intensive and vertically disintegrated[2] establishments at core locations in contrast with more capital-intensive and more vertically integrated establishments in the periphery.

I have shown elsewhere (Scott, 1982; 1988a) that other artisanal industries in large metropolitan areas are often characterized by very similar articulations of functional and locational characteristics. In particular, the tendency for urban production systems to split into two rather distinct elements, one located dominantly in the core and the other in the periphery – with the former marked by many small, labor-intensive establishments intertwined in dense subcontracting networks, and the latter by larger, capital-intensive and more vertically integrated establishments – seems to be a recurrent predisposition of many different industries.

The changing labor force characteristics of the industry

Broad employment trends in Southern California's household furniture industry have already been traced out in Figures 5.1 and 5.2. Superimposed over these trends are a series of dramatic shifts in the demographics of the labor force, which in turn seem largely to have been driven by the peculiar evolutionary trajectory that the furniture production system of Southern California has followed in recent decades. These demographic shifts can be described in detail with the aid of the Public Use Microdata Samples (PUMS) from the population censuses for various years. Unfortunately, the PUMS data are given only for the two-digit definition of the furniture industry, i.e. SIC 25 (furniture and fixtures), which combines SIC 251 (household furniture) and SIC 252 (office furniture) together with several other three-digit categories. That said, SIC 251 currently accounts for a total of 50.8% of all employment in SIC 25 in Southern California, and there seem, in any case, to be sufficient similarities among the different three-digit categories within SIC 25 so that the data are probably reasonably descriptive of tendencies in SIC 251 alone.

Tables 5.3 to 5.5 present changes in various primary characteristics of the labor force in SIC 25 in Southern California from 1950 to 1990. The

Table 5.3　*Employment in SIC 25 (furniture and fixtures) by selected social characteristics in Southern California, 1950; data are given in terms of percentages of total employment*

	Native-born		Foreign-born	
	Male	Female	Male	Female
White	69.9	0.3	13.0	1.7
African-American	3.3	1.0	0.0	0.0
Hispanic	2.9	0.0	5.2	0.0
Asian	2.5	0.0	0.0	0.0
Other	0.0	0.0	0.0	0.0
Total	13,656	220	3,147	303

Source: US Department of Commerce, Bureau of the Census, *Census of Population and Housing*, 1950: Public Use Microdata Sample

Table 5.4　*Employment in SIC 25 (furniture and fixtures) by selected social characteristics in Southern California, 1970; data are given in terms of percentages of total employment*

	Native-born		Foreign-born	
	Male	Female	Male	Female
White	36.4	8.3	4.9	2.7
African-American	4.9	1.1	0.0	0.0
Hispanic	14.4	3.4	17.8	3.4
Asian	0.8	0.4	0.0	0.4
Other	1.1	0.0	0.0	0.0
Total	15,200	3,500	6,000	1,700

Source: US Department of Commerce, Bureau of the Census, *Census of Population and Housing*, 1970: Public Use Microdata Sample

Table 5.5　*Employment in SIC 25 (furniture and fixtures) by selected social characteristics in Southern California, 1990; data are given in terms of percentages of total employment*

	Native-born		Foreign-born	
	Male	Female	Male	Female
White	16.9	6.9	2.4	0.6
African-American	1.0	0.9	0.1	0.1
Hispanic	5.8	2.6	47.6	10.0
Asian	0.3	0.3	2.7	1.4
Other	0.3	0.1	0.1	0.0
Total	11,448	5,057	24,958	5,694

Source: US Department of Commerce, Bureau of the Census, *Census of Population and Housing*, 1990: Public Use Microdata Sample

principal directions of change over this period of time are strikingly clear. In the first place, the labor force has gone from being dominantly native-born to dominantly foreign-born; thus in 1950 the native-born component of the labor force stood at 80.1% whereas in 1990 it was only 35.0%. In the second place, the ethnic character of the labor force has changed from being 85.0% white in 1950 to 73.2% non-white in 1990. And in the third place, among foreign-born workers in the industry, Hispanics are by far predominant (refer to Figure 5.3), and by 1990 foreign-born Hispanic workers alone accounted for as much as 57.6% of the total labor force. Asians, by contrast, represent a minor presence in the industry.

In addition to these three dominant lines of change, a couple of subsidiary transformations of the labor force are observable. Thus, while African-Americans have always been a small minority of furniture workers in Southern California, their numbers have nonetheless declined yet further from a total of 1,405 workers or 4.3% of the labor force in 1950 to 1,010 workers or 2.1% of the labor force in 1990. Also, female partici-pation rates have been increasing steadily over time, with females account-ing for 3.0% of all workers in 1950, and 22.8% in 1990. Information obtained during site visits suggests that there is now a marked internal gender-based division of labor in most furniture establishments, with men assigned to the main shop floor where jobs such as carpentry, frame-making, painting, and assembly are carried out, and women assigned above all to fabric sewing operations and other tasks that do not require heavy materials handling. During the same visits it also became clear that some significant proportion of the immigrant labor force actually consists of undocumented workers.

It is apparent that over the last three or four decades a massive process of substitution of foreign-born Hispanic workers (mainly male but some female) for native-born male white workers has been going on in the household furniture industry in Southern California, most particularly since 1970 which marks the beginning of a great surge of foreign-born workers into the industry (see Tables 5.3 to 5.5). A numerically minor echo of this same trend is reflected in the displacement of African-American workers from the industry. These demographic transformations are no doubt the observable effects of a more fundamental process in which employers over time have steadily replaced a high-wage (and predominantly unionized) labor force with a politically marginal and low-wage labor force. Let us consider some further ramifications of this remark.

In the immediate aftermath of the Second World War, a significant proportion of the workers in the Los Angeles furniture industry belonged to Local 576 of the United Furniture Workers of America (UFWA) (Arroyo, 1979; Cornfield, 1986; 1989). The leadership of the Local at this time was composed mainly of communist sympathizers who were engaged in a protracted political struggle with employers. The historical details of the struggle need not detain us here, but it was eventually resolved by the

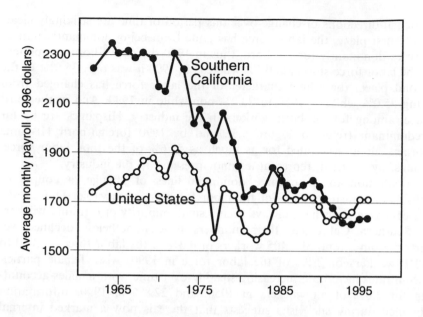

Figure 5.4   *Average monthly payroll (in constant 1996 dollars) in SIC 251,*
for Southern California and the United States (source of data: US
Department of Commerce, Bureau of the Census, County Business Patterns*)*

establishment in the early 1950s of a new organization (Local 1010 of the
UFWA) to take the place of Local 576 and to eliminate communist
influences within the workforce. For a time, Local 1010 remained a significant voice in the industry. However, and especially after the early 1970s,
Local 1010 became less and less able to recruit new members from among
what was now coming to be a dominantly immigrant labor force, or to
protect the wages and working conditions of its members. The Local thus
steadily declined numerically and politically over the following two
decades, and today, with only a few hundred workers on its membership
rolls, it is all but moribund.

As these events were unfolding, average wages paid in the household
furniture industry in Southern California were falling substantially in real
terms. Figure 5.4 traces out the trend in the average monthly payroll (in
constant 1996 dollars) in SIC 251 in the region and in the United States as
a whole from 1962 to 1996. What is strongly evident from the graph is the
high level of wages in SIC 251 in Southern California relative to the United
States over the 1960s and early 1970s. Much of this difference can be
accounted for by the fact that SIC 251 was largely – as it still is – a
traditional Southern labor-intensive industry. However, after about 1972
or 1973 average wages in SIC 251 dropped precipitously in Southern
California so that by the early 1980s they had fallen to the point where
they were equal to or even lower than the average payroll in SIC 251
nation-wide.

The evident historical correspondence between the demographic trans-formations of the labor force as described above, and the observed changes that were simultaneously going on in the political organization and earn-ings capacities of workers, is on the face of it remarkable and is entirely consistent with the notion that employers in Southern California's furni-ture industry have been able to restructure local labor markets in ways that have resulted in steady labor cost reductions. Of course, we must also take account of the fact that over the same period a rather similar process of deunionization and wage cutting was going on in many different industrial sectors throughout the United States, and the observed changes can only partially be correlated with the sorts of labor market transformations that have occurred in Southern California. Despite this reservation, the data laid out in Figure 5.4 reveal an especially and unusually steep decline in average wages in the household furniture industry in Southern California after the early 1970s, and this, as suggested by Tables 5.3 to 5.5, was combined with a concomitant and very sharp rise in the proportion of immigrants in the labor force.

Competitive strategy

Individual producers in Southern California's household furniture industry are thus predominantly small in scale, largely dependent on cheap labor, and given to low- or at best medium-quality production. As the field interviews suggest, moreover, producers deal with one another in trans-actional relationships that only rarely entail something more than arm's-length connections. There is, as a corollary, a notable failure in the industry to build collaborative and cooperative alliances between producers in the interests of achieving dynamic learning effects and superior product quality. A particular sign of the atmosphere of isolation and cut-throat competition in which most producers seem to operate is the inability of the California Furniture Manufacturers' Association – the chief formal organ-ization of producers in the region – to attract more than a small minority of local firms onto its membership rolls; and another is the signal absence of a sense of collective purpose among local manufacturers, apart from the purely negative one of a common opposition to state and local govern-mental regulations. These attributes are tokens of an industry that, like the London furniture manufacturers described by Best (1989), has for the most part opted for a competitive strategy of unidimensional cost-cutting rather than one of collaboration, innovativeness, and quality enhancement. As Salais and Storper (1993) have so strongly emphasized, however, the pro-duction of complex, skills-intensive outputs in flexible product configura-tions calls for sophisticated alliances between interdependent producers, and for a shared culture of understandings about craft and style and consumer tastes.

Insistent cost-cutting has been a dominant competitive strategy in much of Southern California's household furniture industry since the early 1970s, when producers in the region were first faced on a major scale with competition from elsewhere in the United States and the rest of the world. The trend has been accentuated by the environmental and labor regulations that have imposed additional burdens on the Southern Californian industry, and then exacerbated yet further by the prolonged economic recession in the region after the late 1980s. The strategy itself is an understandable *individual and short-run* response to these circumstances, for the immediate gains to be obtained by substituting cheaper for more expensive labor are likely in the minds of producers to outweigh by far the long-term and much less certain benefits of a strategy focused on moving up the quality/price curve, with all that this would demand in terms of new investments, higher labor skills, enhancement of design inputs, and so on. This individual and short-run strategy is, however, self-defeating in the end. It can temporarily alleviate the strain of competition, but any gains made by an individual producer in this manner are subject to eventual negation as other producers move in the same direction, and it also severely curtails any possibility of shifting into skills-intensive forms of production. Moreover, in what is now a *global* race to cut costs, Southern California is at an absolute competitive disadvantage – despite its large immigrant labor force – in the sense that there are always other parts of the world where production costs can be brought down to yet lower levels. With the diminution over time of the buffer effects of transportation costs, this competition has become increasingly intense. The consequence is that chronic stress (alleviated only by occasional cyclical upswings in demand) has become an endemic feature of Southern California's household furniture industry, and it will almost certainly endure so long as the industry pushes further forward in a strategy of competitive cost-cutting.

The alternative strategy of building regional and firm-specific competitive advantage on the basis of skill, quality, and reputation is very much more difficult to attain, not only because it is more risky for individual producers but also because it would entail significant changes in local industrial organization and culture. Despite these obstacles, it probably represents the industry's best pathway to long-term growth and prosperity in the new global competition (Best, 1990; Cohen and Zysman, 1987). The point is underlined by the findings of Steedman and Wagner (1987) who have demonstrated how high productivity and excellence in design have been attained by the German furniture industry (in comparison with more laggardly British manufacturers) through the extensive use of computer numerically controlled machinery combined with intensive apprenticeship and labor training programs. In view of the many barriers that stand in the way of a spontaneous emergence of this developmental pathway in the Southern Californian industry, some active policy stimuli would appear to be imperative, both to foster appropriate forms of industrial restructuring, and to build the institutional infrastructures that are necessary to sustain the regional manufacturing system in a more aggressively creative and innovative posture.

Reinventing Southern California's Household Furniture Industry

Elements of an agenda

Southern California's household furniture industry is thus facing a mounting crisis. To a major extent, the industry specializes in supplying low- or medium-quality products with limited design appeal, mainly to markets in the West of the United States, and it operates under conditions of intense cost competition and with minimal levels of institutional cohesion. There is, to be sure, a small group of extremely imaginative and design-conscious furniture manufacturers in the region (Finegan, 1990; Molotch, 1996), but these represent a definite minority. The burning policy question that needs to be faced is how (if at all) this group can be reinforced and enlarged.

One policy advocacy that is widely in circulation in California at the present time is to ease the regulatory restraints on industry in order to engender a 'good business climate' (see, for example, Council on California Competitiveness, 1992). There can be no doubt, of course, that many of the local regulations that currently weigh heavily on the household furniture industry need to be rationalized and reformed. Deregulation of environmental and labor standards, however, is apt to be an open door to yet further downgrading of the industry, in view of the vicious circle of wage cutting alluded to above. Such deregulation is assuredly not very credible as a method of encouraging the industry to compete in high-quality international niche markets. I shall argue that policy-makers should be grappling with the more fundamental and perplexing problems of constructing a system of regional competitive advantages above and beyond simple cost advantages, and, as a corollary, of supporting the rise of Southern Californian household furniture producers to mastery of wider national and international markets.

Any effort to attain this goal would involve reorganization of the bases of much of the region's household furniture industry, and a major realignment of its relations to the wider urban community. Figure 5.5 provides a highly schematized conception of this alternative industrial system. The figure identifies five main tiers of economic and social activity. At the center is the market, and in the present context, this signifies above all niche markets for high-quality furniture in both Southern California and the rest of the world. The next three tiers all refer to the supply side of the local industrial system; namely, (a) the regional ensemble of household furniture manufacturers as such; (b) the complex of subcontractors and input providers (including services) that sustains the core manufacturing ensemble, and (c) the overarching industrial milieu or 'atmosphere' of the region, and more than anything else, its rich assortment of design activities and complementary craft, fashion, and cultural-products industries (from motion pictures to clothing), all of which offer enormous potential externalities on which the household furniture industry might draw. The fifth and outer tier of Figure 5.5 alludes to diverse agencies and institutions of collective order, some of which actually exist in Southern California at the

Figure 5.5 *A prospective view of a regional household furniture manufacturing system together with an associated set of institutional infrastructures*

present time, some of which are purely prospective in nature, but all of which have important roles to play in any reconstructed household furniture industry in the region.

The manufacturing system and its institutional underpinnings

In what now follows, these points are elaborated at greater length. The discussion proceeds on two main fronts, namely, an exposition of some of the presumed internal and external operating characteristics of a reorganized manufacturing system, and a conceptual map of the social and political underpinnings needed to make that system work effectively.

Toward a reorganized industry   One way in which a shift toward quality-conscious manufacturing for rapidly changing niche markets can be induced is by promoting increased levels of specialization and complementarity on the part of individual producers. By this means, new and more extensive combinations of skills and other industrial resources can be created, and the capacity of the production system as a whole to diversify its products is enhanced. To achieve this goal, producers must generally opt for relatively high levels of vertical disintegration so that they can focus more intently on particular tasks while relying on subcontractors for specialized inputs. But producers will only be inclined to shift in this direction under circumstances where social trust and inter-firm cooperation are well developed, for in the absence of these critical sources of cohesion, producers will not wish to run the risks of increasing their dependence on others.[3] Collaborative regional networks of manufacturers with some form of internal governance are one possible means of creating such cohesion, and a number of experiments are now proceeding in diverse industries (including the furniture industry) in different parts of the world with networks of this kind. For example, Furniture New York is a successful consortium of some 33 designers and furniture manufacturers that has been operating since 1990 with the aid of funding from the New York State Department of Economic Development, and that now engages in globally recognized branding of all participants' products (Brown, 1994; NIST, 1992). The emergence of collaborative networks of manufacturers brings other benefits as well, for it typically enhances information exchange and thus tends to upgrade the learning capacities and innovativeness of all participants.

Localized manufacturing networks provide important kinds of externalities or agglomeration economies for individual manufacturers. Other externalities are generated by the wider milieu within which the regional industrial system operates. As it happens, Southern California encompasses what is almost certainly one of the world's largest clusters of design-intensive industries turning out an enormous variety of commercial-cum-cultural artifacts, and these industries have potentially huge overspill effects on the household furniture sector (see Chapter 11). One of the more pertinent of these from the standpoint of the furniture industry is represented by the large community of interior and furniture designers that is to be found in Southern California. The members of this community are located in and around the wealthier quarters of the region, notably in the area between Hollywood and Santa Monica, with a peak concentration occurring in the vicinity of the Pacific Design Center (see Figure 5.6). Some of these designers work closely with local furniture manufacturers to provide customized products for individual clients, or to create limited editions for high-end retailers. By and large, however, their sphere of operations is radically divorced from the Southern Californian furniture industry as such, and they evidently tend to reach out to suppliers in other parts of the country and other parts of the world in preference to purely local sources.

The same disjunction is observable between the household furniture industry and much of the other craft, fashion, and cultural-products industries in the region. By far the most dynamic of these industries are the

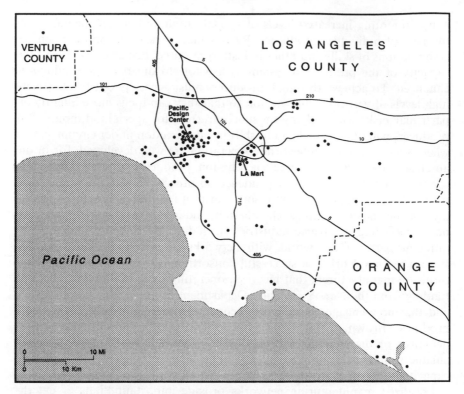

Figure 5.6 *Location of interior and furniture designers in the greater Los Angeles region: also shown are the Pacific Design Center (a major showroom facility serving the furniture and design trades) and the LA Mart (an older and declining furniture showroom facility)*

film and television sectors, but a wide variety of others can also be found in Southern California, including music recording, clothing, jewelry, toys, advertising, automobile design, theme parks, and so on. The more successful of them have projected a certain image of Southern California across the globe, and they are involved in constant packaging and repackaging of the region's (real and imagined) lifestyles, attitudes, and mores for popular consumption. Concomitantly, the region has acquired a definite stylistic and cultural aura resonating with an emphasis on the casual, the informal, and the colorful. This aura, or reputation, then becomes a positive externality, i.e. a commercially exploitable resource, for everyone in the region. However, only a small number of household furniture manufacturers have seen fit to take advantage of this unique resource, and the latent synergies that the industry might tap into by building stronger bridges to other craft, fashion, and cultural-products industries in the region remain remarkably underdeveloped.

Lastly, many opportunities are also available for commercial exploitation of the direct spillover effects and tie-in arrangements that are now a common element of the relations between Southern California's entertainment sectors and other industries. In this manner, makers of products like clothing, cosmetics, toys, soft drinks, and so on, frequently join hands with the film, television, and music recording industries in mutually beneficial ventures. Despite these opportunities, the household furniture industry, again, remains notably detached from its surrounding industrial milieu.

The institutional system   The outer tier of Figure 5.5 presents a number of different organizations and agencies, all of which have important roles to play in the restructuring of the household furniture industry and the subsequent maintenance of the industry in a high-skill, high-quality output configuration. Some of the institutional arrangements referred to in Figure 5.5 are public and quasi-public bodies, whereas others are purely private organizations and associations (in many cases, directly representative of the industry itself). The important point here is that they constitute not a centralized planning apparatus, but a framework of bottom-up supports providing essential services and incentives to the industry, and more than anything else, helping the forces of entrepreneurship and competition to operate more effectively. These arrangements address three main overlapping objectives:

1   To overcome market failures and to enhance externalities by providing resources for tasks such as labor training, technological research, marketing, and export promotion. These are all tasks in which individual firms (especially small firms) are apt to underinvest. Public investment in physical infrastructure for the industry is also of major importance, as represented by the reference in Figure 5.5 to a furniture design and manufacturing zone, which is proposed here as a means of anchoring a cluster of high-quality producers and associated subcontractors and service providers, possibly in association with a household furniture mart or design center devoted to the support of local products.

2   To promote trust, cooperation, and the innovative capacities of producers. This objective can be achieved in part by fostering network forms of industrial organization together with associations that help to sustain fiduciary responsibility in inter-firm relationships and that build commitment to advanced standards of design and craftsmanship. Labor organizations can also play a role in this regard by participating with employers in appropriate transformations of the work environment while simultaneously pressing for improvements in wages and working conditions.

3   To establish regional forums of adjudication (or what Friedmann, 1994, has referred to as 'industry focus groups') in which furniture manufacturers and other relevant parties such as subcontractor associations, labor organizations, local government agencies, banks, and so on, can come together in order to discuss problems of mutual concern and attempt to hammer out long-term region-wide strategies for dealing

with them. Forums of this sort are likely to encourage participants to exercise the option of voice rather than exit, and hence to contribute creatively to the construction of a viable regional cohort of household furniture manufacturers.

None of these objectives can be easily achieved by individual producers working in isolation from one another, for with their necessary sensitivities to price signals and profitability criteria in a competitive world, they are endemically disinclined to make unilateral efforts to secure the *collective* conditions of survival and growth. This is why the argument laid out above leans heavily on the necessity of policy intervention if high performance in Southern California's household furniture industry is to be achieved on a significant scale. Another way of expressing the same point is to say that the creation of competitive advantage in modern regional industrial systems calls ever more insistently for institutional infrastructures that generate beneficial forms of investment, coordination, social cohesion, and trust, and that mitigate free-rider problems.

Conclusion

I have shown how the household furniture industry of Southern California has developed and grown over the postwar decades, and how it has assumed a peculiar locational pattern involving significant agglomeration in central Los Angeles combined with much geographic dispersal throughout the rest of the metropolitan region. I have indicated how the industry appears to be entering an extended period of stagnation and decline due in large degree to its pursuit of short-sighted, cost-cutting strategies and its increasing inability to adapt to the rapidly changing market forces now sweeping across the international economy. Much of the industry is caught in a dog-eat-dog squeeze between two very different kinds of competitive pressures whose force has been magnified by the tightening of domestic markets in recent years. On the one hand, the industry has been damaged by imports from other places where furniture can be manufactured on the basis of much lower overall costs of production; on the other hand, it has been largely unable to match levels of quality attained by another important set of outside competitors who are able to produce furniture of superior consumer appeal based on their command of skilled labor and a reputation for excellence in design. Temporary relief can be expected during periods of cyclical upswing in the local economy, but over the long run the outlook for the industry appears to be decidedly inauspicious as things now stand.

I have therefore put forward a policy agenda that in its broad outlines seems to offer a number of practical possibilities for breaking out of this competitive squeeze, and for reestablishing the household furniture industry in Southern California on an alternative footing. The agenda prescribes a variety of complex maneuvers directed both to certain forms of industrial restructuring and to the mobilization of diverse corporate bodies in an effort to underpin the collective performance of the entire community of household furniture manufacturers in Southern California. It is aimed at the objective of revitalizing labor skills and innovative capacities, of enriching positive regional externalities, and of eliciting strong commitment to the region and its future from all participants in the industry. The ultimate goal is to create a durable groundwork of competitive advantages enabling the Southern Californian household furniture industry to hold its own in the new global competition, and to shift into a high-skill, design-intensive mode of operation. Perhaps the greatest asset that the industry could more or less immediately begin to appropriate resides in its geographic connection to the wider complex of design-intensive industries in Southern California, and hence to an abundance of as yet unexploited creative and commercial synergies.

More generally, the policy agenda that has been advanced in this chapter has implications not just for the redevelopment of the household furniture industry in Southern California, but for the consolidation of the entire regional complex of craft, fashion, and cultural-products industries as a massive and dynamic pole of local economic development effects.

Notes

1 The other four-digit household furniture industries are SIC 2514 (metal household furniture), SIC 2515 (mattresses and bedsprings), SIC 2517 (wood television and radio cabinets), SIC 2519 (household furniture not elsewhere classified).

2 Meaning, specifically, establishments with high levels of subcontracting activity.

3 Schmitz (1993) alludes to a similar point in his account of the transformation of a backward shoe manufacturing industry around Novo Hamburgo in Rio Grande do Sul, Brazil, into a dynamic high-quality agglomeration of interdependent producers. See also Amorim (1994) for a discussion of how the state government of Ceará in northeast Brazil helped to establish a flourishing furniture industry in São João do Aruaru.

PART 3
CINEMA, MUSIC, AND MULTIMEDIA

The two sectors that we have just examined represent classical craft manufacturing industries. Production in these sectors is for the most part secured by production workers, often in settings that are more reminiscent of nineteenth century industrial districts than what we might think of as the wellsprings of an advanced cultural economy. As such, the cultural content of their final products is frequently rather subdued, especially at the low-quality end of the market spectrum. By contrast, the chapters in the present part of the book deal with a series of media industries that are right at the leading edge of cultural production in modern society. We examine first of all the logic and dynamics of the French cinema and its intimate interrelations with the wider urban fabric of Paris, where production activities are overwhelmingly concentrated. We then turn to an analysis of the US music recording industry, with its main centers of creative energy firmly rooted in Los Angeles and New York. Finally, we consider the extraordinarily rapid growth of the multimedia industry in California over the last decade or so, and its peculiar forms of agglomeration in the Bay Area and Southern California. This account of the multimedia industry is complemented by an analysis of the labor market for multimedia and digital visual effects workers in Southern California, and I show how it is shot through with finely grained institutional arrangements that facilitate its operation. Even though cinematic, musical, and multimedia goods and services appear at the moment of final consumption in a form that usually masks the concrete circumstances of their production, they nevertheless originate in complex labor processes grounded in distinctive geographic conditions that almost always leave strong cultural traces in the end results.

6

FRENCH CINEMA I: STRUCTURE, ECONOMIC PERFORMANCE, AND SOCIAL REGULATION

Two major features of the French film industry need to be noted at the outset. One is that it represents a peculiar mix of market operations and centralized social regulation. The other is that, in contrast to the situation in Hollywood, a significant proportion of film-makers in France self-consciously aspire to create final products that attain to the status of high or serious culture. The discussion in this chapter examines the first of these features; the second is broached in the chapter that follows, where the difficult question of *place* and its role in sustaining the cultural idio-syncrasies and the market capacities of the modern French cinema is the center of attention.

Here we focus on the economic structure and performance of the industry (with special reference to the ever shifting production networks and unstable labor markets that are among its principal functional attri-butes), and on the complex regulatory policies that have been constructed around it over the last several decades. We shall also see how both econ-omic structure and regulatory policies are bound up with the geography of the industry, marked as it is by an overwhelming tendency to locational agglomeration in Paris.

This investigative agenda takes on particular significance in the context of the growing competition in cultural-products markets across the globe. The French cinema has been deeply scarred by the tensions arising from this competition, and it has, over the entire postwar period, been subject to an intense and unequal commercial war with the products of Hollywood. Despite the growing competitive pressures resulting from this situation, France's film industry maintains a consistently high level of output thanks to the government's carefully crafted policy of support for the national cinema. At the present time, the industry exists as a multifaceted system of production complemented by a full array of specialized services and skilled workers. It is capable of turning out anything from 100 to 150 feature films a year, some of which are of exceptionally high quality. That said, the French industry's total revenue in 1996 of 4.5 billion francs[1] represents a rather meager 14.9% of the earnings of the US film industry, and its relative commercial status has been declining steadily over the long term. A central problem for the French industry, both culturally and economically, is not just how to continue its resistance to Hollywood, but also how to begin to claim back some of the latter's ever expanding market domain (cf. Court, 1988; de Baecque and Jousse, 1996; Michalet, 1987).

Structure and Performance of the French Film Industry: An Overview

Business organization

The heart of the French film industry is made up of a mass of specialized firms under independent ownership, together with a handful of large media conglomerates or multifunctional entertainment corporations (Creton, 1994; 1997). The latter, in parallel with a world-wide trend, often have interests that extend well beyond the film industry and into television, publishing, music, and other kinds of leisure industries (cf. Benhamou, 1996; Huet et al., 1978; Tasker, 1996), and many of them in turn are being absorbed as subsidiary units into yet larger financial-industrial groups (see Figure 6.1).

The three largest firms in the French film industry can be roughly described as vertically integrated 'majors' somewhat analogous to the so-called Hollywood majors. However, the French majors are actually very much smaller than their counterparts in Hollywood. Two of them, Gaumont (which is independently owned) and Pathé (which is now part of the larger Chargeurs financial-industrial group), date from the very beginnings of the French film industry at the turn of the century; the third, UGC or Union Générale du Cinéma (part of the Compagnie Générale des Eaux group), was established in the aftermath of World War II.[2] Their activities span the entire production–distribution–exhibition chain, but they are not so much integrated in the strict functional sense as connected in loose structures of ownership and association, and their participation in actual film production activities tends increasingly to occur by means of wholly or partially owned subsidiaries (see Figure 6.1). In any case, the monopolistic practices that marked the Hollywood majors in their heyday, and that led in the late 1940s to the forced divestiture of their exhibition facilities, have never become a significant problem in France, and the disputes that occasionally do occur between the majors and independents (e.g. over distribution or exhibition) can usually be resolved within the special arbitration framework of the CNC (Centre National de la Cinématographie). The French majors are not involved to anything like the same degree as their Hollywood equivalents in direct financial participation in the production activities of independents. As I shall observe later, the greater functional distance between the majors and the independents in France can be ascribed substantially to the fact that the latter have comparatively easy access to alternative sources of financial support.

Film production units in France, no matter whether they are subsidiaries of larger corporations or independents, tend to be very flexible and fast-

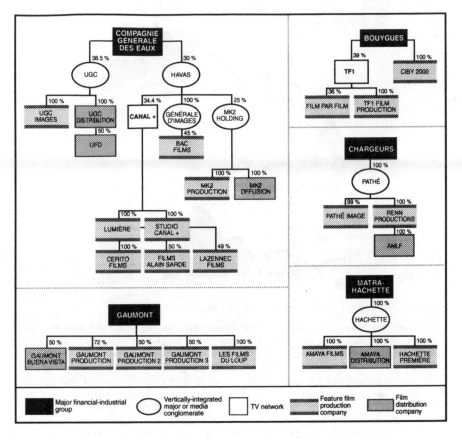

Figure 6.1   *Major corporate groups involved in the French film industry: numbers indicate percentage ownership (CNC, 1997, with amendments based on company reports and interviews)*

moving. They rarely own much in the way of physical equipment and facilities; rather, their stock-in-trade is the conception, organization, and execution of film projects. In smaller independents the actual *producer* of any film is usually also the PDG (président-directeur général or CEO) of the firm; in larger subsidiaries the producer is more likely to be a paid employee. Producers assume the responsibility for overall project management, including raising the necessary financial resources and securing distribution and marketing services. Increasingly, these tasks involve co-production deals. On any given project, the producer also normally enters into a critical partnership with a director who is in most cases taken on as an employee of the production company for as long as may be needed to bring the project to fruition. The director is in charge of the artistic execution of the film and on occasions may also be the scenarist. Under French law, the director is the sole and inalienable owner of the intellectual property rights to the film, though not of the film itself, *qua* object of

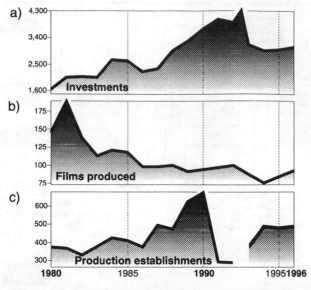

Figure 6.2   *Major trends in the French film industry, 1980–96*

The figure shows (a) total domestic and foreign investments in French film production, in millions of constant 1996 francs; (b) total number of feature films produced (100% French productions plus co-productions with French majority investment); (c) number of film production establishments in the Paris region in industry category 86.02 (production of films for cinema and television) until and including 1992, and in category 92.1C (production of films for cinema) thereafter (sources of data: CNC, CNC Info, Bilan Annuel, Paris: Centre National de la Cinématographie, and unpublished information provided by GARP (Groupement des ASSEDIC de la Région Parisienne)

commerce, which is in most instances the property of the production company (Benghozi, 1989). By the same token, it is the director who controls the final cut of the film and not the production company as is ordinarily the case in the United States. The producer and the director work collaboratively on all major decisions concerning the actual film shoot, including casting of the principal roles and selection of other key personnel.

Industry trends, establishment characteristics, and employment

The data laid out in Figure 6.2 indicate that the French film industry has grown modestly over the last couple of decades despite some major fluctuations in the recent past. To be sure, the number of films made has declined since the early 1980s, but total investments in production have expanded fairly steadily over the same period of time; and while some overinvestment occurred in the late 1980s and early 1990s (stimulated by policy measures to be discussed below), followed by a severe shake-out

Table 6.1   *Frequency distributions of establishment size for industrial categories 92.1C (production of films for cinema) and 92.1D (technical services for cinema and television), Paris region, December 1995*

Employment size category (permanent workers only)	% of establishments 92.1C	92.1D
1–4	70.5	55.5
5–9	17.5	20.5
10–19	6.8	14.1
20–49	3.5	6.4
50–99	0.9	2.3
100–199	0.2	0.5
200–499	–	0.5
500+	–	0.5
Total establishments	458	220

Source: unpublished data provided by the Groupement des ASSEDIC de la Région Parisienne

after 1993, the dominant long-run trend of restrained expansion now appears to have been reasserted. Of late, foreign capital has hovered at between 20% and 30% of total investments. In 1994, the average French film cost a total of 27.2 million francs ($5.2 million) as compared with $34.3 million for an average US film (Bonnell, 1996). Figure 6.2 also indicates that production establishments in the Paris region have grown in number over the last couple of decades, though the shake-out of the early 1990s took a severe toll on them. A major change in the official French industrial classification in 1992 means that the line representing total production establishments in Figure 6.2 is broken into two incommensurable segments. The first of these represents producers of films for both cinema and television; the second refers only to producers of films for cinema. Despite the fact that the establishment data shown in Figure 6.2 concern only the Paris region, they can be taken to be approximately representative of the industry in France as a whole since they constitute some 85% of the national aggregate.

Frequency distributions of establishment size in the Paris region are arrayed in Table 6.1. The data presented here concern both the film production industry as such (officially, sector 92.1C: production of films for cinema) and the technical services industry (sector 92.1D: technical services for cinema and television) which includes activities like sound recording, special effects, editing, coloring, and so on. Individual establishments in both sectors are notably small, with 88.0% of establishments in 92.1C employing fewer than 10 workers, and 76.0% in 92.1D employing fewer than 10. In both cases, these employment figures refer only to permanent workers, though establishments do periodically take on significant numbers of temporary employees. The data given in the table underestimate the total number of establishments in sectors 92.1C and 92.1D in the Paris region, for they do not take account of functioning establishments whose sole personnel consists of the PDG, who is not classified as a paid employee. A recent report published by the CNC (1997b) puts the actual number of production establishments in France as a whole in 1995 at 797, of which something of the order of 677 are probably located in the Paris region (see also Virenque, 1990). The somewhat greater representation of medium-sized and large establishments in 92.1D as compared with 92.1C is presumably a reflection of the former sector's higher levels of capitalization and its concomitantly superior command of internal economies of scale.

Total employment of *permanent* workers in sectors 92.1C and 92.1D in the Paris region was 2,374 and 3,401 respectively in 1996, according to unpublished statistics provided by the Groupement des ASSEDIC de la Région Parisienne. Rannou and Vari (1996) suggest that the approximate number of *temporary* workers in the industry at any one time (not including actors and writers) can be obtained by doubling the figure for permanent workers. By this rule of thumb, there were roughly 4,748 temporary workers in 92.1C and 6,801 in 92.1D in the Paris region in 1996. The number of permanent and temporary workers employed by the film industry and related cinematographic and television technical services in the Paris region can therefore be roughly estimated at 17,324. By way of comparison, the US Department of Commerce reports in *County Business Patterns* that there were 129,863 employees in 4,416 establishments in SIC 781 (motion picture production and services) in Los Angeles County, California, in 1994.

Distribution and markets

Distribution of both domestic and foreign films is carried out by many different firms in France, though most of this activity is dominated by the three majors together with various distributors of foreign (largely American) films. The top 10 distributors in the country are identified in Table 6.2, which also shows their market share in 1996. In all, these 10 distributors account for almost 90% of France's film distribution trade. Two of them, Gaumont-Buena Vista and UFD (UGC-Fox Distribution), represent joint ventures between French majors and US companies. Four are purely French holdings, i.e. AMLF (a subsidiary of Pathé), Michel Gauchon, Bac Films, and Metropolitan Film Export. The rest are American subsidiaries.

The distribution of French films is well developed within the borders of France itself, but is much less effective in other countries, and exports of French films are negligible (Coulot and Téboul, 1989; Martin, 1995). Whereas more than half of the earnings of Hollywood films are now accounted for by exports, only 375 million francs (about 7% of the revenues raised by domestic film theater entries) were generated by French film exports in 1995 (CNC, 1997b). Most of these exports are directed to other European countries, with Germany, Italy, and Belgium in the lead

Table 6.2   *Top 10 film distribution companies in France, 1996*

Distribution company	Market share (%)
Gaumont-Buena Vista	19.8
UIP	14.0
AMLF	13.2
Columbia Tri-Star Films	7.6
Warner France	6.7
UFD	6.6
Polygram Film Distribution	6.4
Michel Gauchon	5.4
Bac Films	5.1
Metropolitan Film Export	3.2
Total	88.0

Source: *CNC Info (Bilan Annuel, 1996)*, Paris: Centre National de la Cinématographie

(Unifrance, 1996). Only 11.7% of total export revenues are raised in the United States, and French films account for a fraction of a percentage point of all film theater entries in that country. French films in the United States are distributed by American companies such as Miramax, Sony Classics, and New Line (Balio, 1997).

On the domestic market, the aggregate revenues of French films from all sources (i.e. film theater entries, television, and video) have tended to grow over the last decade or so, but with severe declines occurring in the theatrical exhibition market over the 1980s. A peak of film theater entries and revenues in France was attained in 1982, to be succeeded by a steady decrease down to the early 1990s, with a slight rise thereafter (Figure 6.3). This problem is compounded by the fact that total film theater entries in France have been marked by a falling market share for French films and a *rising* share for American films. By 1996, French films were bringing in only 37.5% of total domestic audiences whereas American films attracted 54.4%. The irony is that television, which is at once a serious competitor to theatrical exhibition and itself a very imperfect substitute for the big screen, has helped to give a new lease of life to French cinema over the 1980s and 1990s (Lazar, 1995; Tixier, 1992). In part, this is due to government policy which obliges television networks to invest in feature film production; in part, it is also a result of the enormous popularity of feature films on French television (Flichy, 1991). In 1996, as many as 1,513 feature films were broadcast over France's public and private television networks, with the privately owned pay-TV channel Canal Plus accounting for 29.7% of the total (CNC, 1997a). According to Farchy (1992), there are now more than 20 television viewers per feature film shown on TV for every one film theater entry in France. Moreover, French law mandates that 60% of all films shown on TV must be of European origin, and of these, 40% must be

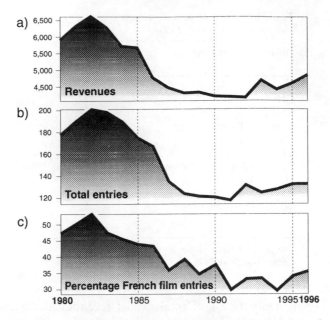

Figure 6.3   *French film theater revenues and entries, showing (a) total revenues in millions of constant 1996 francs, (b) total entries in millions, and (c) percentage of entries accounted for by French films (source of data: CNC, CNC Info,* Bilan Annuel, *Paris: Centre National de la Cinématographie)*

French. However, in a bid to protect theatrical exhibition, the law also limits the number and scheduling of feature films for television broadcast, and prescribes specific time delays after the first release of any film before it can appear on TV. The market for video recordings of feature films has been somewhat slow to develop in France compared with North America and other parts of Europe, though it is now beginning to show signs of life, and in 1995 as many as 4,145 different feature films were available on video, 43.8% of them being French (CNC, 1997a).

Toward a two-tier system?

It would seem that something like a two-tier production system is now starting to emerge in the French film industry.

On the one hand, there is a distinctive and numerically dominant small-budget film producing sector – a sector that is essentially artisanal in its production methods and business practices. This sector turns out films destined mainly for limited domestic markets (comedies being one of the staples). It is also the sector within which the French *auteur* convention of film-making is most highly developed, and films in which this convention is conspicuously on display (those of Eric Rohmer or Jean-Luc Godard being familiar examples) often find their way onto selected international exhibition circuits. Some of the films made in this sector, such as Serreau's *Trois Hommes et un Couffin* (subsequently remade in Hollywood as *Three Men and a Baby*), even enjoy a commercial success that goes far beyond the initial expectations of their financial backers.

On the other hand, there is a commercially more dynamic sector, still not entirely distinguishable from the former, which can be partially characterized as the predominant representative of *la qualité française* (a term that roughly signifies films with dense production values, often with strong literary or historical overtones, and with lead roles assumed by major stars). Firms in this sector are represented by the three majors together with production companies such as Bac Films, Hachette Première, Renn Productions, Studio Canal Plus, and other producers with strong commercial backing (recall Figure 6.1). Many of the films that emerge from this sector are characterized by relatively large budgets, as in the case of Berri's *Germinal* or Rappeneau's *Le Hussard sur le Toit*, which at a cost of 172 and 176 million francs, respectively, are the most expensive purely French films ever made. Various efforts are also under way among firms in this sector to produce films that are explicitly calculated to appeal to foreign markets, either by seeking out co-production partners in other countries or by actually making films outside France, sometimes even making them directly in English. However, as Adriani (1993) and Prédal (1996) have argued, some of the latter practices may well turn out to be deleterious in the end for the French film industry. The most ambitious and the most overtly non-French of all these internationally oriented films is Besson's *The Fifth Element*, recently released by Gaumont, which has proven to be a huge commercial success, but which serves in the end as a testament to Hollywood more than it does to French cinema. I shall return to this point in Chapter 7.

Social Regulation and Institutional Infrastructures

The imperative of social regulation

Given that the film industry is one of those distinctive sectors of modern capitalism where both economic and cultural interests are significantly at play, it is no surprise to find that in France, with its long traditions of industrial Colbertism and its approach to culture as a national imperative, the cinema should be subject to intense regulatory scrutiny. There is indeed virtually no corner of the industry that is not touched in one way or another by the visible hand of the state.

Above and beyond the idiosyncratic traditions of French society, there is a further factor that must be examined in relation to this regulatory activity. As I argued in Chapter 2, complex economic aggregates (such as national or urban economic systems) can never successfully reproduce themselves through time on the basis of purely atomized market relations. Aggregates like these can virtually never operate effectively without some minimal collective underpinnings (whether governmental or civil), and in many cases their economic performance can actually be enhanced where markets are supplemented by appropriate institutional arrangements. Even in the Hollywood film industry, which on first examination looks like the essence of freewheeling market capitalism, there is considerable collective order in the form of influential business associations (with many direct linkages to national and local centers of political decision-making), powerful professional guilds, indurated social networks, conventionalized behaviors, and mechanisms for public provision of supportive infra-structures and subsidies, all of which help in various ways to strengthen the bases of the industry's competitive advantages. In the French film industry, the urge to collective order is imbued with added urgency both because of the foreign competition which over the last few years has decimated other European film industries, and because of a generalized political will in France to preserve the national cultural identity and patrimony. This will was notably apparent in the GATT negotiations of 1993 where, arguing for the need for a 'cultural exception', France and its European partners succeeded in a push to exempt audiovisual products from a regime of free international trade. This exemption has allowed France, at least for the time being, to pursue its unique system of social regulation of the film industry. Detailed information about the workings of this system can be found in numerous publications (e.g. Bonnell, 1978; 1996; CNC, 1993; Dibie, 1992), and only the most general overview of its *modus operandi* will be provided here.

The role of the CNC

French governmental oversight of the film industry dates from the Vichy period during the Second World War, and above all from the founding of the CNC in 1946 as a quasi-autonomous administrative body at first under the tutelage of the Ministry of Information, subsequently passing over to the Ministry of Industry, and finally in 1959 coming under the nominal control of the Ministry of Culture. The current regulatory structure has thus emerged cumulatively over the postwar decades, though its main lineaments were put into place by two particularly activist ministers of culture, namely, André Malraux (1958–69) and Jack Lang (1981–6 and 1988–93) (CNC, 1996; Farchy and Sagot-Duvauroux, 1994).

Currently, the CNC acts as a sort of grand coordinating body for French policy in regard to the film industry, and it engages in a remarkable diversity of actions. It supports Unifrance Film International which seeks to promote French films in foreign countries; it contributes significantly to the annual Cannes Film Festival (see Benghozi and Nénert, 1995; Billard, 1997); it regulates labor markets by managing a system of professional certification; it is in partnership with the Ministries of Culture and Education in helping to support one of the two national French film schools, i.e. FEMIS (Institut de Formation de l'Image et du Son).[3] It also has an

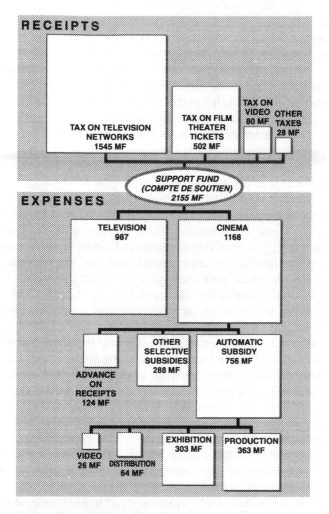

Figure 6.4   *Monetary flows through the CNC's support fund in 1996:
numbers represent millions of francs; areas of white rectangles are
proportional to receipts/expenses (CNC,* La Politique Française de Soutien
au Cinema, *Paris: Centre National de la Cinématographie, 1997)*

affiliated agency, the CST (Commission Supérieure Technique de l'Image
et du Son), which provides advice and guidance to the industry on questions of technology and equipment, and it runs a small program that helps
to subsidize research by private firms on new technologies. Above all, the
CNC operates a central support fund for the film industry by managing an
extensive system of levies and monetary reallocation within the entire
audiovisual-cinematographic complex (see Figure 6.4).

Money for the CNC's support fund is raised in two main ways. One is
represented by a tax of approximately 11% on all film theater tickets sold
in France. Given the current dominance of American films over French

films at the box-office, this tax obviously falls more heavily on the former than it does on the latter. The other source of income is an imposition of 5.5% on the revenues of television networks. Additional minor sums come from taxes on video sales and rentals, and from miscellaneous other sources. The money raised in these ways is then redistributed through the support fund in aid of both cinema and television production activities, though only the former case is of concern here.

There are, of course, strict rules that must be followed before any film can gain support from the fund. These appertain above all to the film's language, the nationality of key creative and technical workers, and the country in which it is produced. The largest part of the support money is distributed through a so-called automatic subsidy that is awarded to producers in proportion to the 11% tax raised on tickets sold for their previous films. Various kinds of automatic subsidies are also available to film distributors, exhibitors, and video producers (Figure 6.4). A second major line of support involves a reimbursable advance on receipts; this is a selective award for which producers must compete, and which in addition offers special opportunities for directors making their first film. Further selective subsidies are available for modifying and improving film scenarios and for developing film music.

Several other fiscal arrangements mandated by the government divert yet more money into film production. Thus, on top of the 5.5% tax on revenues that television networks must contribute to the CNC's support fund, they are obliged to allocate a further 3% (and in the special case of Canal Plus, 9%) to the production or prepurchase of French films. In response to this requirement, all major television networks in France have now set up subsidiaries devoted to feature film production. The government has also established a system of tax shelters, known as SOFICAs (Sociétés de Financement des Industries Cinématographiques et Audiovisuelles), to encourage private investment in film production, as well as a special scheme designated IFCIC (Institut pour le Financement du Cinéma et des Industries Culturelles) providing loan guarantees to facilitate the raising of private investment funds by producers.

There is, as well, an emerging political effort at the European level to build continent-wide synergies and competitiveness in the film industry (Dibie, 1992; Finney, 1997). The Eurimages scheme was established by the Council of Europe in 1988 with the objective of encouraging collaboration on film projects among member countries. The European Union's MEDIA II program (following on the heels of an earlier MEDIA I program) seeks to fund projects that will contribute to the enhancement of business expertise in both the film and television industries. Also, in 1990, the French Ministry of Culture established a special fund in support of coproductions with Central and Eastern European countries. The results of these different European-level programs appear to have been at best marginal to date, though Finney (1997) offers a modestly optimistic analysis of the potentialities of the Eurimages scheme.

Regulation and organization of employers and workers

In addition to the CNC, a number of civil organizations play a role in coordinating the activities of employers and workers in the French film industry. These organizations are nearly all located in Paris. They contribute to the overall system of social regulation by representing the concerns of their members in various forums of decision-making, by helping to circulate critical information among large segments of the industry as well as providing various additional services, and by engaging with one another in collective bargaining about key contractual issues.

Employers' associations   One of the more important of these is the Fédération Française des Producteurs de Films et de Programmes Audiovisuels. The Federation is a syndicate of employers' associations in the film and television industry, and it includes in particular the Chambre Syndicale des Producteurs et Exportateurs de Films Français, the main collective mouthpiece of film production companies. In addition, the Fédération Nationale des Industries Techniques du Cinéma et de l'Audiovisuel brings together several employers' associations in technical industries such as special effects, equipment supply, film processing, and studio rental. Specialized organizations representing distribution and exhibition companies are also strongly developed. Coordination among all these groups is provided by the Bureau de Liaison de l'Industrie Cinématographique.

Clearly, all of this organizational structure means that industry representatives are able to bring considerable lobbying pressure to bear on the government in general and on the CNC in particular.

Local labor markets and workers' associations   Workers in the French film industry are also active on the organizational front. Directors – who occupy an ambiguous position between management and labor – are represented by various independent associations, chief among them being the Association des Auteurs-Réalisateurs-Producteurs. More conventional forms of union organization are well in evidence on both the creative and the technical sides of the industry. Several different unions representing creative workers are allied together within the Fédération Nationale des Syndicats du Spectacle, de l'Audiovisuel, et de l'Action Culturelle, one of whose main constituent groups is the Syndicat des Artistes Interprètes, which is the primary actors' union. Technical workers are mainly represented by either (a) the Syndicat National des Techniciens et Travailleurs de la Production Cinématographique et de la Télévision or (b) the Syndicat Général des Travailleurs de l'Industrie du Film. The chief function of these workers' unions is to negotiate wage contracts with different employers' associations, as well as to argue for film workers' interests in the wider political arena. Information gained in interviews with union representatives suggests, however, that only a minority of eligible workers are formal union members, and the labor unions in France's film industry evidently

Table 6.3   *Occupations subject to a*
regime of professional identity cards
issued by the CNC

Director
First assistant director
Continuity clerk
Unit manager
Director of production
Director of photography
Camera operator
First assistant camera operator
Production designer
First assistant production designer
Sound engineer
Assistant sound engineer
Film editor
Assistant film editor
Head make-up artist

Source: CNC (1993)

have little of the power and reach of the Hollywood guilds. One reason for this phenomenon, above and beyond the comparatively low levels of worker unionization that prevail in France generally, may possibly be found in the very effective regulation of labor markets for film industry workers carried out by the CNC and other government bodies. These arrangements may well have blunted film workers' incentives to join more aggressively together in pursuit of their joint interests.

In the first place, there is a complex occupational division of labor between workers in the film industry, and in France this is managed in part by administrative fiat. For any film subsidized by the CNC (which is to say virtually all films made in France by French production companies) workers in key occupational categories must be officially certified. Certification is undertaken by the CNC on the basis of a system of professional identity cards issued to workers in relation to their educational qualifications, experience, and nationality, though according to Rannou (1992) the system is now apparently breaking down under conditions of increased labor market instability. The occupations nominally regulated by the CNC are listed in Table 6.3. All of them concern personnel in the domains of directing, management, photography, production design, sound, and make-up, though the most junior employees in these occupations are now exempt from regulation. Also exempt are scenarists, actors, composers, musicians, stunt performers, costume designers, carpenters, electricians, and workers in various other technical trades.

In the second place, all workers in the industry, whether regulated by the CNC or not, face extremely unpredictable labor market conditions and are subject to frequent bouts of unemployment over the course of the year (CNC, 1997a; Debeauvais et al., 1997; Menger, 1991). Since the mid 1980s this instability has been intensifying, and today two-thirds of all work in

Table 6.4 *Sources of investment
finance for French films, 1996*

Source of finance	%
CNC:	
Automatic support	8.3
Advance on receipts	4.9
Television networks:	
Prepurchases	31.7
Co-production	10.3
SOFICAs	4.8
French producers	24.2
Foreign investors	10.2
Distributors' advances	5.5
Video rights	0.1
Total investments (million francs)	3,286.8

Source: *CNC Info (Bilan Annuel, 1996)*, Paris:
Centre National de la Cinématographie

the French film industry is temporary (Rannou and Vari, 1996). In mitigation of this circumstance, however, most of the temporary workers in the
industry are covered by a special government-sponsored unemployment
scheme (the so-called *Intermittence du Spectacle*) which, subject to certain
conditions, allows them to move in and out of different jobs at irregular
intervals while also collecting unemployment benefits in periods when they
are not working. This arrangement is obviously an important asset to the
industry as a whole, for it helps to maintain the supply of skilled workers
at reasonable cost while allowing producers maximum flexibility in regard
to hiring and layoff decisions – a crucial advantage in any industry where
profitability is dependent on the ability to maintain low fixed overheads
and to avoid long-term labor contracts (Faulkner and Anderson, 1987).

Lastly, labor training, especially on the technical side of the industry, is
still to a significant degree based on an informal on-the-job training model,
though formal training is becoming more common. In a study of French
film directors carried out by Thonon et al. (1990), it was found that 44% of
all directors questioned had received some sort of formal film education,
with the percentage being significantly greater among younger as compared
with older directors (see also Prédal, 1993). Formal education is provided
by the two publicly supported film schools in Paris, as well as by a number
of private schools and university programs.

A Preliminary Evaluation

The data presented in Table 6.4 show that subsidies and policy-driven
investments now account for about 60% of all of the capital currently
flowing into the French film industry. These measures have helped to

preserve the industry's integrity, and in particular, they have guarded it against the depredations of foreign competition. They have also helped to counter some of the negative effects – cultural as well as economic – of television on the film industry by encouraging a new symbiosis between the two. French commentators frequently but disingenuously claim that these policy measures involve little or nothing in the way of direct government expenditures. That is literally correct, in the sense that the monetary subsidies to the film industry do not actually pass through treasury coffers, but it is wrong in essence given that these subsidies would not occur in the absence of various official mandates.

In spite of its labyrinthine qualities, the structure of administrative support and associational representation in the French film industry represents an effective and well-lubricated system. By leaving detailed production outcomes open to the play of many decentralized decision-makers, the system of regulation in place also allows for the kind of bottom-up approach to industrial development that is so widely advocated nowadays by regional and urban economic development theorists (cf. Stöhr, 1990). It has most certainly preserved the French cinema as a going concern and as an important cultural force in the modern world (Creton, 1997), but as I shall argue in the next chapter, it can be criticized on the grounds of its essentially defensive as opposed to offensive posture.

Notes

1 In 1996 the average exchange rate of the French franc in terms of one US dollar was 5.12.

2 Total earnings in 1996 for Gaumont were 1,236 million francs, for Pathé 1,841 million, and for UGC 1,447 million.

3 The other being the Ecole Nationale Supérieure Louis Lumière, which depends on the Ministry of Education.

7

FRENCH CINEMA II: PLACE, CULTURAL GEOGRAPHY, AND COMPETITIVE ADVANTAGE

Organization and Location of the Industry

The division of labor and agglomeration

Film production necessitates the bringing together of an enormous array of different trades, skills, aptitudes, and sensitivities under coordinated managerial and aesthetic control. Any single project not only entails the raising of funds and overall program management but also calls into play the tasks of (a) pre-production (e.g. scenario development, casting, set and costume design), (b) shooting (e.g. camera-work, lighting, acting, make-up), (c) post-production (e.g. editing, special effects, sound engineering). Among other things, needed equipment and studio space must also be found and rented.

In France, the teams of firms (including freelance workers) that form in relation to specific film projects almost always come together on an *ad hoc* and temporary basis. The French film industry, in short, like many industries that face unpredictable market conditions, is characterized by a proclivity to vertical and horizontal disintegration, that is, to overall fragmentation as a strategy for achieving production flexibility (cf. Piore and Sabel, 1984; Storper and Christopherson, 1987). True, as Faulkner and Anderson (1987) and Moriset (1995) have suggested in their investigations of the American and French film industries, respectively, successful groups of firms and individuals may constitute quasi-recurrent production net-works over a limited series of projects, but they rarely endure unchanged for long. This pervasive condition of functional disintegration and rela-tional variability in the industry means that production companies need to have easy access to a wide variety of specialized firms and workers so that they can constantly adjust and readjust their activity networks. As I argued earlier, this sort of situation often results in patterns of locational agglo-meration, especially where inter-firm transactions are frequent, small in scale, non-repetitive, and labor-intensive, as they tend to be in the French film industry. Agglomeration is further intensified where local labor markets are also unstable, for the need constantly to rematch workers and jobs puts a premium on overall proximity.

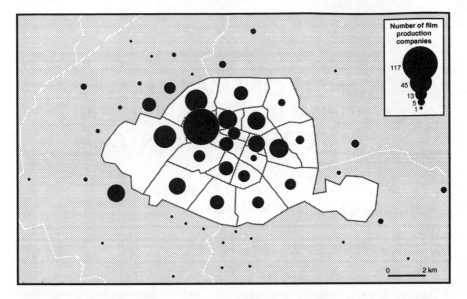

Figure 7.1   *Location of film production companies in the Paris region (based on address data in* Annuaire du Cinéma, Télévision, Vidéo, *Paris: S.N. Bellefaye, 1997)*

Empirical patterns of location

Agglomeration is very marked indeed in the French film industry. Almost all firms in the sector are located in the Paris metropolitan region, and a significant proportion of these are concentrated in one particular district close to the center of the city. This remark may be amplified by means of detailed empirical description of the spatial organization of three critical subsectors, namely, (a) production companies, (b) creative talent and casting agencies, and (c) film studios. The first two of these subsectors are tightly agglomerated. The third is more widely dispersed, with the larger studios tending to spread out into suburban locations in the Paris metropolitan region, but it can also be seen as the exception that substantiates the rule.

Production companies are particularly transactions-intensive in their modes of operation, and in view of their critical importance within the industry as a whole, they may be expected to exhibit a very strong disposition to locational convergence and spatial centralization within the wider metropolitan environment. This expectation is borne out by Figure 7.1, which shows that producers are heavily concentrated in and around the eighth *arrondissement* in the west center of Paris, a pattern that they share with other media and communications sectors as represented by talent agencies, advertising firms, recording companies, and television and radio broadcasting services. The locational concentration of film producers in this manner has been persistent over the whole postwar period, though

Table 7.1   *Film production companies and their locational incidence in the Paris region*

Year	Number of production companies in the Paris region	% in eighth *arrondissement*	% in City of Paris
1997	642	18.2	77.9
1987	667	29.7	82.5
1977	458	38.4	83.0
1967	437	55.6	90.4

Source: calculated from address data in *Annuaire du Cinéma, Télévision, Vidéo*, Paris: S.N. Bellefaye, 1997

there has also been a complementary process of spatial drift of companies into inner suburban areas (especially into the western reaches of the metropolitan area), presumably in response to rising land values in the center of Paris (see Table 7.1). Nevertheless, the eighth *arrondissement* with 18.2% of all production companies in the Paris region in 1997 remains by far the dominant pole of attraction for the industry, while over three-quarters of producers in the region can still be found within the bounds of the city of Paris itself.

Agencies representing creative talent (actors, writers, directors, etc.) are marked by a similar locational pattern. These agencies function as trans-actional nodes, trading above all on costs and uncertainties in the exchange of information in the labor market. Figure 7.2 depicts the locational distribution of creative talent and casting agencies in the city of Paris. It should be emphasized that the agencies shown here serve not just the film industry but the entire spectrum of arts and entertainment sectors, and for this reason, their distributional pattern is subject to a number of hetero-geneous pushes and pulls. Even so, their locational concentration in and around the eighth *arrondissement* is plainly evident. By helping to reduce the frictions of information flow, these agencies contribute significantly to the overall agglomeration economies available to the film industry in the greater Paris region.

An important but contrasting element of the production system is represented by film studios. These are essentially independently owned sound-stage operations, not to be confused with the notion of 'studio' common in the USA, meaning a Hollywood major. Studios are hired out to production companies by the day or week. Unlike other elements of the production system, their locational pattern is governed more by their capital- and land-intensive characteristics than it is by their transactional relationships. They need to be broadly accessible to film production teams within the wider metropolitan region, but their demands for space to house their often ample facilities also push them toward the periphery where relatively cheap land is available. The locations of all 77 studios to be found in the Paris region are identified in Figure 7.3. These studios are as a rule multipurpose in the sense that they serve a variety of different sectors

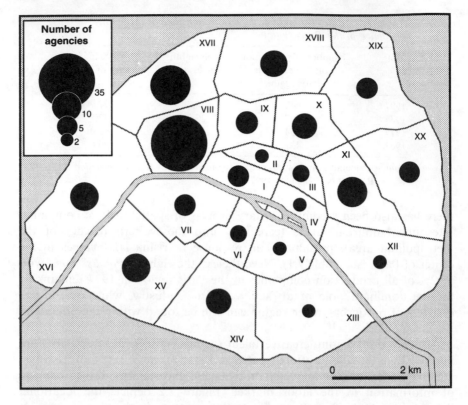

Figure 7.2   *The location of creative talent and casting agencies in the city of Paris (based on address data in France Telecom,* Les Pages Jaunes, *1997):* arrondissements *are numbered*

including film and television production, advertising, photography, and so on. Figure 7.3 shows that their locations are rather evenly distributed across the central part of the region, but with a tendency to align themselves along the perimeter of the City of Paris and with a clear projection out into far suburban areas. Moreover, studios closer to the center of Paris are invariably small and offer limited facilities, whereas those in the suburban periphery are large and embody multiple sound stages. There is, indeed, a positive and statistically significant relationship between the total sound-stage area available at any given studio and its distance from the center of Paris[1] – a recurrence, no doubt, of the widely observed inverse correlation in metropolitan systems generally between land price and the land area consumed by individual users. Most studios are nowadays highly specialized on the leasing out of sound stages, but some, especially larger studios in suburban locations, may offer additional services such as carpentry for set construction, equipment rental, or post-production work, on either a vertically integrated or an inside contracting basis. A few studios have come to be nuclei of small clusters of independent technical

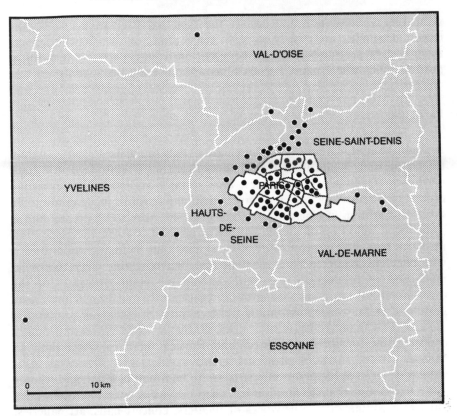

Figure 7.3   *Location of film studios in the Paris region: each dot represents*
one studio (based on address data in Annuaire du Cinéma, Télévision,
Vidéo, *Paris: S.N. Bellefaye, 1997)*

industries, but there is nothing in France to compare with the sizable
agglomerations that Nicolas (1997) has described around the Pinewood
and especially the Shepperton studios just outside London.

A number of the French studios operating today date from the early
decades of the century and were the production sites of some of the great
Poetic Realist films of the 1930s and 1940s, with their justly celebrated set
designs. Among them are Eclair Studios at Epinay-sur-Seine and the
Studios de Boulogne at Boulogne-Billancourt (Collomb and Patry, 1995).
Certain other legendary studios in the Paris region, notably Billancourt and
Joinville, have disappeared over the last decade or so under the double
pressure of rising land values and falling demand for indoor film shooting
facilities. In fact, as the New Wave cinema came into vogue in the late
1950s, with its dominant aesthetic of simplicity, spontaneity, and natural
décor, indoor shooting declined drastically (cf. Crisp, 1993; Frodon, 1995),
and studio fortunes have begun to pick up again only recently, partly
because of rising demand by television producers (Barbu, 1992). Even

given this circumstance, and despite the fact that French cinema is now largely dominated by post-New-Wave sensibilities, studios remain subject to significant pressure because of competition from cheaper Eastern European facilities where many French films are currently being shot.

Paris, the Place

It might be said, without undue circularity, that the distinguishing characteristic of French film is its Frenchness. This trait is embodied in a hallmark set of resonances, attitudes, and gestures rooted in the everyday fabric of French society and given distinctive form in a continually evolving tradition of cinematic art. Yet if the Frenchness of French film is somehow a reflection of French society at large, it is Paris, the place, that mediates the whole process of distillation, and that so frequently infuses it with concrete character. Paris is at once the matrix within which the social machinery of production is entrenched and the main repository of the diverse cultural resources that are both consciously and unselfconsciously mobilized in the conceptualization and execution of cinematic projects.

Paris, like many other capital cities, is the locus of an extraordinary concentration of artistic, literary, and musical abilities. According to Menger (1993), 75.5% of all French creative artists and 70% of all individuals engaged in the performing arts are to be found in Paris, and what is more, the degree of concentration has been increasing over the recent past. Paris also contains dense networks of theaters, concert halls, art galleries, museums, architectural monuments, and other major arenas of collective cultural consumption, all of which help to sustain active appreciation of and involvement in the arts. These endowments, together with its long traditions of aesthetic and intellectual accomplishment, make Paris one of the leading centers of cultural life in the modern world, and all the more so in view of the cross-fertilizing effects that constantly flow back and forth between the different forms of artistic activity that it harbors. The cinema draws with special intensity on the cultural milieu of Paris, as exemplified by the ways in which it ramifies with the theater, the musical and literary worlds, and the fashion industry. At the same time, the prevailing social and cultural ethos is one that prompts film-makers to resist the absolute subordination of the final product to commercial values, a circumstance that helps to shore up the artistic ambitiousness of French cinema, but one that also provides important clues as to the dynamics of the ever intensifying competitive pressures that it faces in regard to Hollywood films. The result is a cinema noted by and large for its intelligence and emotional depth, as an expression not just of the talents of the scenarists, directors, and actors who are on the front line so to speak of cinematic creation, but also of the excellence of the industry's workers in areas such as set and costume design, photography, lighting, and editing. Equally, Paris has long been a center of influential film criticism, kept alive today by magazines like *Les Cahiers du Cinéma, Le Film*

Français, and *Positif*, and it is noted for its unparalleled population of devoted cinephiles. The appetites of this audience are maintained at a high level of discernment by what is certainly the widest menu of films on offer at any given moment to the public in any city in the world. In the vocabulary of the business economist these remarks translate into the equivalent proposition that the film industry of Paris enjoys the triple competitive advantages of a milieu (a) that generates a constant stream of vibrant cultural externalities, (b) that harbors a large pool of suitably skilled and adapted workers, and (c) that constitutes a discriminating home market (cf. Porter, 1990).

As important as these assets may be, they are apt to be inert until energized and reproduced through an actually working production system. This remark is particularly pertinent in the case of the French film industry whose fragmented and transactions-intensive mode of operation continually remobilizes and refashions the specialized human and cultural resources of the city as production occurs; and precisely because the film industry *is* caught up in complex divisions of labor – meaning that constantly revolving groups of individuals are brought into active engagement with one another in the world of work – new and unexpected combinations of these resources are forever being created in the very act of production. Concomitantly, the same processes of interaction often engender spontaneous learning effects. These effects then accumulate, as it were, within the alveolate agglomeration of the city. The French film industry is undoubtedly typified by mechanisms of informal knowledge creation akin to these. More importantly, perhaps, the industry is also subject to a complementary dynamic: one focused more on the maintenance and transformation of workers' sensibilities (forms of empathy, feeling, awareness, imagination, expressiveness, and so on) than on the genesis of cumulative technical advances, and which become manifest in final products in distinctive but variable cultural codes, styles, conventions, fashions, and all the rest.

The job-specific sensibilities of film industry workers are, of course, partly a reflection of their formal and informal training. They also grow, however, out of processes of acculturation in different realms of daily life together with the forms of habituation and socialization that tend to occur on the job, and that help to endow workers such as actors, directors, or set designers with instinct-like capacities to proceed with the tasks of cultural performance and improvisation, much as in the notion of practice outlined by Bourdieu (1980). This point suggests that at least an element of the creative energies that develop in some cultural-products industries can be seen as an endogenous property unleashed by (but also hemmed in by) the procedural routines of production. We might say, building on the work of Miège et al. (1986), that as culture is industrialized so, for better or worse, the production of culture itself tends increasingly to reside in teams of specialized workers (i.e. in divisions of labor) which to a varying extent begin to substitute for the individual artist in the traditional senses of the term (cf. Moulin, 1983). Where production is agglomerated, the very same processes are liable to result in a type of geographic lock-in as manifest in the appearance of place-specific forms of product identity (a special sort of 'authenticity') that are then exploitable as localized monopoly assets (Molotch, 1996). An echo of the same point can perhaps be discerned in Marcel Pagnol's decision in 1932 to open his own film studio in Marseille so as to escape from the conventional urbanities of Parisian film-making and to pursue more effectively his search for a cinema reflecting the social attitudes and mannerisms of the French Midi, or, for that matter, in the efforts made by some American cineastes to create an alternative cinema by deliberately choosing *not* to work in Hollywood.

From Survival to Competitiveness

In any cultural-products industry there is always a tension between the economic logic of the production system and the cultural imperatives of aesthetic and intellectual accomplishment (cf. Bordwell et al., 1985), and it is sometimes suggested that the purely business and practical aspects of film-making are an impediment to its full artistic realization. In fact, every art must come to terms with the historically contingent conditions that define its range of possibilities and its limitations, and in this sense the business and practical aspects of making films (even *films d'auteur*) must be seen as intrinsic components of the entire creative process of cinematography in modern capitalism and not its necessary antithesis. It must be added at once that the traditions of the French cinema, and the legally sanctioned artistic authority of the *auteur* in any final product, tip this tension-filled relation in the direction of a more personalized, more recondite cinema, one that makes fewer concessions to the average viewer than we are accustomed to from the dream factories of Hollywood. A notable symptom of this state of affairs is the evident reluctance of French film-makers to work within formulaic genres and standardized plot structures (Denat and Guingamp, 1993; Gauthier, 1993; Jeancolas, 1995). The result is a cinema that is high in general quality, but that is frequently less successful in purely commercial terms, and which, partly on account of its cultural idiosyncrasies, finds it difficult to penetrate export markets except among a minuscule cosmopolitan elite. Even on its home terrain, French cinema has been fighting a losing battle against American films though, significantly, the battle has been more successful in Paris than it has been in the provinces.[2] The net result is a certain debilitation edging toward a mood of crisis in the contemporary French cinema, and a palpable search among the new generation of young directors now coming to the fore for wider contact with popular audiences (Chalvon-Demersay, 1994; Luong, 1996; Prédal, 1996). It is important to reflect in this context on what French economic and cultural policy may have done to create these problems, and what remedial action, if any, might be taken.

There can be little doubt that without the strong policy intervention of the last few decades, French cinema would probably have declined as severely as it has in Italy, Germany, and (until quite recently) Britain. As noted, this policy has been accomplished by means of an intricate combination of financial subsidies, induced investments, television broadcasting quotas, managed labor markets, and the many and varied services provided by the CNC to the film industry. These measures have been applied, moreover, in a way that is sensitive to the need for organizational flexibility in the industry. Notwithstanding these achievements, the policy system that has been patched together over the years has consisted more of a set of defensive maneuvers than it has of a frontal attack on the problem of building industrial dynamism and expanding into new markets. It has succeeded in blunting the worst effects of foreign competition, essentially by propping up domestic market share and by dramatically reducing entrepreneurial risk, but it has been notably less forthcoming in helping to shape new competitive strategies or to create new synergies of a type that might promote superior levels of economic performance. Even if the CNC makes gestures in this direction through its various programs of assistance, these are in practice much less than effective given the current competitive conjuncture. A further problem with some of these policy measures is their plainly regressive effects on the distribution of income and consumer benefits (cf. Benhamou, 1996). In 1996, 28.4% of all film theater entries in France were accounted for by individuals in upper socio-economic categories (who represent 21.9% of the total population of France) while just 18.3% of entries were accounted for by individuals in lower socio-economic categories (who represent 24.3% of the total population) (CNC, 1997a). At the same time, the latter group is much more likely than the former to watch television. Hence, by diverting significant resources from television to cinema, current policy tends to subsidize the cultural preferences and practices of upper socio-economic groups at the expense of lower.

This is not the place to enter into the intricate arguments that now come into play about income distribution versus national cultural goals and objectives. Nor is it the place to attempt to devise a detailed bill of specifics purporting to provide a prescription for the commercial regeneration of French cinema. Any new policies that need to be formulated, and any concrete actions that need to be taken, can only be worked out in the first instance, not in relation to an abstract *a priori* blueprint, but on the basis of detailed self-assessment by those most directly involved in the industry together with appropriate political debate. With this cautionary note in mind it is nonetheless appropriate to explore some broad strategic lines of a credible first encounter with the problem. I suggest, in particular, that the theoretical ideas on urban and regional development advanced earlier in this book offer some fruitful lessons. These ideas suggest a number of promising approaches to the task of reinforcing regional dynamism, hinging above all on collective efforts to intensify agglomeration economies and relational synergies. Three main lines of reflection would appear to be of particular pertinence to the French film industry in this respect.

First, there seems to be a deficit in the French film industry of those Schumpeterian forms of commercial and technological innovation that we frequently find in other densely agglomerated industrial complexes. What we observe, rather, is a series of cycles of the birth and demise of firms with rather limited forward advance in matters of best business practice. By and large, firms themselves are too small to invest significant resources in R&D, and there is relatively little in the way of public spending devoted to the upgrading of productive practices in the industry at large. It is certainly the case that the CNC and numerous professional and trade associations all play a certain role in respect to this issue, but for the most part their activities are either seriously underfunded (the budget for the CNC's new technologies program being just 15 million francs a year) or focused on the circulation of fairly routine if not largely second-hand information. There is in fact a shortfall in basic and applied research, not just on commercial and technological matters, but also on the creative side of the industry (e.g. on the aesthetic possibilities of new computer graphics and multimedia technologies). One potential line of redress would be to overhaul existing organizations, enabling them to become more robust centers of innovation and knowledge creation. Another might be to establish entirely new institutional foci with tight links to the industry as a whole and capable of playing a role in the film industry somewhere between that played by, say, IRCAM (Institut de Recherches, Coordination Acoustique Musique) in regard to French contemporary music and INA (Institut National de la Communication Audiovisuelle) in regard to French television.

Second, a pervasive problem of the French film industry, as of all the national European film industries, is that it is unable to command the overall economies of scale that the Hollywood industry enjoys. As a result, Hollywood films can almost always undercut European films on a marginal cost basis even on European markets. One strategic response to this kind of competitive dilemma is for European film-makers to focus even more intently than they have in the past on consumer satisfaction through the production of high-quality films. Another response is conceivable in terms of a more resolute search, if not for a pan-European cinema, at least for a stronger functional integration of individual national film industries in ways that make more constructive use of the differential strengths of each (cf. Jäckel, 1996). Admittedly, the rather limited programs of the Council of Europe and the European Union have thus far not produced startling results. However, the rising incidence of more spontaneous forms of business cooperation in Europe, especially at the inter-regional level (cf. Keating, 1998; Scott, 1998), provides some indication that different segments of the industry in major centers of cinematic production like Paris, London, and Rome may yet be induced to join forces in the quest for a larger and more internally variegated amalgam, and hence a potentially more competitive film industry. An obvious advantage of any putative European cinema, as such, is that it would by definition be international.

Third, the French film industry is patently weak in the areas of export promotion and marketing, and this problem becomes all the more significant when the search is on for economies of scale within the production system. In some degree, the poor performance of French films on foreign markets can be ascribed to linguistic barriers, but these are probably not the irremediable impediment to the development of non-French-speaking audiences that many individuals in the industry currently believe they are (cf. Finney, 1997). Even in the United States the occasional small successes of foreign-language films (e.g. Chinese, German, Italian, as well as French) suggest that there is a modest but lucrative latent market there, while the difficulties faced by many British films until recently on American markets would seem to indicate that the problem is less a simple matter of language than it is one of insufficient prior marketing and publicity work in preparing potential audiences to deal with alternative cinematic idioms. In any case, the language problem is likely to diminish significantly with further progress in the computerization of dubbing procedures, including digital reconfiguration of actors' lip movements (Martin, 1995). Although Unifrance and cultural attachés in French consulates all over the world make valiant efforts to advance the cause of French cinema in foreign countries, there is no adequately financed or coordinated effort at the present time to develop a global business strategy for the French film industry, whether it be in the area of market research, promotional effort, or physical distribution.

There is, of course, no easy solution to these latter problems, as evidenced by the failure in 1985 of Gaumont-Columbia's joint venture, Triumph Films, initially established to distribute French films in the USA (Coulot and Téboul, 1989). Moreover, while foreign distributors of French films can be expected to make some effort – in their own interests – to promote individual films, they are certainly not going to underwrite the costs of wider export market penetration by French cinema as a whole. Much, however, might be achieved by more extensive pooling of resources of individual French companies as well as by joint marketing efforts (both public and private) covering not only films but also a range of other distinctive French products such as fashions, perfumes, wines and liqueurs, gastronomic products, tourist services, and so on. In the production arena, too, a greater effort might be made to play the global card by paying more heed to the susceptibilities of wider foreign audiences, though the challenge here is to develop alternative forms of expression while simultaneously retaining the individuality and credibility of French cinema as such. Certainly, any attack on wider markets by means of wholesale mimicry of Hollywood (as in the case of *The Fifth Element*) is probably doomed to undermine more than it is to promote French cinema as such. Over and above questions of authenticity and standards of cultural judgment, this remark can be justified by invoking the general theory of industrial districts which suggests that because of increasing returns effects, the long-term survival of any industrial agglomeration is more likely to be secured by meaningful differentiation from a dominant competitor than it is by imitation.

Few of these suggestions could in all probability even be broached without also considering some reform of the CNC's mission. A major question in view of the discussion above is whether or not money currently held in the Center's general support fund should be shifted from providing subsidies to producers and into assistance for more aggressive foreign distribution and marketing efforts. The net result of any such action, at least in the short run, would no doubt be a drop in the annual output of films, though the cuts would presumably hit hardest at the bottom end of the quality spectrum where producers are often, in any case, more concerned about obtaining financial subsidies than they are with actually attracting audiences. Over the longer run, if the right formula could be found – and this would no doubt include, among other things, some beneficial heightening of the entrepreneurial risk faced by production companies together with some growth in the size and commercial capacity of larger firms – there are many indications that a more vigorous industry could emerge. However, since an unintended consequence of any policy system that involves the selective distribution of largesse is to create quasi-rentier groups (Throsby, 1994), any effort at significant reform of the CNC is likely to be politically contentious.

Whatever future shape French policy might assume in regard to the film industry, there is a convincing case in favor of the view that continued collective action is essential both to preserve the industry as a going concern and to help it build new business muscle (Benghozi and Sagot-Duvauroux, 1994). Quite apart from the economic interests that are at stake here, the French film industry is also an institution embodying cultural values and perspectives that well merit concerted public support. That, indeed, is a political judgment that French society has already made, firmly and unambiguously. By the same token, the complaints of the Motion Picture Association of America about corresponding restraints on free trade are entirely correct but completely miss the point, which is that cultural products, being as much about individual and social forms of self-identity as they are about sales and profits, have an *intrinsically* political meaning. It may be added that the regulatory system which has maintained the French film industry so forcefully as a bastion of alternative cinematic culture to Hollywood represents a service whose benefits resound well beyond the frontiers of France.

Conclusion

In these two chapters I have attempted to show how significant aspects of the French film industry can be understood in terms of the complex interplay between a functionally disintegrated system of production, a notably activist regulatory environment, and the specific geographic locale of Paris. The whole forms a dynamic network of interdependencies generating a constant stream of beneficial externalities that function as critical foundations of the industry's competitive advantages and creative capacity. Many different kinds of industries in the modern world are characterized by similar functional and spatial attributes, but in the case of cultural-products sectors the concomitant analytical issues are especially intricate on account of the reflexive interactions that occur between the milieu, the workings of the industry, and the aesthetic and semiotic content of final products. In particular, because the outputs of cultural-products industries are usually marked by such an intimate relation to their place of origin (endowing them as it does with an often inimitable cachet), the latter is of special significance in any investigation of their design dynamics and market trajectories.

In France, a long tradition of public support for the cinema has helped to maintain it as a viable economic sector and as a lively and popular art. Yet despite the evident success of French policies and administrative arrangements in regard to the film industry – most notably as a line of defense against foreign (i.e. American) competition – they should probably at this stage be subject to wide review. More than anything else, an argument can be made for building a more dynamic and visionary partnership between the industry and government, and for devising new institutional modalities for the promotion of innovation, scale economies, and export and marketing capabilities so as to complement the creative talent that abounds in contemporary French cinema with a more potent business and commercial platform.

Cultural products now account for steadily rising shares of modern business activity and international trade, which means in turn that selected cities and regions find it increasingly possible to prosper on the basis of their ability to build competitive advantage in cultural-products sectors. The paradox is that precisely at a time when these developments are moving swiftly forward, the French film industry continues to show unmistakable signs of competitive weakness. Accordingly, one of the major challenges that the industry faces is not just to rebuild and recapture lost domestic audiences but also to construct the conditions for an effective assault on significant niches within international markets. France already possesses major assets in its long and distinguished tradition of cinematography, its large pool of skilled technical and creative workers, and its still robust film production capacities. The challenge thus has some degree of realizability, especially no doubt within the more commercial segment of what I referred to earlier as an emerging two-tier system in the French film industry. Whatever changes this may or may not imply in terms of the content and style of French films, it is almost certainly not achievable without some significant reinforcement of the industry's collective order as an agglomeration of interdependent producers and careful reconsideration of the policy environment within which it is implanted. The likely alternative to determined action – the deepening ghettoization of French cinema – is neither culturally desirable nor economically inevitable.

Notes

1 For a total of 32 studios for which data could be found, the statistical relationship between sound-stage area A_i (m^2), for the ith studio and its distance from Paris D_i (km) can be written $A_i = 19.11\exp(1.98D_i)$, $R^2 = 0.59$. Data for this exercise were taken from CST (1996) and various business directories.

2 Unpublished data made available by the CNC show that in 1996, 48.9% of theater entries in Paris were for American films, whereas in the rest of the country the figure was 55.7%.

8

THE RECORDED MUSIC INDUSTRY IN THE UNITED STATES

There are few sectors that can more dramatically illustrate the theme of the convergence between the economic and the cultural in modern life than the recorded music industry, which not only is a major economic force in its own right, but also supplies a final product that has virtually no other interest to the consumer than its aesthetic and semiotic content. It is, in the terms of Bourdieu (1971), a purely symbolic good, though its roots go deeply into an everyday world of business decisions and productive labor (cf. Leyshon et al., 1998). My strategy in the present chapter is to steer a course that moves backward and forward between these two polarities while emphasizing a third or intermediate perspective that focuses on the production system as the creative field within which the changing forms and symbolic content of recorded music are generated. At stake in this issue is the central question of locational variations in creativity and their effects on the ability of producers in different places to contest wider markets.

The Recorded Music Industry: Structure and Performance

Products and sales

In 1997, total domestic sales of recorded music in the United States were valued at $12.2 billion (RIAA, 1997). This figure exceeds the domestic sales of the motion picture industry in the same year by some $1.5 billion. Reliable information on the income of American recording companies from exports (both visible and invisible) is difficult to obtain, but a perusal of the financial reports of major corporations suggests that their overall export market may well be equal in size to the domestic market (see also Burnett, 1990). The industry has grown rapidly over the last few decades, and in real terms, its domestic sales increased by 160.1% between 1987 and 1997.

By far the greater part of the industry's revenues from domestic markets comes from sales of compact disks (83.3% of total sales) followed by cassettes (13.5%), (RIAA, 1997). The residue is made up by music videos and a rapidly vanishing output of vinyl single and long-playing records. The main categories or genres of music produced in these ways are rock, country, rhythm and blues, and pop, representing 32.5%, 14.4%, 11.2%, and 10.1%, respectively, of total market share in 1997. Other more specialized genres include folk, Latin, gospel, jazz, world music, serious music, and so on.

Corporate organization

As is common in other media sectors, the recorded music industry is organized into a handful of large corporate entities, or majors, together with a great many so-called independents, most of which employ only small numbers of people (Hesmondhalgh, 1996; Sanjek, 1988). Both majors and independents face an overall market that is notorious for its instability and unpredictability, and the market is made all the more volatile by a consistently massive oversupply of output relative to consumer demands (Alexander, 1994; Baker, 1991; Hirsch, 1969). As a consequence, there is rapid turnover among smaller independents, especially as barriers to entry and exit are low (Monopolies and Mergers Commission, 1994).

The majors are all represented by highly capitalized multinational firms whose interests typically extend across a diversity of media, consumer products, and electronics sectors (Barnett and Cavanagh, 1994; Lovering, 1998; Sadler, 1997; Wallis, 1990). These firms are marked by constant mutation as they go through rapid successions of mergers, demergers, and acquisitions. At the present time, five principal corporate entities dominate the recorded music industry both in the United States and in the wider international arena. These are Bertelsmann AG (headquartered in Germany), the EMI Group (Britain), the Seagram Company Ltd (Canada), Sony Corporation (Japan), and Time-Warner Inc. (United States), all of which, in addition to their many other interests, have a commanding presence in the US music industry by reason of their specialized artist management, music publishing, recording, record pressing, and distribution divisions.

Time-Warner, for example, has extensive holdings in motion picture production, publishing, broadcasting, and consumer products, as well as a full range of music industry divisions. A schematic overview of Time-Warner's principal music industry properties is laid out in Figure 8.1. The nucleus of these properties is represented by the Warner Music Group and its stable of affiliated record labels including Atlantic, Elektra, Rhino, Sire, and Warner Brothers Records. The Group also has a number of joint ventures with independent labels, and each of the Group's affiliated labels in turn has its own dependent affiliates, joint ventures, and agreements. All of the affiliated labels are associated through common corporate ownership with WEA Inc. (which in turn owns record manufacturing and distribution facilities) and the Ivy Hill record packaging and sleeve printing company. Even though Time-Warner's music industry interests appear in Figure 8.1 as though they constitute a vertically integrated line of production activities, they are in practice more like a loose coupling of quasi-independent units under a single ownership umbrella than an unbroken production

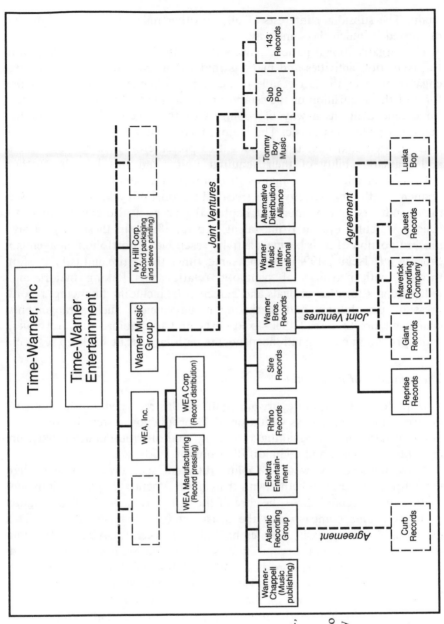

Figure 8.1 *Principal music industry interests of Time-Warner Inc. (sources: Disclosure Inc., Laser Disclosure Database; National Register Publishing, Who Owns Whom, Directory of Corporate Affiliations; Time-Warner Company Report and Fact Book, 1998; and conversations with Warner Music Group representatives)*

chain. The subsidiary interests of all the other music industry majors are organized in much the same way.

This organizational pattern reflects the strategic repositioning in regard to production activities and markets that the music industry majors have engaged in over the last couple of decades. This has primarily taken the form of the acquisition or the establishment of joint ventures with successful independents as a way of coping with the excessively unpredictable market for recorded music. The majors have gone about this task, moreover, in ways that have usually sought to preserve the managerial cultures and maneuverability of their acquired units, and this has the further advantage of allowing the majors to monitor and exploit different market segments with great effectiveness (recall the model of cyclical change in the music industry as presented in Chapter 3), just as it also enables them to keep a watchful eye on rising talent (Rowe, 1995). In these ways a significant portion of their business activity resembles a portfolio management process (cf. Negus, 1998). At the same time, the entire industry is shot through with networks of symbiotic relationships linking majors and independents together in deals and agreements, including financing, record pressing, distribution, and marketing arrangements. Such arrangements enable majors to spread their fixed costs and to stabilize their revenues, while providing many small independents with large-scale back-up services.

The structure of production

This pattern of corporate organization in the recorded music industry intersects in complex ways with a physical production system in which the different tasks of music-making, recording, and distribution are broken up into intricate social and technical divisions of labor.

A schematic overview of the many different specialized activities that make up the industry together with their main functional interrelationships is laid out in Figure 8.2. At the core of the structure depicted in this figure is the recording company and the artists who are signed up to it. The recording company itself operates basically as a central A&R (artist and repertoire) recruitment organization and as the publisher of finished recordings. Around this core lies a constellation of distinctive economic and culture-producing functions ranging from song writing and the provision of musical instruments on the one side, to manufacturing and promotion and distribution on the other. At various intermediate stages come such other essential components of the production process as legal services, music publishing, recording studios, producers, sound engineers, and various accessory services. To these may be added a number of specialized operations not shown in Figure 8.2 such as record mastering, video production, graphic design, sleeve printing, packaging, and so on.

The central unit of ownership and control around which both majors and independents are structured is a record label (or labels), and other functions may be integrated or not along with this fundamental activity.

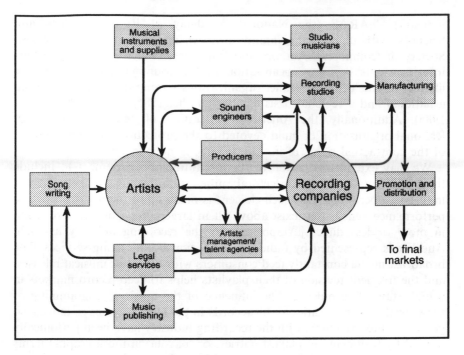

Figure 8.2   *A schematic overview of specialized activities in and around the recorded music industry, showing their main functional interconnections*

Full-blown functional integration, however, is less common today than it was in the past, a feature that the record industry shares in common with the motion picture industry. Even in the case of the majors, specialized affiliated divisions usually operate nowadays as more or less autonomous decision centers. Thus, the different activities delineated in Figure 8.2 generally assume the operative form of independent firms or freelance workers in vertically disintegrated relation to one another (or quasi-disintegrated relation where contractual association prevails, as in the case of artists signed up to record companies). An advanced level of vertical disintegration, of course, represents a classic means of dealing with market uncertainty by making it possible for a high order of transactional flexibility to occur within the production system.

The institutional environment

In many different industrial sectors it is common to find a number of overarching organizations and associations providing regulatory services for their members and seeking to promote their interests. The recorded music industry is no exception to this statement. Its principal institutional supports in the United States are the Recording Industry Association of America (the main trade and lobbying association for the recording industry), NARAS (the National Academy of Recording Arts and Sciences, with its annual Grammy awards), and ASCAP (the American Society of Composers, Authors and Publishers, which is the largest performing rights licensing organization in the country), though there are literally dozens of other smaller organizations serving the industry on both a national and a regional basis (cf. Baskerville, 1985; RIAA, 1997; Ryan, 1985). Additionally, the American Federation of Musicians is a professional organization or guild devoted to the protection and enhancement of the contractual rights of its 120,000-strong membership.

We may extend this notion of the institutional environment to include those elements of the parasectoral milieu that intrude actively on the industry's operations. One such element is made up of the networks of live performance venues that exist above all in large cities, and often function in more or less direct juxtaposition to the recording industry as such. Another is represented by radio and television broadcasting services. The broadcast media constantly feed consumers with the latest musical releases, and the frequent revision of their playlists helps to keep record markets in a high state of turbulence. The influence of the musical programming of these media on the creation of hit records in the United States is, indeed, so great that their relations with the recording industry have been periodically tainted by trafficking in playlist entries, or 'payola' in more graphic terms (Chapple and Garofolo, 1977; Segrave, 1994). To these broadcast media we must add the many printed news media associated with the industry, *Billboard* being the most prominent.

The Locational Pattern of the Recorded Music Industry in the United States

A brief descriptive geography of music-making and recording

Before we deal directly with the locational structure of the recording industry as such, it will be useful for us to examine something of the geography of its basic raw material, namely, composers and performers of music.

The *US Census of Population* informs us that there were 148,020 professional composers and musicians in the United States in 1990, divided in the ratio of two to one between males and females, respectively. These individuals are widely distributed across the whole country. If we confine our attention to metropolitan areas, we find that the relation between the number of composers and musicians y_i and total population x_i in the ith such area can be written as the simple regression equation $y_i = 0.000064x_i^{1.1605}$, with $R^2 = 0.88$ and $n = 248$. The parameters of this equation signify that the number of composers and musicians in any place generally represents a minute but fairly constant proportion of the total population, with mild increasing returns effects being observable in the very largest metropolitan areas. The single most notable exception to this rule of proportionality is Nashville, Tennessee, which with just fewer than one million inhabitants in 1990 had a total of 3,351 composers and musicians, giving it the highest ratio of these professionals to total population in the entire country. This peculiar geographic distribution of composers and musicians across the United States stands in strong contrast to the locational structure of the recording industry as such (see next paragraph), a circumstance which suggests that only limited functional overlap occurs between these two sets of activity taken in their entirety.

In fact, the map of recording companies in the United States (see Figure 8.3) reveals a pattern that bears a notably uneven relationship to the underlying geography of population. The pattern is dominated by three main agglomerations of recording companies corresponding to the metropolitan areas of Los Angeles, New York, and Nashville, and for the rest it comprises a widely dispersed arrangement of establishments, with some local points of focus in cities such as Atlanta, Austin, Chicago, Miami, San Francisco, and Seattle, but with many other large cities appearing simply as blanks. Recording companies shown in Figure 8.3 are classified either as majors and their affiliates or as independents. The figure comprises 72 companies in the former group and 235 in the latter. Almost all of the majors and their affiliates are located in Los Angeles, New York, and, to a lesser degree, Nashville. Of the independents, 51 occur in Los Angeles, 44 in New York, 9 in Nashville, and 151 in the rest of the country. While the number of majors and affiliates shown is probably quite accurate, there can be little doubt that the number of independents accounted for represents a serious undercount (in this regard, see the discussion of Table 8.1 below). There is no authoritative source of information that can be used as a basis for checking these numbers,[1] and given the extremely short lifespan of most independent recording companies, precision would in any case always be somewhat elusive. Nevertheless, an impartial check of the accuracy of the relative *geographic* distribution of recording companies as shown can fairly easily be carried out. This operation consists simply in comparing the frequency distribution by zip code aggregates of the locations of independents as taken from the *Recording Industry Sourcebook* (Cardinal Media Industries, 1998, the data source for Figure 8.3) with an equivalent distribution taken from an alternative source published by Pollstar (1998). Even though the listings of companies in these two publications are frequently quite divergent (a symptom of the difficulties of establishing an authoritative inventory of companies), the two frequency distributions are virtually identical. It would seem reasonable, then, to treat the independent companies depicted in Figure 8.3 as a geographically representative sample of the total population of such companies in the United States as a whole.

An initial explanatory sketch

What accounts for the peculiar geographic pattern shown in Figure 8.3, and above all for the observable inclination to locational agglomeration on

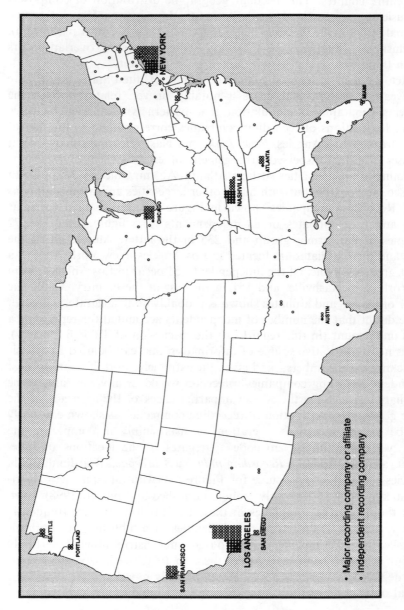

Figure 8.3 *Main locations of (a) majors and affiliates and (b) independent recording companies in the United States (source of address data: Cardinal Media Industries, 1998)*

the part of recorded music companies? At the outset, we should note that Los Angeles, New York, and Nashville were all marked by a number of positive historical conditions favorable to the initial growth of local recording industries. Both Los Angeles and New York are the sites of long-standing and highly developed motion picture and broadcasting industries that provided – and still provide – a symbiotic context for a flourishing music business, especially for producers of the more commercial forms of recorded popular music that are the staples of these two centers. Nashville for its part began its development as a hub of the music business in the 1920s when it became a center of country music broadcasting and live entertainment. It subsequently attracted a significant number of both major and independent recording companies as this largely regional musical culture gained commercial favor with wider audiences after the Second World War (Peterson, 1975; 1997; Peterson and DiMaggio, 1975).

These remarks help us to understand something of why Los Angeles, New York, and Nashville became associated with the recorded music industry, but they do not provide us with much more. Above all, they gloss over an issue that is of major analytical concern in the present context, namely, how virtually all industrial agglomerations eventually develop and grow (and thus consolidate their geographic foundations) in ways that are often quite independent of any initial locational conditions that may have been in effect, and how agglomeration as such actually comes to play an intrinsic part in its own regeneration. Reference back to Figure 8.2 enables us to begin the task of elucidating this issue. As already noted, this is an industry that has strong proclivities to functional disintegration so that it commonly assumes the profile of a transactions-intensive complex of interrelated activities. Both horizontal and vertical transactions in the industry, moreover, tend to be small in scale, frequent in occurrence, and highly idiosyncratic, and they also regularly involve prolonged personal encounters between many different individuals. Circumstances like these in and of themselves are apt to encourage locational agglomeration as a mechanism for preventing the space–time costs of system operation from spiralling out of control. As a corollary, and especially where strong market instabilities are present (as in the case of the recorded music business), the clustering together of many different types of firms and specialized workers in one place provides all participants in the industry with a form of social insurance in the sense that clustering will almost always guarantee a relatively high probability of finding just the right kind of input within easy access at just the right time (cf. Veltz, 1997).

In support of these broad points, we may observe that the geographic distribution of recording companies shown in Figure 8.3 is closely duplicated in similar maps for other critical recording industry activities. The maps are not presented here since they all essentially convey information identical to that contained in Figure 8.3. They show that for major supporting functions in the recording industry, such as music publishing, artists' management, music attorneys and legal services, and recording studios, the same pattern of agglomeration (in Los Angeles, New York, and Nashville) is dominant. Even the physical manufacturing or pressing of records is also characterized (in terms of number of establishments) by concentration in the three main music recording centers, though the occasional large mass-production facilities owned by the majors are generally to be found at scattered locations in the Midwest and other parts of the Northeast of the United States. The agglomerative propensities of recording companies are evidently so strong that they can be observed at the submetropolitan level too. The music recording industry in Los Angeles is densely clustered in a narrowly confined area in and around Hollywood (see Chapter 11); and a similar phenomenon occurs in New York with recording companies clustered predominantly in central and southern Manhattan.

Even in the preliminary and rather static sense in which I have thus far identified agglomeration in the recorded music industry, it can be seen as a fountainhead of important economic externalities that yield increasing returns effects and that strengthen local competitive advantages. Above all, agglomeration and its benefits for producers are greatly reinforced by the cultures, conventions, learning effects, and innovative impulses that typically spring into being in nodal centers of economic activity. These advantages are further bolstered where effective distribution services to the wider world are available, and in the case of record distribution in the United States a particularly aggressive system of distribution prevails (a system dominated again by the majors but also serving the independent sector).

Beyond the three main agglomerations that characterize the geography of the US recorded music industry there are also the minor clusters identified earlier, together with numerous individual establishments spread out across the country. Many of the companies to be found at these other locations represent outliers of the mainstream segment of the popular music industry; others are a reflection of the presence of local musical cultures that offer specialized recording opportunities (cf. Carney, 1994). These local cultures comprise long-standing traditional forms of music as well as purely recent growths, as in the cases of the music of Detroit–Motown in the 1960s, the commercial Latin music of southern Florida that has developed since the 1970s, the Seattle sound of the early 1990s, or the contemporary music of the Vietnamese immigrants of Orange County and San Jose, California.

Popular Music and the Creative Field

In Chapter 3 I developed an extended argument about creativity and innovation in the cultural economy, and I argued that dense production agglomerations are especially likely to be sites of insistent originality and inventiveness. The argument was based on a conception of the creative field as a dense network of social and economic interactions that under certain conditions continually destabilize patterns of cultural work and that help to engender new insights and sensibilities among the participants in any given sector.

These remarks point to a simple and testable hypothesis. If there is indeed a relationship, as suggested, between creativity and agglomeration in the recorded music industry, we should expect to observe a non-linear increasing returns relation between the size of any music industry agglomeration and its ability consistently to produce records that appeal to consumers, holding constant the effects of other complicating variables. The notion of consumer appeal is, of course, difficult to operationalize in empirical terms, but I shall measure it here in terms of hit records. More specifically, the dependent variable that is now subject to analysis is defined as the number of hit single records produced in any given agglomeration in any given year. I propose to examine this hypothesis by means of a test based on data culled from *Billboard*'s Hot 100 charts, a source that has the advantage for our purposes of representing the commercial mainstream of popular music, but that is not overwhelmingly dominated by the major labels (cf. Belinfante and Johnson, 1983). The information published in the Hot 100 charts includes an identification of the original company issuing each record, and on this basis it is then usually possible to determine the location of the company by US metropolitan area (and to eliminate those few companies whose records enter the US charts, but which are located outside the country). This process, it should be remarked, turns out to be extremely time-consuming, and it was not successful in every individual case.[2] The presumption here – made on the basis of the preceding discussion – is that the location of the original recording company is the best index of the general geographic environment or creative field out of which any record arises, even if actual recording sessions are very occasionally conducted at distant studios. That said, the test to be carried out remains silent about the specific social mechanisms that link the environment and the production of hit records together, and thus while a negative result will assuredly disconfirm the hypothesis, a positive result will only inform us that the relationship is at best consistent with the offered explanation. In addition, the Hot 100 charts track just one segment of the music business, and thus any results that we may obtain here need to be seen as providing at best a partial window onto an extremely diverse industry.

We proceed with data taken from the Hot 100 charts for the years 1995, 1996, and 1997. For each of the specified years, the total numbers of records making an appearance on these charts were 348, 342, and 474, respectively. In 1995, 55.7% of these records were produced by majors and affiliates as defined earlier; in 1996, the percentage was 58.2%; and in 1997 it was 54.0%. The majors and affiliates, as we know, are overwhelmingly located in Los Angeles and New York, which may perhaps be taken as evidence in favor of our hypothesis. However, given their ability to command the services of mega-stars, together with their enormous productive resources and distributing capacities, their disproportionate success might easily be (and probably is) a function of their scale as much as it is of their location.

A more searching test of the hypothesis can be carried out by concentrating on the performance of independent record companies. The relevant information for this purpose is laid out in Table 8.1. For each of the years 1995, 1996, and 1997, the table shows:

1   The number of Hot 100 hits produced by independent companies in Los Angeles, New York, and other parts of the US (including Nashville), together with a residual category representing companies whose location could not be traced or which are foreign-owned.
2   The number of independent companies actually located in Los Angeles, New York, and the rest of the United States, as indicated by the *Recording Industry Sourcebook*.
3   A corresponding set of indices of representation for Hot 100 hits, with the index in any given case being defined as p_{it}/P^*_{it}, where p_{it} is the proportion of Hot 100 hits produced by independent companies at location i in year t, and P^*_{it} is the proportion of independents at location i in year t. A value of the index greater than one signifies an overrepresentation of hits relative to the total number of companies; a value less than one signifies the opposite.

Two further points need to be registered in regard to Table 8.1. One is that the number of independent companies shown for any year is taken from the *Recording Industry Sourcebook* for the succeeding year, on the supposition that the listings will already be somewhat out of date by the time they are published. The other is that the number of independent companies indicated in Table 8.1 appears to decline drastically from 1996 to 1997. While there was a small downturn in the music business at that time, the explanation for this apparent sudden shift lies elsewhere. In fact, it is due to a concerted effort on the part of the *Recording Industry Sourcebook*'s editorial staff in 1997–8 to weed out a buildup of company listings that were no longer valid. In view of this, it may well be that the data presented are biased, though one could plausibly argue that most of this bias is likely to take the form of an overstatement of the presence of companies in Los Angeles and New York in 1995 and 1996 due to a propensity for listings in large places to overaccumulate in the absence of systematic sorting and sifting. Since this particular bias, if it exists, runs counter to the power of the hypothesis-testing procedure put into effect below, we shall press on. Recall the crucial point that the data taken from the *Sourcebook* do not appear to have any geographic bias.

Let us consider now the most important part of Table 8.1, i.e. the indices of representation for Hot 100 hits for the three designated geographic areas in 1995, 1996, and 1997. Los Angeles and New York quite clearly have unusually high levels of representation; the index for the rest of the United States is unusually low (and note, in passing, that if we were to eliminate

Table 8.1 *Independent record companies: absolute and relative incidence of Hot 100 hits by location*

Year	Number of Hot 100 hits produced by independent companies				Number of independent companies			Indices of representation for Hot 100 hits		
	Los Angeles	New York	Other US	Location unknown or foreign	Los Angeles	New York	Other US	Los Angeles	New York	Other US
1995	58	48	31	16	198	148	295	1.37	1.53	0.49
1996	59	48	28	8	195	141	277	1.37	1.55	0.46
1997	57	106	40	16	51	44	140	1.29	2.79	0.33

Sources: Record Research, Inc., *Joel Whitburn's Billboard Music Yearbook*, 1995, 1996, and 1997; Cardinal Media Industries, Inc., *Recording Industry Sourcebook*, 1996, 1997, and 1998

Nashville from this category, the index would be even lower). The indices for Los Angeles and New York are consistently some three to four times greater than those for the rest of the United States, and in 1997, New York's index actually shot up to a value more than eight times greater than that for the rest of the country. The evident deduction is that independents in Los Angeles and New York have a very significantly higher probability of producing a hit record than independents elsewhere. One might conceivably counter this remark with the observation that many independents in the rest of the country are probably not especially in the business of trying to produce Hot 100 hits, but that, if true, would only underline the argument being offered here. Recording companies in Los Angeles and New York tend to specialize in the creation of Hot 100 hits precisely because these centers offer a far more propitious environment for this sort of enterprise than any other place in the country, i.e. an environment that enables them to produce a massive flow of finely honed musical novelties that rise rapidly in the hit parade without a corresponding explosion of basic costs. The majors and their affiliates no doubt benefit from the same environment, and this, in combination with their scale advantages, presumably leverages their competitive advantages to very high levels indeed.

One further nuance in these data needs to be explored. A cursory examination of the Hot 100 charts suggests that hits tend to come in clumps such that a recording company's probability of making a hit increases sharply if it has already had a hit earlier in the same year. In order to eliminate as much as possible of this contagion effect, the indices of representation were recalculated by expressing Hot 100 hits in terms of independent companies with *at least one* hit in any given year. As indicated in Table 8.2, the results of this operation run parallel to those presented in Table 8.1, except that, if anything, the apparent significance of Los Angeles and New York as breeding grounds for hit records relative to the rest of the US is slightly accentuated.

These results suggest that the hypothesis enunciated above has a fair degree of robustness, and that commercially effective forms of creativity in the recorded music industry are indeed positively related to agglomeration. As already intimated, however, the results do not in any sense provide unambiguous evidence of a connection between the creative field and the production of hit records, for they still do not help us pinpoint any more closely the relative significance of the different elements that appear to constitute this field. In this regard it remains an open question as to what particular role within the geographic milieu is played by such specific factors as the availability of a skilled labor supply, the interactive work environment, the innovative stimuli that flow from dense and multifaceted agglomerations, or even simply the presence alongside the independents in Los Angeles and New York of the many large recording companies offering important channels of dissemination for the output of the former. What is evident is that these two centers are disproportionately endowed with the capacity to produce successful records, and this capacity needs

Table 8.2   *Independent record companies: absolute and relative incidence of Hot 100 hits expressed in terms of companies with at least one hit*

Year	Number of independent companies with at least one Hot 100 hit				Indices of representation for companies with at least one Hot 100 hit		
	Los Angeles	New York	Other US	Location unknown or foreign	Los Angeles	New York	Other US
1995	35	27	17	9	1.43	1.48	0.47
1996	31	24	11	8	1.47	1.58	0.37
1997	23	35	15	12	1.45	2.56	0.34

Sources: as for Table 8.1

probing much more deeply in future research efforts in order to reveal its detailed inner logic and dynamics.

Conclusion

I have presented a general description of the organizational and geographic features of the US recorded music industry, paying special attention to its massive locational buildup in many-sided agglomerations in New York, Los Angeles, and, to a lesser extent, in Nashville. I have also tried to elaborate further on the concept of the creative field in terms of those webs of association and interdependence that constitute the basic social framework of productive activity, and which, together with the wider milieu, exert strong influences on forms and rates of innovation. A hypothesis to the effect that densely agglomerated creative fields are likely to show strong increasing returns effects as expressed in the disproportionate commercial success of final products has been tested, with encouraging results.

The preliminary nature of this work should once again be stressed. Two of the lines of research opened up here call particularly for further elaboration. First, the notion of the creative field needs vastly more conceptual and analytical development in order to highlight the individual effects of specific variables (business organization, the division of labor, local labor markets, location, and so on) on market outcomes. Second, a more varied and nuanced set of empirical cases must be investigated before the hypothesis-testing exercise attempted above can be generalized with any degree of confidence. My analysis has been pitched at an aggregate level that in practice conceals many important subtleties in the geography of musical recording. More work is needed on the production of music within specialized genres, and on market segments other than the one represented by *Billboard*'s Hot 100, to see if the results presented here can be replicated at these more detailed and hence more sensitive levels of analysis.

Notes

1 Neither of the two standard industrial categories – SIC 3652 (prerecorded records and tapes) and SIC 7929 (entertainers and entertainment groups) – that touch on aspects of the recording industry and musical performance offers any information explicitly on recording companies as such.

2 The main sources of information used to locate companies were business directories (both hard copy and electronic), the internet, and telephone conversations with record industry representatives.

9

THE MULTIMEDIA INDUSTRY: FROM SILICON VALLEY TO HOLLYWOOD

California's Industrial Atmosphere

Over the last several decades California has been one of the major engines of innovation and growth within the American economy at large. Its job creating powers have been remarkable across all major sectors of production, even in manufacturing which in much of the rest of the United States has been under considerable stress since the end of the 1960s. To be sure, the deep downturn in federal defense spending that occurred over the late 1980s and early 1990s had a deeply negative impact on much of the state's economy, though the aftershocks of this crisis have now been largely surmounted. This resurgence in itself is potent testimony to the state's underlying economic vigor and resilience.

Two main groups of sectors in the state stand out as being particularly vigorous and resilient, and both of them have demonstrated notable growth over the entire period since World War II. The first of these comprises a wide variety of high-technology industrial sectors but above all semiconductors and computers together with systems design and software engineering. The second is focused on a group of design-intensive consumer-oriented and cultural-products industries such as motion pictures, television programming, and music production, the marketability of whose outputs depends in different ways on elements of fashion, entertainment value, and creative content. The multimedia industry has emerged over the last decade or so at a critical point of intersection between the high-technology sectors on the one hand and the cultural-products industries on the other.

The geographical distribution of high-technology and cultural-products industries in California coincides closely with two main metropolitan areas, namely the San Francisco Bay Area (comprising the six counties of Alameda, Contra Costa, Marin, San Francisco, San Mateo, and Santa Clara) and Southern California (comprising the five counties of Los Angeles, Orange, Riverside, San Bernardino, and Ventura). Indeed, the locational occurrence of the two groups of industries is even more specialized than this, for they tend to converge together into specialized industrial districts, two of which (Silicon Valley and Hollywood) have come to be universally emblematic of the industries they contain (Saxenian, 1994; Storper, 1989).

It is in these contextual conditions that the multimedia industry of California has risen to prominence in recent years. This is an industry that has come into being only over the last decade or so; but it has grown with great rapidity, and California's multimedia firms today occupy a premier position in the United States if not the world. As in the case of the biotechnology industry, the multimedia sector appears to flourish most actively where a pre-existing and well-developed base of appropriate knowledge and skills is already in place (Zucker et al., 1994). The multimedia industry draws extensively on the resources and capabilities of both high-technology industry and the media industries in general. Specifically, it combines elements of both Silicon Valley, in that it depends directly on computer technology and programming expertise, and Hollywood, in that it depends on a well-developed capacity to present visual, verbal, and aural material in dramatic and imaginative forms. In this chapter, I propose to examine in some depth the nature of these dependencies and to trace out the organizational and locational dynamics of the industry in the state at large. As I engage in this exercise, I shall offer a number of observations about the relative competitive advantages and prospects of the Bay Area and Southern California as centers of multimedia production. I shall also suggest a number of policy measures that are likely to be of importance in any effort on the part of state or local authorities to consolidate the industry's acquired lead in California.

The Multimedia Sector: Toward a Definition

The first problem that one encounters in any attempt to study the multimedia industry is to identify its essential characteristics in terms of its sectoral composition and representative products. This is a particularly difficult task because the boundaries of the industry (like many other industries in their nascent stages) are extremely fluid and its outputs very variable in form and substance (Collaborative Economics, 1994; Cotton and Oliver, 1993). The task is all the more perplexing since there is as yet no official designation of the multimedia industry in the Standard Industrial Classification.

At the outset, the most basic types of enterprise in the industry are represented by *title developers*, i.e. firms that create multimedia programs. Another group of firms, referred to as *title publishers*, is responsible for issuing and marketing titles and, sometimes, for financing title development. Quite frequently, developers and publishers are separate entities; on other occasions, both functions are combined within one firm. Developers and publishers are usually quite small in size, although larger firms, some with thousands of employees, are also present in the industry. A third segment of the industry involves physical distribution of final products, but this particular function lies outside the purview of the present investigation.

The content of multimedia titles ranges across the gamut from action games through business and commercial applications to encyclopedias and data bases. Individual titles are delivered to final consumers on CD-ROMs or computer diskettes, or via on-line systems, and they are then run interactively on personal computers. Developing a multimedia title is much like making a feature film. It entails a series of project-driven organizational and work tasks in which teams of temporary employees, subcontractors, and skilled freelance workers (artists, writers, actors, animators, photographers, musicians, programmers, researchers, etc.) are brought together under the management of a producer.

How, we may ask, are these activities expressed in an actual structure of production and commercialization? Figure 9.1 represents an effort to portray the main elements of the multimedia industry in its wider functional context. Let us review the different structural levels indicated in Figure 9.1, while noting that there are also important interconnections between each of the levels.

1   The technical foundations of the multimedia industry reside in complex machinery and hardware, specifically, computers and communications systems together with an assortment of components and peripherals.
2   Access to this base is provided by means of software engineering. One of the major functions carried out at this level is the creation of authoring tools allowing multimedia producers to perform specific operations (such as animation or hypertext manipulations) using the machinery and hardware base.
3   The core of Figure 9.1 comprises the multimedia industry in the narrow sense, lying at the center of a group of overlapping circles representing the basic media, i.e. (a) visual media, such as motion pictures, television, or graphics, (b) print media, such as books, magazines, newspapers, directories, or statistical materials, and (c) audio media, such as taped voice-overs, musical recordings, or radio. These media can assume conventional analogue forms (like celluloid film or books), or they can to an increasing degree be digitized and stored electronically, which then also makes it possible to consume them in interactive form. The multimedia industry comes into existence at points of intersection between the basic media, in conjunction with full digitization and interactivity. However, as digitization diffuses through all the media, it becomes more and more difficult to distinguish them from one another or from an essential multimedia core.
4   As a corollary of the preceding remarks, the outputs of the multimedia industry are quite heterogeneous, and further product differentiation is to be expected in the future as multimedia techniques penetrate all forms of human communication. In addition to the product types mentioned earlier, many new applications of multimedia technologies are constantly emerging, ranging from health service provision to multiperson social interactions within virtual reality spaces.

Most multimedia firms tend to be rather small and specialized, but any and all combinations of the activities described in Figure 9.1 can be found

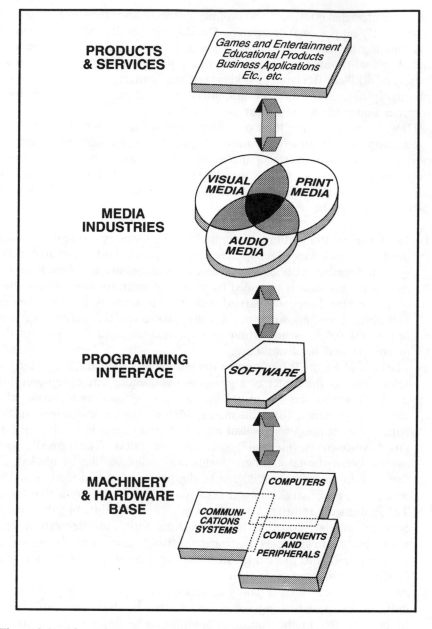

Figure 9.1   *The multimedia industry in functional context*

within individual units of production. There is also a growing trend for large media conglomerates to position themselves within the multimedia sector, either by taking over existing firms or by setting up internal multimedia divisions. This trend can be observed in such sectors as publishing, music production, broadcasting, and so on, but it is perhaps most

Table 9.1   *Employment size distribution in a subset of multimedia firms in California*

Employment size category (full-time employees)	Firms no.	%
0–9	130	49.8
10–19	45	17.2
20–49	32	12.3
50–99	20	7.7
100–249	21	8.0
250–499	4	1.5
500–999	2	0.8
1000+	7	2.7
Total in subset	261	100.0

Source: Samsel and Fort (1995)

active at the present time in the motion picture industry of Hollywood where the established studios are aggressively entering the multimedia business as a way of extending their core competencies and of adding further value to their traditional in-house production activities.

Thus, the multimedia industry is extremely fluid, and its structure is no doubt likely to change drastically over the next decade or so. A common view that emerged in a series of field interviews with industry representatives is that the industry has been evolving over the last few years from a dominant concern for techniques of multimedia programming (important as these may continue to be) to a dominant concern for content and substantive production values.

The Multimedia Industry in California: A Preliminary Description

I now provide a preliminary empirical description of the enterprise characteristics, product markets, and locational structure of the multimedia industry in California. Because of the paucity of published data on the industry, much of this initial exploratory work is based on an analysis of information culled from the *Multimedia Directory*, edited by Samsel and Fort (1995). This source lists a total of 912 multimedia firms in the United States of which 431 (i.e. 47.3%) are in the state of California, though as I indicate later, the actual number of multimedia firms in the state is probably at least twice this amount. The *Directory* also provides information on employment for a subset of Californian multimedia firms, and this information is arrayed in the frequency distribution given in Table 9.1.

Product markets

Table 9.2 provides a list of the main products made by Californian multimedia firms as reported in the *Multimedia Directory*, and it shows, too, the

Table 9.2   *Product markets served by subsets of multimedia firms in California*

Type of product market	% of firms		
	California	Bay Area	Southern California
Games (action and/or adventure)	38.2	41.8	44.9
Educational games	37.5	41.3	35.3
Self-enhancement	35.6	28.1**	47.6**
Education (K-12)	31.9	32.1	32.1
Business applications	25.3	30.6**	19.3**
Interactive television	21.5	20.9	26.2
Information repositories and kiosks	17.1	21.4*	12.8*
Graphics	16.2	15.3	15.0
Special applications	14.1	14.3	14.4
Vocational education	13.1	14.3	10.2
University education	13.1	12.2	13.4
Merchandising applications	12.2	12.2	12.8
Clip media and fonts	8.7	8.2	9.6
Number of firms in each subset	431	198	188

Numbers within pairs that are marked by an asterisk are significantly different from one another by a test of the difference of proportions; one asterisk designates the 95% level of confidence, two asterisks designate the 99% level. The types of market niches mentioned are not necessarily mutually exclusive.

Business applications   Multimedia titles for use in a variety of business situations including personnel training, product promotion, problem-solving, management education, and so on.
Clip media and fonts   Pictorial and audio materials and typographic fonts in electronic format. These items are then used as inputs to other media and multimedia products.
Games (action and/or adventure)   Interactive games for entertainment.
Education (K-12)   Multimedia titles for use in schools.
Educational games   Interactive games for educational purposes.
Graphics   Graphic services for use in multimedia production, including services of artists and animators (both manual and computerized).
Information repositories and kiosks   Directories, data bases, guides, etc., and electronic terminals for public use (such as automatic teller machines or shopping mall guides).
Interactive television   Interactive multimedia content and delivery systems using broadcast or cable television technologies.
Merchandising applications   Product presentations and sales via interactive media.
Self-enhancement   Multimedia titles that offer the individual consumer courses of instruction on everything from gardening to personal fitness.
Special applications   Problem-solving and consultancy services.
University education   Multimedia titles for use in university instruction.
Vocational education   Multimedia titles for job training and skills enhancement (in fields such as carpentry, car repair, computer programming, paralegal work, nursing, etc.).

Source: Samsel and Fort (1995)

percentage of firms engaged in making each type of product. The data are presented for the state as a whole, as well as for the Bay Area, and Southern California. Note, however, that the *Directory*'s classification of multimedia products is rather idiosyncratic, and it emphatically underplays the important Hollywood connection. At a later stage I shall rectify the analytical deficiencies that flow from this state of affairs by considering more ample data from a questionnaire survey of Californian multimedia firms.

The most common products shown in Table 9.2 are games, self-enhancement titles, educational materials, and business applications, but a broad spectrum of other kinds of multimedia outputs is also produced in the state. Notice that Bay Area firms are significantly more specialized than Southern Californian firms in multimedia products for business purposes (namely, business applications and information repositories and kiosks). Southern Californian firms are more specialized in self-enhancement products, which are frequently tied to the entertainment field. This description, provisional and limited as it may thus far be, informs us that California's multimedia industry is made up of a number of separate though overlapping subsectors. In addition, the evidence to hand so far provides a hint that the business and commercial applications subsector is relatively more developed in the northern half of the state, whereas the entertainment-related subsector is more developed in the southern half. The staple middle ground of the industry as represented by games and educational products has a more or less equal geographic incidence over the two halves of the state.

Locational patterns and relationships

The majority of California's multimedia producers are concentrated in the state's two dominant metropolitan regions, i.e. the Bay Area and Southern California. Table 9.3 indicates that the former region contains some 45.9% of all of California's multimedia producers and the latter 43.6%. Outside these two centers, only San Diego (which can be considered as a sort of outlier of the Southern Californian complex) has any significance as a locus of production.

Figures 9.2 and 9.3 provide detailed bird's-eye views of the intra-regional geography of multimedia production in both regions. In the Bay Area (Figure 9.2), producers are located in a series of subclusters stretching along Route 101 from suburban Marin County in the north through San Francisco and San Mateo Counties to Santa Clara County in the south. Figure 9.2 also reveals the existence of a small number of producers scattered through Contra Costa and Alameda Counties to the east of San Francisco Bay. In Southern California (Figure 9.3), the spatial outlines of the industry coincide for the most part with those of the Los Angeles entertainment complex running from Burbank through Hollywood to Santa Monica, with a notable buildup of multimedia firms occurring in the latter area. Small but important accretions of multimedia producers are also to be found in the San Fernando Valley to the northwest of the main complex, and in Orange County to the south.

These peculiar inter- and intra-regional locational patterns can presumably be accounted for – at least in part – by the localized external economies that issue forth when firms of a particular type agglomerate together in geographic space. Certainly, the vigorous growth of the multimedia industry in the Bay Area and Southern California is related to the

Table 9.3   *Distribution of a subset of multimedia firms in California by geographic area*

Region and county	Number of firms
Bay Area	
Alameda	19
Contra Costa	9
Marin	30
San Francisco	54
San Mateo	33
Santa Clara	53
Total Bay Area	198
Southern California	
Los Angeles	160
Orange	22
Riverside	1
San Bernardino	1
Ventura	4
Total Southern California	188
Rest of California	
Fresno	1
Madera	1
Monterey	3
Placer	1
Sacramento	2
San Diego	26
San Luis Obispo	1
Santa Barbara	2
Santa Cruz	6
Shasta	1
Solano	1
Total rest of California	45
Grand total in subset	431

Source: Samsel and Fort (1995)

prior existence in the two regions of large computer, software, and entertainment industries and the consequent presence of ready-made pools of technologies and skills directly relevant to the needs of the multimedia sector.

Consider Table 9.4 which shows 1992 employment levels for the Bay Area and Southern California in SIC 357 (computer and office equipment), SIC 737 (computer and data processing services) and SIC 781 (motion picture production and services), together with a number of derivative four-digit sectors. The data reveal that both regions have significant employment in computer manufacturing and software services, but with the Bay Area leading clearly in both of these instances. The main occurrences of SIC 357

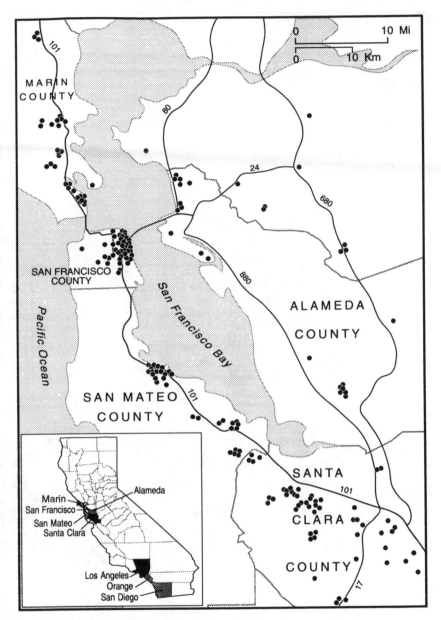

Figure 9.2 *Multimedia firms in the San Francisco Bay Area: inset shows California counties (Samsel and Fort, 1995)*

and SIC 737 are in fact tightly focused on Silicon Valley (Santa Clara County), one of the world's most innovative high-technology regions. Silicon Valley is also the home of such major high-technology firms as Intel (semiconductor devices), Apple (computers), and Silicon Systems (computer graphics), all of which have played, and continue to play, a major role in the

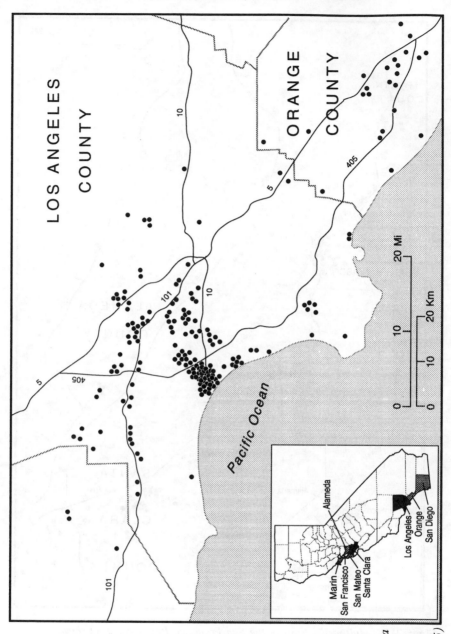

Figure 9.3 *Multimedia
firms in Southern
California: inset shows
California counties
(Samsel and Fort, 1995)*

Table 9.4 Employment in the computer, software, and motion picture industries in the Bay Area and Southern California, 1992

Region and county	SIC 357 Computer and office equipment	SIC 3571 Electronic computers	SIC 737 Computer and data processing services	SIC 7371 Computer programming services	SIC 7372 Pre-packaged software	SIC 781 Motion picture production and services	SIC 7812 Motion picture and video production	SIC 781 Services allied to motion pictures
Bay Area								
Alameda	5,506	2,700	9,130	2,360	3,268	158	140	0
Contra Costa	306	175	3,430	983	683	148	69	79
Marin	0	0	3,164	831	1,763	699	353	346
San Francisco	0	0	4,937	1,626	413	1,126	825	269
San Mateo	1,225	438	9,269	1,733	1,454	783	58	720
Santa Clara	38,553	22,984	24,230	8,300	5,608	495	211	278
Total Bay Area	45,590	26,297	56,724	16,105	15,247	3,409	1,655	1,692
Southern California								
Los Angeles	4,201	4,201	28,539	7,739	2,937	128,466	44,470	80,998
Orange	10,928	5,410	15,407	3,000	2,307	622	319	289
Riverside	0	0	356	74	0	56	0	0
San Bernardino	0	0	1,314	98	750	69	55	0
Ventura	902	750	2,211	1,065	90	516	180	339
Total Southern California	16,401	10,361	47,827	11,976	6,084	129,729	45,024	81,626

Source: US Department of Commerce, Bureau of the Census, *County Business Patterns*

multimedia industry as such.[1] By contrast, Southern California has dramatically more employees in motion picture production and services than the Bay Area (cf. Collaborative Economics, 1994). Southern California (and more specifically Hollywood) is an internationally dominant force in the creation of commercialized entertainment products, including motion pictures, television programs, and music, just as it is also the center of a number of adjunct industries and services like animated films, special effects, film editing, script writing, sound recording, and so on. The multimedia industry seems to have emerged in Southern California mainly as an appendage to the Hollywood entertainment complex, and its growth has been boosted by the fact that major motion picture studios like Disney, Fox, MCA/Universal, MGM, and Time-Warner are now actively establishing major positions in the industry. The recent entry by Sony Electronic Publishing and Dreamworks SKG into multimedia production has further boosted its development in Southern California.

Indeed, multimedia technologies are in turn beginning to prompt major transformations in the traditional entertainment industries of Southern California. To take just one example, these technologies have helped in significant ways to revitalize the animated film industry of Los Angeles, which by the mid 1980s (with one or two notable exceptions like Disney and Hanna-Barbera) seemed to be waning rapidly (Scott, 1984). The multimedia revolution has not only greatly widened the markets served by animation companies but also induced a significant reskilling of animated film workers by inducing a shift away from manual ink-and-paint operations toward technology- and design-intensive computer-based animation. This has encouraged significant repatriation back to Los Angeles of animated film production activities which were formerly subcontracted out to firms in cheap labor countries in East and South East Asia.

Firm Origins and Employment

Specifications of a sample survey

In view of the serious limitations of the data scrutinized in the previous section, a mail questionnaire survey of the multimedia industry in California was carried out over the summer of 1995 with a view to eliciting more detailed information on the industry's characteristics and dynamics. The population of firms contacted in this survey consisted of all 431 firms with Californian addresses listed in the *Multimedia Directory* together with an additional 444 firms whose addresses were culled from a large number of different business and telephone directories. In total, then, 875 firms were included in the population. This expanded data base refers to a group of firms that should properly be referred to as multimedia *and* digital visual effects producers since it includes firms that provide computerized inputs to the motion picture industry, such as animation and special effects, though we shall continue here to designate them as multimedia producers, for the

Table 9.5 *Sample data on dates of founding of multimedia firms in California*

Period	% of firms founded in period
1950–9	1.3
1960–9	1.9
1970–9	4.4
1980–4	12.0
1985–9	24.7
1990–	54.4
Number of respondents	158

sake of brevity. Each firm in the expanded data base was sent a questionnaire, and a second questionnaire was mailed a few weeks later to those firms that did not reply in the first round. In all, 158 usable questionnaire returns were received back, representing 18.1% of the population, which is a rather satisfactory response rate for this kind of survey. More importantly, the sample of 158 responses compares well against certain known features of the population. A Kolmogorov–Smirnov test demonstrates that the distribution of sampled firms by county is not significantly different (at the 99% level of confidence) from that of the population. The same test further indicates that there is no significant difference between the frequency distribution of full-time employment in sampled firms and the frequency distribution of employment as given in Table 9.1.

Origins of California's multimedia firms

The sample data laid out in Table 9.5 suggest that the vast majority of extant multimedia firms in California were established after the mid 1980s. A few firms in the sample were founded before this period, but most of them began life as something other than multimedia producers. No significant differences are observable between the Bay Area and Southern California in terms of the founding dates of sampled firms. This result is somewhat unexpected in view of the apparent preponderance of technology over content in the earliest stages of the development of the industry, implying that the industry probably emerged in the Bay Area before it did in Southern California (though the precise historical beginnings of the industry remain to be deciphered).

We can learn much about the functional roots of the multimedia industry in California by looking at the original functions of firms that were in existence before they became multimedia producers. As many as 38.6% of the firms in the sample are of this sort. Table 9.6 documents the prior production activities of these firms in the state as a whole as well as in the Bay Area and Southern California. Despite the diversity of activities listed in Table 9.6, almost all of them entail forms of experience and know-how that are highly relevant to the multimedia industry in terms of the

Table 9.6   *Original production activities of sampled firms not engaged in multimedia production at the time of their foundation*

Type of activity	% of firms		
	California	Bay Area	Southern California
Computer products: wholesaling or retailing	16.4	22.7	15.4
Graphics/photography	16.4	22.7	7.7
Motion picture/TV/video production	16.4	4.6**	34.0**
Computer industry	9.8	13.6	3.9
Print media	6.6	13.6*	0.0*
Software/systems design	6.6	13.6*	0.0*
Toys and games	6.6	0.0	11.5
Education	6.6	4.6	7.7
Audio/music production	4.7	4.6	3.9
Special effects	1.6	0.0	3.9
Miscellaneous	8.2	0.0	11.5
Number of respondents	61	22	26

Numbers within pairs that are marked by an asterisk are significantly different from one another by a test of the difference of proportions; one asterisk designates the 95% level of confidence, two asterisks designate the 99% level.

programming of software, the development of content, or the distribution of final products. Bay Area firms are significantly more likely than those in Southern California to have originated in the print media and software/systems design sectors; they are also more likely (but at less than the 95% confidence level) to have been engaged in graphics or photography activities. Southern Californian firms have a conspicuously higher probability of having been involved in motion picture/TV/video production before they shifted into the multimedia sector.

A further body of data on the origins of California's multimedia industry was obtained from respondents by means of a question on the prior employment and occupations of firm founders. The responses to this question are systematized in Table 9.7, in regard to which the reader should note that the number of cases refers not to individual firms but to individual founders (of which there are many more than firms since a firm can have multiple founders). Once more, the data reveal that transitions into the multimedia industry tend to occur from positions that are close in functional terms to the core tasks of multimedia production. At the top of the list of prior occupations comes sales and marketing, signifying not only the common need for this type of experience in running a multimedia firm, but also, and probably more importantly, the circumstance that a high proportion of California's multimedia firms specialize in products for business and commercial applications. Symptomatically, there is a much higher probability of firm founders in the Bay Area having been originally engaged in sales and marketing occupations than is the case in Southern California, just as founders in the Bay Area are also more likely to have been employed in the computer industry or in software/systems design.

Table 9.7   *Prior employment/occupation of founders of multimedia firms*

Employment/occupation	% of cases		
	California	Bay Area	Southern California
Sales and marketing functions	12.4	17.6**	6.0**
Multimedia industry and consulting	11.2	11.2	10.9
Motion picture/TV/video production	11.2	4.8**	22.8**
Computer industry	8.1	11.2	7.0
Software/systems design	8.1	10.4	4.0
Graphics/photography	8.1	7.2	8.0
Writing/journalism/editing	3.9	2.4	4.0
Education	0.4	5.6	7.0
Audio/music production	0.2	2.4	2.0
Miscellaneous	29.1	27.2	28.7
Number of cases[1]	258	125	101

Numbers within pairs that are marked by an asterisk are significantly different from one another by a test of the difference of proportions; one asterisk designates the 95% level of confidence, two asterisks designate the 99% level.

[1] Sampled firms provided data for up to four founders.

Founders of multimedia firms in Southern California are not surprisingly much more likely to have been employed in motion picture/TV/video production than founders of Bay Area firms.

Employment characteristics of California's multimedia firms

We have already noted that California's multimedia firms are usually quite small in size. The median firm in the sample employs just nine full-time workers, though there is considerable variation around this central tendency.

Face-to-face interviews with multimedia industry representatives elicited the information that a common employment strategy is to maintain a small cadre of full-time workers and to use part-time and freelance workers as buffers as the need for labor rises and falls. Within sampled firms, there are 1.4 part-time workers and 3.5 freelance workers for every 10 full-time workers on average. There is, too, a statistically significant inverse relationship between the ratio of part-time workers or freelancers to full-time employees and the number of full-time workers employed in any firm.[2] Smaller firms evidently have a much greater propensity than larger firms to vary their intake of labor by means of part-time and freelance workers. In brief, smaller firms engage in markedly flexible employment practices, a response, we may surmise, to the many market uncertainties that attend this particular sector of production and that encourage employers, especially smaller employers, to fine-tune their use of labor relative to the temporal irregularities of the production cycle. Larger firms, by contrast (and recall that there are many fewer of them), seem to confront uncertainty more by a

Table 9.8   *Major skill categories of workers in sampled firms*

Skill category	% of labor force		
	California	Bay Area	Southern California
Creative	44.4	39.4	42.2
Technical	26.8	30.6	22.8
Business	21.9	25.6	20.2
Number of respondents	147	65	62

strategy of bundling titles into a portfolio of market offerings, allowing them to achieve a degree of stability, and thus to harvest economies of scale. These remarks suggest that in principle it should be possible to identify a trade-off function for any given level of market uncertainty between variable labor inputs and overall full-time employment per firm in the multimedia industry.

Workers in California's multimedia industry are on the whole highly skilled, and average salaries for full-time workers are of the order of $50,000 a year, according to the questionnaire returns. Some 41.7% of the labor force consists of females. The main kinds of labor skills demanded by employers fall into three broad categories, namely, creative (content development), technical, and business or managerial. As Table 9.8 reveals, creative workers are preponderant over the other two types, though the latter are not unimportant. Bay Area firms have proportionately more technical workers than Southern Californian firms. An echo of this observation can be found in the fact that questionnaire respondents in the Bay Area claimed a significantly greater predisposition to generate their own authoring tools than respondents in Southern California. The former indicated that 43.0% on average of the authoring tools that they use are developed in-house, whereas the equivalent figure for the latter is 28.8%.

Industrial Organization and Agglomeration

Firms and products

Of all the multimedia enterprises that responded to the questionnaire, 72.0% are independent firms, while 28.0% are owned by parent companies. The vast majority of these parent companies are themselves media firms, in sectors such as motion pictures, television programming, broadcasting, music production, and publishing (cf. MacDonald, 1990). Most of the parent companies are American in origin, but a small number of multimedia production facilities in California are affiliated with Japanese and European enterprises.

Questionnaire respondents were asked to report in detail on their output profiles by appropriately marking a lengthy checklist of different products.

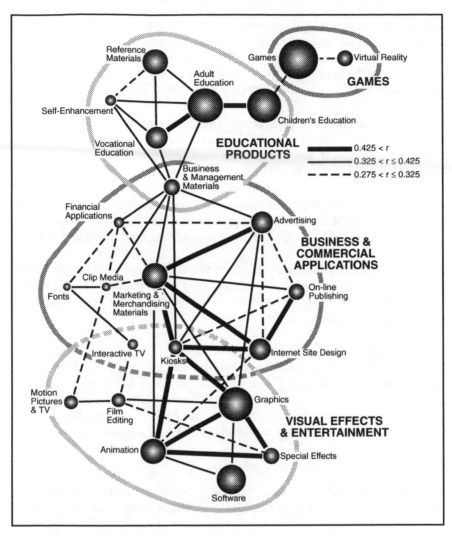

Figure 9.4 *Cluster analysis of multimedia products and market niches, based on questionnaire data: areas of circles are proportional to the number of firms in the associated activity*

The checklist includes not only the items designated in Table 9.2, but also a number of additional product types, e.g. in the business and commercial domain, and especially in the entertainment segment of the industry (animation, film editing, special effects, and motion pictures/TV). In view of the extensive body of information obtained in this exercise, a cluster analysis of firms' production activities was performed, the results of which are presented in Figure 9.4. Cluster analysis is a method that operates over a matrix of correlation coefficients in the search for significantly inter-related groups of variables.

In order to reduce the visual complexity of Figure 9.4, only correlation coefficients greater than 0.275 (a value that considerably exceeds the 99% significance level) are represented. Four distinctive clusters make their appearance in the figure, and the empirical meaning of each can be assessed by reference to the variables contained within it. They are:

1   A distinctive cluster of firms focused on games production. This cluster is relatively isolated in functional terms from the rest of the multimedia industry, though it contains a large number of firms.
2   An equally distinctive but more heterogeneous cluster made up of firms that specialize in educational products.
3   An extremely heterogenous cluster of firms engaged in business and commercial applications of multimedia techniques. Many of the firms belonging to this cluster are in essence advanced producer service providers.
4   A cluster that is clearly identifiable in terms of its focus on digital visual effects and entertainment products, and that includes a significant complement of firms specializing in software development and programming activities.

Note that clusters 3 and 4 overlap to a degree that makes it difficult to distinguish them clearly from one another at the margins. Figure 9.4 suggests that the multimedia industry, so far from being monolithic in structure, is in fact made up of many different elements representing a complex constellation of subsectors. With the passage of time, the internal differentiation of the industry is doubtless likely to deepen and widen.

External relations of multimedia producers

The multimedia industry, like many of the other craft, fashion, and cultural-products industries in California, is deeply embedded in a mesh of both global and local relationships. On the one hand, multimedia producers located in California sell widely to markets across the United States and the world. On the other hand they also participate in dense and tangled networks of purely localized transactions at the level of their day-to-day operations.

Subcontracting relations in the Californian multimedia industry are especially confined in their spatial range. Questionnaire respondents provided information on the main categories of work that they regularly subcontract out. Table 9.9 provides a summary of the 14 principal types of subcontracting activity revealed in this manner, though an extraordinary variety of other types were also cited. It was found that firms subcontract *out* work that is on average equal to 22.8% of their total sales, and they take *in* work that is equal to 32.3% of total sales. These are high figures in comparison with many other industries (cf. Scott, 1993a), and they no doubt express the critical need for flexibility in the multimedia industry. Table 9.10

Table 9.9   *Major types of work subcontracted out by multimedia firms in California*

Type of work	Frequency of mention by questionnaire respondents
Artwork and illustration	77
Programming and software services	64
Writing and editing	32
Content research	28
Cinematography/video	25
Musical composition and performance	25
Sales and marketing	20
Animation	16
Game design	13
Special effects	13
Public relations	8
Packaging	6
Voice over	4
Live action	3

Table 9.10   *Californian multimedia firms: spatial patterns of subcontracting activity*

Origin	Destination			
	Bay Area	Southern California	Other California locations	Rest of the world
Bay Area	79.3	6.0	1.1	11.9
Southern California	5.0	69.6	1.5	15.2
Other California locations	24.0	35.5	12.8	12.8

The data show average percentages of the value of work subcontracted out between specified origins and destinations for sampled firms.

shows dramatically that in the Bay Area and Southern California most of the work subcontracted out by multimedia firms involves purely intra-agglomeration linkages. In both cases, more than two-thirds of all such linkages are with local firms. Concomitantly, the same table reveals that only small amounts of subcontract work flow between the two agglomerations.

Another important type of external relationship among multimedia firms involves joint venture activities, and as we might anticipate in an industry that needs to draw on many widely varying forms of know-how, these are well developed. One-half of all firms sampled have at least one joint venture relationship, and in many cases they have multiple affiliations (Table 9.11). By far the majority of the joint ventures recorded by sampled firms comprise links to large media firms in sectors ranging from motion pictures to publishing. In this manner, many multimedia producers gain access to the expertise of established primary media firms (notably in the areas of content and distribution), while by the same token, media firms are able to tap into the highly specialized skills of the multimedia industry.

Table 9.11   *Californian multimedia firms: frequency of joint venture activities*

Joint ventures per firm	Frequency of occurrence (%)
0	50.0
1	16.9
2	13.1
3	7.7
4	6.2
5	0.8
6+	5.4
Number of respondents	130

Table 9.12   *Geographic distribution of joint venture partners of Californian multimedia firms*

Multimedia firms in	Joint venture partners in:					
	Bay Area	Southern California	New York City	Rest of the world	Location unspecified	Total joint ventures
Bay Area	8	1	6	15	59	89
Southern California	2	18	7	14	35	76
Other California locations	1	2	0	20	16	25
Total joint ventures	11	21	13	35	110	190

Data are presented as number of joint ventures.

Surprisingly perhaps, only a small number of the joint ventures brought to light in the questionnaire survey comprise links between multimedia firms and high-technology firms.

Joint ventures in the multimedia industry are almost as restricted in their spatial range as subcontracting was shown to be. Table 9.12 indicates the main geographic features of the joint ventures enumerated in the sample. The data demonstrate anew that multimedia firms in California have strong roots in the local economy. In the case of Bay Area firms, 26.7% of all joint ventures are with local firms (note that the percentage is calculated strictly on the basis of joint ventures where the location of the partner is known). In the case of Southern Californian firms the corresponding figure is 43.9%. Relationships between Bay Area firms and Southern Californian firms are again somewhat restrained. There is, however, a relatively large amount of joint venture activity in the multimedia industry between California and New York City (Table 9.12). On detailed inspection, we find that most of these joint ventures involve linkages between Californian multimedia firms and large traditional publishing houses like Harper-Collins, the Hearst Corporation, McGraw-Hill, Random House, Simon and Schuster, and others. The questionnaire survey also revealed the existence of a number of joint ventures between Californian multimedia producers and Japanese and European firms.

Trajectories of regional development

The entire preceding discussion has demonstrated that the state of California is endowed with a vigorous and many-sided multimedia industry. Most of the firms in the industry are concentrated in two major agglomerations of approximately equal size located in the Bay Area and Southern California. New York, we may note, also has a large multimedia industry (most of it located in Central and Lower Manhattan), but within the country as a whole the New York industry ranks a very distant third after the two Californian agglomerations.

Virtually all of the different subsectors that make up the multimedia industry can be found at significant levels of development in both the Bay Area and Southern California (cf. Table 9.2). That said, some important emerging contrasts have also been shown to exist between the two regions. Firms in the Bay Area are significantly more specialized in technology-intensive forms of production, with a much greater emphasis on tool development and programming capabilities than Southern Californian firms. Bay Area firms are also significantly more likely to specialize in multimedia products with business and commercial applications (as well as in products connected to the print media and graphic design). By contrast, Southern Californian multimedia firms are far more prone than Bay Area firms to be involved in entertainment and communications activities. These contrasts are palpably inscribed in the current make-up of the two agglomerations as well as in their historical genesis (cf. Tables 9.6 and 9.7).

If regional growth is indeed driven by increasing returns effects and agglomeration-specific learning processes, as theory suggests, then there is a reasonable expectation that these contrasts will grow sharper with the passage of time. Moreover, in spite of the relative proximity of the Bay Area and Southern California to one another, the multimedia industries in the two regions appear to be rather disconnected. And contrary to views that one occasionally hears expressed among industry representatives, there is also very little locational shift of multimedia firms between the two regions (see Table 9.13). In short, the multimedia industries in the Bay Area and Southern California seem to be moving along rather different trajectories of development, and this has a number of implications, as we shall now note, for the shape and form of regional economic development policy in regard to the industry.

Policy Predicaments and Institutional Order

The collective traits of regional industrial complexes

The multimedia industry of California, then, is spatially organized into two main agglomerations which display certain tendencies to functional divergence. These agglomerations are not just inert or locationally contingent assemblies of producers; to an important degree they are marked by

Table 9.13   *Original locations and present locations of Californian multimedia firms*

Original location		Present location		
	Bay Area	Southern California	Other California locations	Number of respondents
Bay Area	88.7	2.8	8.5	71
Southern California	1.5	84.1	14.5	69
Other California locations	33.3	0.0	66.6	3
Rest of the world	50.0	35.7	14.3	14
Number of respondents	72	65	20	157

Data are presented as percentages summing to 100% across the rows.

collective patterns and processes such that the fortunes of all individual producers are intrinsically interlinked. To pick up on ideas that have been more fulsomely expressed at other points in this book, four broad sets of phenomena underlie the tissue of interdependencies that can typically be found in any industrial agglomeration. These are:

1 The multifaceted social division of labor through which firms transact with one another for specialized products and services, often on a detailed customized basis. This phenomenon is enhanced where market relations are complemented by definite forms of collaboration, trust, and information sharing (Lorenz, 1992).
2 The multifaceted local labor markets representing repositories of knowledge, skills, and agglomeration-specific habits, together with the public and private institutions that provide education and training for the local labor force.
3 The informal (but cumulatively important) learning effects that are generated within the transactional networks linking producers together.
4 The social superstructures and physical infrastructures (ranging from local cultures and conventions to community development banks and special types of industrial parks) that help to undergird the performance of all producers. One of the major advantages of the multimedia industry in the state of California is its functional and locational propinquity to the high-technology milieu of Silicon Valley and the creative design culture of Hollywood, and its concomitant ability to draw on the competitive advantages embodied in these location-specific assets.

These four interlocking features of the collective order of industrial agglomerations constitute essential foundations for regional economic innovativeness and competitiveness. Precisely because these phenomena *are* collective in nature – as well as being in several important respects resistant to spontaneous supply via normal market mechanisms – they are legitimate and pressing objectives of public policy. California's multimedia industry has already achieved a position of competitive leadership by reason of its acquired early mover advantages, and the increasing returns effects that commonly accrue to regionally concentrated forms of economic development will doubtless help to keep the industry in this position. However, in the absence of serious attention to regional policy issues there is always some danger that the industry will falter, or (as a result of systemic lock-in effects) that it will be diverted into dysfunctional development paths. The danger is all the more sharp in that multimedia industries in a number of other parts of the world can count precisely on forms of public support that are calculated to boost their regional competitive advantage, thus potentially allowing them to challenge California's lead.

The public sphere: achievements and deficits

In California, the main collective responses to the needs of the multimedia industry that have occurred up to the present time have been the formation of a number of civil and quasi-public organizations (especially in the Bay Area) with the objective of coordinating local development efforts.

Two such organizations merit explicit mention here. One is the Multimedia Development Group (MDG) in San Francisco, a business and professional association with some 500 members, most of whom are located in the northern half of the state. The main objective of the MDG is to facilitate exchanges of information among its members, and to represent the industry as a whole whenever relevant political issues are raised. The other is the ambitious and far-sighted Bay Area Multimedia Partnership, also located in San Francisco, and which represents an alliance between a series of private-public organizations such as the Bay Area Economic Forum and Joint Venture: Silicon Valley (after which it is in part modeled) and private industry groups. The partnership was formed in early 1995, and it is seeking aggressively to implement a many-sided regional development agenda for the multimedia industry in the Bay Area, including programs to foster technological research, labor training, inter-firm collaborative networks, and market research. Among its plans is a project to establish four multimedia centers in different parts of the Bay Area to facilitate the implementation of its programs. One of these centers is the already operational Digital Village – itself a private–public partnership established at the College of Marin's Indian Valley Campus in Novato in 1994 – which mounts symposia, seminars, and training courses, and offers a job placement service. The Bay Area Multimedia Partnership is also proposing to set up a Multimedia Institute that will work closely with the Alliance of Motion Picture and Television Producers to provide training for multimedia workers.

The multimedia industry of Southern California has been less forward in developing joint expressions of its regional identity and needs, though this political passivity seems now to be waning. There are in Los Angeles, as in the Bay Area, active chapters of the International Interactive Communications Society and the Association of Computer Machinery's Special Interest Group on Computer Graphics where much useful information about new developments in the industry is exchanged (see next chapter). Los Angeles has also become the venue for the annual E^3 exhibition (i.e. Electronic Entertainment Expo), a major multimedia trade show featuring electronic, entertainment, and educational outputs, which is an important focal point for demonstrations of new products and technologies. Local governments in Southern California are becoming aware of the job creating potentialities of the industry and various trial balloons are currently being floated about appropriate forms of municipal participation in the promotion of the industry in the region. In addition, both the Bay Area and Southern California are extremely well endowed with a diversity of educational institutions that are now beginning to play an important role in training students for careers in the multimedia industry.

Notwithstanding these evolving expressions of collective order in and around the multimedia industry of California, much remains to be accomplished, especially perhaps in such matters as the development and diffusion of basic technologies, the more systematic shaping of labor skills in response to local needs, and the formation of appropriate support programs for small experimental producers. One kind of initiative that has occasionally proven to be useful in stimulating local economic development effects in other parts of the world has been the establishment of multipurpose centers to attend to general industry needs, either as a public service or on some revenue-generating basis. There is in practice a wide variety of such centers ranging, for example, from the municipally funded industrial service centers of the Third Italy (Bianchi, 1992), through institutions like the Steinbeis Foundation of Baden-Württemberg (Cooke and Morgan, 1990), to the Gemopolis experiment mentioned in Chapter 4. A somewhat analogous development in the multimedia industry can be observed in New York, where the city government, in partnership with a number of corporate sponsors, has recently inaugurated the New York Information Technology Center. The Center will eventually house up to 350 companies in what is hoped will become a major focus of multimedia development on the East Coast of the United States. A similar sort of venture in either the Bay Area or Los Angeles (with appropriate representation on the part of such constituencies as multimedia producers, employees' associations, local government, and academia) would undoubtedly have important repercussions on the future of the industry in California, though considerable thought and effort would need to be invested in the details of its design and operation.

Lastly, there is an urgent policy task to be accomplished in ensuring that the individual development efforts currently proceeding in the Bay Area and Southern California are at least in some minimal way coordinated with one another. There is a particular need to safeguard against the possibility that the public energies now being mobilized in the two regions to promote their multimedia industries do not turn into wasteful development races.

There is also a concomitant opportunity to build a series of regional joint ventures to assure that public resources are optimally deployed within the state as a whole and that all local assets are effectively combined into a coordinated effort of development.

Looking Forward

California's multimedia industry is currently second to none in size, innovativeness, and developmental potential. Not only is the industry larger and more advanced than it is in any other area of comparable geographic extent, but it also draws enormous strength and vitality from its roots in the computer and software industries of Silicon Valley and from its rapidly developing connections to Hollywood and the wider cultural-products industries of Los Angeles. Like the industries that typify these two celebrated poles of economic growth, it too tends to cluster in dense transactions-intensive complexes made up of many small- and medium-sized producers working together in tightly knit social divisions of labor and drawing on regional external economies. At the same time, the commercial reach of the industry is effectively world-wide.

In the normal course of events, the burgeoning multimedia industry of California can be expected to grow vigorously over the coming years. We may expect, too, that it will become increasingly differentiated in its internal structure as multimedia techniques and sensibilities continue to permeate all forms of cultural transmission and human interaction and as multimedia market niches expand in number. One probable effect of this latter trend will be the continued emergence of multimedia industries in many different parts of the world and a persistent pattern of regional specialization based on product differentiation. In all probability, the observed divergences of the industry in the Bay Area and Southern California will continue to sharpen. The Bay Area multimedia industry may be expected to consolidate its existing advantages as a relatively technology-intensive sector producing outputs with a strong business and commercial orientation. The industry in Southern California for its part will undoubtedly continue to forge ahead on the basis of its foundations in what is incontestably the most advanced entertainment and fantasy creating industrial complex in any part of the globe.

These capacities and prospects of the industry in California should not, however, be viewed with complacency. Even in the best of all possible worlds, well-thought-out efforts of public policy and collective action can help to anchor the industry's early start in the state and to enhance its innovative and job creating potentials. Given the intensifying currents of global competition, and the rise of a new economic strategic order where firms develop mastery of markets not just as a function of their individual competence but also on the basis of the competitive advantages of their local milieu, disciplined public policy attention to the needs of California's multimedia industry is essential if it is to preserve its lead over the long run. At a minimum, this comment points in the direction of the importance of detailed efforts to shore up agglomeration economies in both the Bay Area and Southern California combined with an effective alliance between the northern and southern parts of the state in the wider interests of all.

Notes

1 We should not forget, however, that a certain number of key entertainment firms (like Broderbund, LucasArts Entertainment, and Colossal Pictures) are also an important element of the Bay Area multimedia complex.

2 The relationship is described in the following two regression equations:

(a) $\log(P/X) = 0.16 - 0.4982\log(X)$, $R^2 = 0.41$, d.f. = 91
(b) $\log(F/X) = 0.68 - 0.5396\log(X)$, $R^2 = 0.33$, d.f. = 106.

The terms P, F, and X are, respectively, the number of part-time, freelance, and full-time workers in any given firm.

10

MULTIMEDIA AND DIGITAL VISUAL EFFECTS WORKERS IN SOUTHERN CALIFORNIA

As I pointed out in the previous chapter, the multimedia industry in Southern California is deeply intertwined with the digital visual effects industry, and both of them are in turn closely connected to the motion picture and television industries. In particular, computer graphics technologies are rapidly unifying the fields of multimedia, animation, and special effects in Southern California, and Hollywood feature films and television programs now routinely depend on ancillary high-technology image-processing operations for their commercial success (PMR, 1997). The inseparability of multimedia and digital visual effects in the region is even more pronounced when we come to focus on local labor markets, for workers move with considerable fluidity from firms in the one subsector to firms in the other. It is therefore this larger conception of the industry – i.e. the multimedia *and* digital visual effects industry – that will predominate in the present chapter, where our chief concern is the local labor markets that have formed around the industry in Southern California and the ways in which they structure professional performance.

The remarkable dynamism of Southern California's multimedia and digital visual effects industry, as noted earlier, is closely related to the region's overwhelming and long-standing importance as a center of the entertainment industry. As such, Southern California represents the country's most densely developed concentration of specialized workers in such domains as story writing, visual dramatization, and scenario production. It is a place, too, where multimedia content providers can always find a ready supply of subcontract services in film and video production, photography, graphic art, script writing, musical composition, acting and voice-over, and so on. Even so, and in view of the recent mushrooming of the multimedia industry in the region, many firms are currently reporting an acute shortage of workers with computer graphics skills and other forms of multimedia expertise. On the basis of the body of information described in the previous chapter, I provisionally estimate the number of establishments in the multimedia and digital visual effects industry in the Los Angeles region at 382. Sample data indicate that the median size of these establishments is roughly nine employees. The total number of employees in the industry is quite unknown and would be extremely difficult to assess without more complete information on the frequency distribution of employment by establishment.

I shall in the first instance attempt to systematize and comment on a large amount of questionnaire survey data about this new and important sector of employment. In so doing, I shall also be alluding to a more general line of inquiry concerned with patterns of space–time filtering of workers through the urban production system and associated questions of the social structure of local labor markets in metropolitan environments (Scott, 1984; 1992a; 1992b). More generally, the present investigation seeks to complement the overall argument presented in this book by offering a number of systematic empirical insights into the operation of this specific local labor market within the dense spatial agglomeration of Southern California's wider entertainment complex.

A Framework of Investigation

The study of local labor markets is almost always greatly hampered by a dearth of pertinent statistics. It is usually quite difficult to find information about the personal and occupational characteristics of workers on an individual basis, especially for cases where there is a requirement that the data be coded, in addition, by location and sector of employment. Obviously, the best way to obtain micro-data of this sort is by direct questionnaire methods, which, however, and under the best of circumstances, are invariably expensive and time-consuming. A particular problem in the present context is actually identifying a target population of individuals to be surveyed. Even where this problem can be resolved, the major obstacle of actually delivering questionnaire forms to workers remains. One possible line of attack is to distribute questionnaires to workers at their place of employment, but this approach runs up against the difficulty of securing cooperation on the part of each firm's management; and it is in any case subject to peculiar biases because this method typically results in returns being clumped by firm, a problem that is exacerbated when only a few firms can be induced to participate in the survey, above all when some of them are unusually large in size (Scott, 1992b). The alternative method of surveying workers at their place of residence faces the even more daunting problem of constructing at the outset an unbiased list of home addresses. A third approach is to gain access to potential respondents through employee organizations such as unions or guilds, though again strong biases may be expected to enter into any resulting survey when these organizations account for only a fraction of all employees in the selected industry.

Unfortunately, there is no organization in Southern California that claims or even seeks to represent all multimedia and digital visual effects workers in the region; and there is none that comes close to embracing a majority of these workers. That said, there are various interest groups in the region whose members are either employed in the industry or actively seeking jobs in it. Two of these are of particular significance here, both because they are fairly large in size and because, taken together, their membership appears to provide a fairly good representation of employment structures in the industry. Each of these groups is a local chapter of a wider international society. They are:

- *IICS (International Interactive Communications Society)*   The objectives of IICS are to provide information, professional support, and skills development for individuals across the spectrum of the interactive arts and technologies business. Its membership is recruited broadly from professionals in multimedia, computing, telecommunications, education, on-line services, media, publishing, and entertainment. In total, the IICS has 34 individual chapters throughout the world. When this particular study was initiated in the summer of 1996, the Los Angeles chapter had a membership of 612.
- *SIGGRAPH (Association of Computing Machinery's Special Interest Group on Computer Graphics)*   Like IICS, SIGGRAPH is dedicated to providing information, professional assistance, and training, but to a rather more narrowly defined membership. This is focused primarily but not exclusively on computer graphics specialists. There are 26 chapters of SIGGRAPH world-wide. The Los Angeles chapter had 820 members when the present project started.

Despite the fact that IICS members are drawn from the entire spectrum of occupations in the industry (including business and financial operations, production management, writing, and so on), while SIGGRAPH tends to be rather more technically oriented, there is some overlap of membership between the two. Neither of the two organizations provides an exhaustive or unbiased window onto local labor markets in the multimedia and digital visual effects industry, but combined together they probably yield as comprehensive a picture as it is possible to obtain at the present time with limited resources. The advantage of basing the study on two different but complementary organizations is that the information they offer provides a degree of focus that would otherwise assuredly be lacking if we looked only at one of them in isolation from the other.

With the full cooperation of the officers of the local chapters of IICS and SIGGRAPH, a standard questionnaire was mailed to all members over the second half of 1996. The total number of responses received back from IICS was 171 (a response rate of 27.9%) and from SIGGRAPH 159 (a response rate of 19.4%). These response rates are fairly representative for this kind of survey, though the sharp and statistically significant difference between the two rates obtained here remains inexplicable. In the absence of any definitive information on the social characteristics of the underlying population of workers, we have no way of assessing what specific biases may exist in the questionnaire returns, though it is probably safe to assume

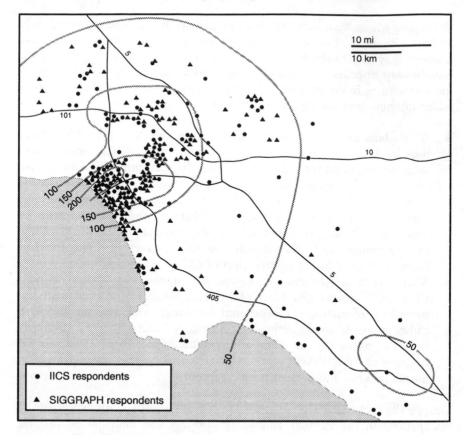

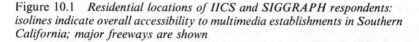

Figure 10.1   *Residential locations of IICS and SIGGRAPH respondents: isolines indicate overall accessibility to multimedia establishments in Southern California; major freeways are shown*

that bias of some sort is present. In view of this warning, I shall refrain in this study from premature generalization of the survey results. Even so, the main findings, taken simply on their own terms, tell us much about at least significant fractions of the labor force in this blossoming industry in Southern California, and they are generally consistent with information gathered in a parallel series of some 25 face-to-face interviews focused on local labor market issues with representatives of multimedia and digital visual effects firms in the region.

A Concise Geographic and Demographic Profile of Questionnaire Respondents

In Figure 10.1 I have mapped out the residential locations of all question-naire respondents together with a set of isolines indicating the generalized spatial pattern of the multimedia and digital visual effects industry in Southern California. The residences of questionnaire respondents are depicted individually in Figure 10.1. Any given isoline in this figure represents a locus of points with identical levels of accessibility to employment places in the industry. Accessibility is defined here as Σd_j^{-1}, where d_j is the distance from any arbitrarily given point to the jth establishment in the industry. The analysis was restricted to just Los Angeles and Orange Counties as there is little or no occurrence of the industry in the rest of the region.

Figure 10.1 clearly highlights the locational concentration of the multimedia industry in and around Santa Monica and the western part of the City of Los Angeles together with an axis that extends eastward and northward through Hollywood and Burbank and then turns back toward the west through the San Fernando Valley. A very minor outlier of the industry can be observed in Orange County to the south. The figure reveals the existence of a remarkable spatial correspondence between the distribution of respondents' residences and the general locational structure of workplaces. This same observation is corroborated by questionnaire data which indicate that the median commuting time for IICS respondents is 15 minutes, and for SIGGRAPH respondents 20 minutes. In fact, this kind of tight spatial relationship between employment places and the residential locations of workers is in general a persistent feature of local labor markets in the large metropolis, even in Los Angeles which is often (mistakenly) seen as being a more or less fluid commuting shed across its entire extent.

Questionnaire respondents can be represented for the most part as a rising cohort of successful professionals in which women play a noticeable and presumably increasing role. A total of 39.9% of IICS respondents and 29.1% SIGGRAPH respondents are female. As shown by Table 10.1, most of the individuals who returned a questionnaire are in their thirties, the median age being 39 for IICS and 37 for SIGGRAPH respondents. (It is likely that workers in the industry as a whole are actually somewhat younger than these figures would suggest, and we should be alert to some possible bias in the sample here.) Both groups of respondents are overwhelmingly dominated by whites, with Asians, Hispanics and African-Americans representing disproportionately small percentages of all respondents (Table 10.2). Annual salaries are high; the median salary for IICS respondents is $55,000, and for the more technically oriented SIGGRAPH respondents is $70,000.[1]

Only about a quarter of all respondents were actually born in Southern California. The remaining three-quarters were for the most part born not only outside of the region but also outside of the state. Of IICS respondents, 6.1% were born in a foreign country, with the corresponding figure for SIGGRAPH being 21.2%. Most of these foreign-born came from Asia, Canada, and Europe. The relatively high proportion of foreign-born in the workforce is no doubt in part a reflection of the reported shortage of computer graphics skills in both California and the country at large.

Table 10.1   *Age of questionnaire respondents*

Age	IICS (%)	SIGGRAPH (%)
20–24	0.6	2.6
25–29	8.5	14.1
30–34	20.1	28.2
35–39	22.6	18.6
40–44	19.5	13.5
45–49	16.5	9.6
50–54	4.3	7.1
55–59	4.9	2.6
60–64	2.4	1.9
65+	0.6	1.9
Number of usable responses	164	156

Table 10.2   *Racial and ethnic characteristics of questionnaire respondents*

Racial/ethnic category	IICS (%)	SIGGRAPH (%)
White	92.4	88.0
Asian	1.3	7.7
Hispanic	4.4	1.4
African-American	1.9	2.8
Number of usable responses	158	142

Employment and Recruitment Patterns

The sectoral distribution of employment

A classification of individual sectors in which questionnaire respondents are employed is laid out in Table 10.3. A clear majority (79.0%) of all questionnaire respondents are employed in a core group of sectors, with the balance being employed in sectors that are at best only marginally connected to the multimedia and digital visual effects industry (see Table 10.3).

Core sectors are multimedia (in the narrow sense), motion pictures/TV/ video, special effects, animation, and so on. Note that the IICS respondents are heavily concentrated in the multimedia sector as such, whereas SIGGRAPH respondents tend to gravitate more to a nexus of sectors involving motion pictures, special effects, and animation, where their high levels of computer graphics skills are in particularly high demand at the present time. Non-core sectors of employment reported by respondents are education, the defense industry, legal services, health services, and miscellaneous industries. Even in these non-core sectors, however, respondents tend to occupy jobs that in one way or another involve multimedia skills and techniques.

Table 10.3   *Sectors of employment of questionnaire respondents*

Sector	IICS (%)	SIGGRAPH (%)	Combined (%)
Core sectors			
Multimedia	42.4	12.6	27.6
Motion pictures/TV/video	11.1	14.0	12.5
Special effects	0.0	20.3	10.1
Animation	0.7	17.5	9.1
Software design	5.6	5.5	5.6
Multimedia consulting and training	6.9	1.4	4.2
Advertising	5.6	2.1	3.9
Telecommunications	2.8	2.1	2.5
Graphic design	2.1	2.1	2.1
Printing and publishing	2.8	0.0	1.4
Total core sectors	80.0	77.6	79.0
Other sectors			
Education	8.3	4.9	6.6
Defense industry	2.1	9.1	5.6
Legal services	2.8	0.7	1.8
Health services	0.7	2.8	1.7
Miscellaneous	6.3	4.9	5.6
Total other sectors	20.2	22.4	21.3
Number of usable responses	144	143	28

There is, in addition, some filtering of individuals from non-core to core sectors, with education and the defense industry being the most common points of origin. Thus (combining data for both IICS and SIGGRAPH), 30.8% of the 26 respondents who reported that their job previous to the current one was in education, shifted into core multimedia and digital visual effects sectors, as defined. The corresponding figure for the 12 respondents whose previous job was in the defense industry is 25.0%. The questionnaire data indicate that once individuals are employed in core sectors, any subsequent job shifts tend to be virtually entirely within the core itself.

Employment, occupations, and computer skills

Almost all questionnaire respondents are currently employed in full-time jobs (Table 10.4). A very significant number (20.3%) of IICS respondents are engaged in freelance activities, whereas only 7.3% of SIGGRAPH respondents are so employed. The much higher percentage of SIGGRAPH respondents occupied in regular salaried employment can no doubt be explained in terms of the demand for firm-specific human capital in the motion picture, special effects, and animation industries (in which SIGGRAPH respondents are mostly employed), where firms like Disney

Table 10.4   *Some general employment characteristics of questionnaire respondents*

Variable	IICS		SIGGRAPH	
	Value of variable	Number of usable responses	Value of variable	Number of usable responses
% employed	94.7	168	98.0	158
% employed full-time	85.8	163	96.6	146
% working freelance	20.3	157	7.3	155
Median length of time with current employer (years)	2.0	157	2.0	140
Median length of time in multimedia work (years)	3.0	161	4.4	148

Table 10.5   *Occupations of questionnnaire respondents*

Occupation	IICS (%)	SIGGRAPH (%)
Owner/senior management	24.8	7.3
Business/financial/sales	18.5	4.7
Production/direction	26.1	20.7
Programming/technical support	12.1	25.3
Animator/graphic designer	7.0	38.0
Writer	5.1	0.7
Other	6.4	3.3
Number of usable responses	157	150

Interactive, Dreamworks SKG, Sony Pictures, and Warner Digital insist upon high levels of intra-firm teamwork and product designs that are safeguarded by copyright and trademark provisions. Such firms are thus likely to prize a captive labor force whose work habits can be molded and overseen more easily than those of freelance workers. For both respondent groups, the median length of current job tenure is 2 years. IICS respondents claim to have been employed in the industry as a whole for 3.0 years, with SIGGRAPH respondents claiming 4.4 years. In addition, over their entire employment experience in the multimedia and digital visual effects industry, IICS respondents have worked for an average of 2.8 firms, and SIGGRAPH respondents for an average of 3.4 firms. These figures suggest that there is some modest but not excessive employment instability in the industry.

The occupational characteristics of questionnaire respondents are laid out in Table 10.5. The only occupation noted in Table 10.5 that requires further commentary here is the production/direction category, which refers to occupations (at various levels of seniority) where the main responsibility for design, organization, and execution of multimedia and digital visual effects work (including website construction) resides. Specialized programming and animation/graphic design occupations are broken out as distinctive categories in their own right in Table 10.5. In practice, there are rarely sharp divisions of occupational function in the multimedia and digital visual effects industry, and the information laid out in the table needs to be interpreted with a high degree of flexibility.

For the most part, the data shown in Table 10.5 are unsurprising. Most workers in the industry are engaged in central production, direction, programming, animation, and graphics occupations. A distinction that is becoming increasingly evident between IICS and SIGGRAPH respondents as the present discussion moves forward also emerges. The former group is patently more entrepreneurial and business oriented, in the sense that it is marked by a relatively high proportion of owners, managers, and individuals in business/financial/sales occupations, whereas the latter group is much more focused on technical occupations like programming, animation, and graphics. This distinction between the two groups of respondents may be further elaborated in terms of their differential command of computer skills. Almost two-thirds of all respondents indicated that they had some computer programming proficiency, with the two most commonly known languages for IICS respondents being HTML (39.2%) and Lingo (22.8%), and for SIGGRAPH respondents C/C++ (40.1%) and HTML (37.0%). HTML is an easily learned and widely used language for building web pages; Lingo is a medium-level programming language with applications in the areas of both graphics and business; and C/C++ is a fundamental programming language requiring significant technical expertise on the part of the user. Once again, then, the two groups emerge with significant overlap, but with IICS veering to the less technical, and SIGGRAPH to the more technical side of the industry.

Spatial mobility and job recruitment

As I have already intimated, most of the questionnaire respondents were born outside Southern California. Even more significantly, roughly half of all respondents received their highest level of education outside the region and, for the most part, outside the state. Furthermore, 3.8% of IICS and 6.1% of SIGGRAPH members were educated in a country other than the United States. These data signify, once again, that the multimedia and digital visual effects industry in Southern California is highly dependent on human capital imported from elsewhere. Nevertheless, once they enter the Southern Californian labor market, workers in the industry tend to become quite rooted in the region. Thus, of all respondents (i.e. the majority) who stated that their current job is not the first job they have ever held, as many as 83.0% indicated that the previous place of employment was located in Southern California.

Job recruitment patterns in the multimedia and digital visual effects industry are displayed in Table 10.6, and they are much alike for both groups of respondents. Observe that the data in the main body of the table are defined as percentages of employed workers only (i.e. excluding

Table 10.6   *Method of recruitment of questionnaire respondents to their current jobs*

Recruitment method	IICS (%)	SIGGRAPH (%)
Friends or organizational contacts	37.2	43.3
Contact initiated by employer	22.7	23.9
Contact initiated by employee	12.7	14.2
Advertisement	17.3	9.0
Job fair	1.8	5.2
Employment agency	8.2	2.2
School placement	0.0	2.2
Number of cases for above variables	110	134
Number of founders of firms or self-employed	28	11
Number of usable responses	138	145

founders of firms and the self-employed). By far the greatest proportion of all workers in the industry are recruited either on the basis of information provided by friends or organizational contacts, or by means of direct communication between the employer and the prospective employee. Advertising also accounts for a modest share of actual recruitment in the industry, with a perhaps anomalously high frequency among IICS respondents. These results are broadly consistent with the labor market recruitment methods in the Los Angeles and Bangkok jewelry industries as revealed by Tables 4.3 and 4.6; in all cases, personal networks play a major role in helping to match employees with employers.

Education, Training, and Professional Organizations

Education and training

Table 10.7 reveals that the majority of questionnaire respondents have attained to high levels of educational qualification. Most respondents have at least a four-year college degree, with significant numbers also having acquired master's degrees. About half of all respondents graduated with their highest degree in 1985 or later.

The educational majors completed by questionnaire respondents are laid out in Table 10.8. If we gloss over the by now familiar differences between IICS and SIGGRAPH respondents, the data presented in this table indicate that most respondents have received educations that are highly appropriate for careers in the multimedia and digital visual effects industry. Well over 50% of them majored in such fields as film, graphics, business, and computer science, while significant numbers of the rest majored in engineering, fine arts, social science, and liberal arts. Educational pathways into the industry are thus multiple, but nevertheless rather clearly focused on a core set of artistic, business, or technical skills most relevant to the industry's needs.

Table 10.7 *Highest level of education attained by questionnaire respondents*

Level of education	IICS (%)	SIGGRAPH (%)
High school	0.6	3.2
Two-year college	7.2	12.3
Four-year college	38.6	49.0
Master's degree	45.2	27.7
Doctoral degree	8.4	7.7
Number of usable responses	166	155

Table 10.8 *Educational majors completed by questionnaire respondents*

Major	IICS (%)	SIGGRAPH (%)	Combined (%)
Film, theater, TV, broadcasting	27.5	13.4	20.7
Graphics, computer graphics, animation	3.8	25.5	14.2
Business	20.6	6.7	13.9
Engineering, mathematics, science	6.3	19.5	12.6
Computer science	5.0	14.1	9.4
Fine arts, architecture	6.3	12.1	9.1
Social sciences	10.0	4.0	7.1
Liberal arts, languages	9.4	3.4	6.5
Education	5.0	0.7	2.9
Law	4.4	0.0	2.3
Medicine, health care	1.9	0.7	1.3
Number of usable responses	160	149	309

There is also a remarkable wealth of relevant educational and training establishments in the region. Of those respondents who took their highest degree in Southern California, as many as 34.0% graduated from the University of California, Los Angeles, followed by the University of Southern California (13.9%), California State University, Northridge (9.0%), and Art Center Pasadena (5.0%). The remainder graduated from some 24 different colleges and universities scattered throughout the region.

Additionally, 70.2% of IICS respondents and 55.3% of SIGGRAPH respondents indicate that they have taken at least one part-time course in multimedia or computer techniques since graduation. The lower figure for SIGGRAPH respondents is no doubt a function of their already relatively high level of technical expertise upon graduation. The institutions providing the part-time courses taken by respondents are exhibited in Table 10.9. Respondents were asked to name these institutions in an open-ended fashion, and the answers are arrayed in Table 10.9 simply by number of mentions, i.e. without any attempt to correct for multiple mentions by any one respondent. Some of the institutions noted in the table are conventional

Table 10.9   *Institutions (in Southern California only) from which*
questionnaire respondents have taken part-time courses in multimedia
techniques, arranged by number of mentions

Institution	IICS	SIGGRAPH	Combined
Colleges, universities and professional schools			
University of California, Los Angeles, Extension	36	57	93
Learning Tree University	3	4	7
Art Center Pasadena	4	1	5
University of California, Irvine	3	2	5
New Horizons	2	2	4
California State University, Long Beach, Extension	0	4	4
Santa Monica College	0	4	4
Orange Coast College	0	2	2
The Learning Annex	0	2	2
Mount Sierra College	0	2	2
California State University, Northridge	2	0	2
University of Southern California	0	2	2
West Coast University	2	0	2
Miscellaneous colleges etc.	21	18	39
In-house training or product vendor programs			
Silicon Studio	14	4	18
Alias	5	0	5
AVID	0	2	2
Microsoft	0	2	2
Miscellaneous programs	15	13	28
Professional associations (including user groups)			
American Film Institute	12	23	35
SIGGRAPH	9	0	9
IICS	2	5	7
Los Angeles MacIntosh Users' Group	2	3	5
Society of Motion Picture and Television Engineers	0	2	2
Women in Film	0	2	2
Director's Guild of America	0	2	2
Miscellaneous professional associations	3	9	12

colleges and universities, others are private establishments providing in-house programs or vendors offering special training, and yet others are professional associations of different kinds (including unions and guilds). The miscellaneous categories shown in the table represent bundles of institutions that received only one mention each. The information in Table 10.9 informs us that there is a rather surprisingly large number and diversity of possibilities for part-time training in the multimedia and digital visual effects industry in Southern California, with the University of California at Los Angeles again leading the way.

The abundance of educational and training opportunities offered in the region for those seeking careers in the multimedia and digital visual effects industry suggests that there is a significant degree of institutional respon-siveness to the current high demand for relevant skills and aptitudes in

Table 10.10 *Affiliations of questionnaire respondents with professional associations, guilds, and unions, arranged by total number of mentions*

Association, guild, union	IICS	SIGGRAPH	Combined
SIGGRAPH	18	–	–
IICS	–	8	–
Society of Motion Picture and Television Engineers	10	9	19
International Alliance of Theatrical and Stage Employees (various locals)	10	0	10
Bar associations	7	0	7
Women in Film	7	0	7
Women in New Technologies	5	14	19
International Television Association	5	14	19
Institute of Electrical and Electronics Engineers	2	6	8
International Animated Film Society	2	3	5
Los Angeles MacIntosh Users' Group	5	0	5
Writers' Guild of America	3	0	3
Director's Guild of America	130	155	285
Miscellaneous			

Southern California. If there is a labor shortage in the industry at the present time, this is perhaps less a function of the absence of basic instructional infrastructures than it is a consequence of the sudden recent surge in the demand for appropriately trained labor. The danger in responding to this shortage by increasing the number of educational and training programs in the region is that it is apt to result in a long-term over-supply of labor. The main objectives of policy in this regard should be not so much to expand the number of programs as to improve the quality of those that exist, while ensuring that minority groups are able to gain better access to them.

Professional organizations

Questionnaire respondents were asked to list in open-ended format all the professional associations, unions, and guilds to which they belong. The answers to this query are tabulated in Table 10.10 which is arranged simply in terms of the number of times each organization was mentioned.

Table 10.10 suggests that multimedia and digital visual effects workers are notably gregarious on the professional front. Respondents are joined together in webs of intersecting affiliations in a wide variety of formal organizations (including IICS and SIGGRAPH), as well as in many different informal support groups. Note that 18 IICS respondents claimed to be members of SIGGRAPH, while 8 SIGGRAPH respondents claimed to be members of IICS, a finding which suggests that while there is some redundancy in the survey data reported here, it is also fairly limited. In general, the organizations noted in Table 10.10 play an important role in the local labor market. They provide corporate representation of their members' interests, they offer training programs of various types, and they ensure that critical information about new technologies, skills, job opportunities, and so on, circulates rapidly through the local labor market. Recall from the earlier discussion that a significant proportion of questionnaire respondents obtained their current jobs by means of organizational contacts.

The Local Labor Market and Regional Economic Development

The labor market for workers in the multimedia and digital visual effects industry in Southern California is highly distinctive in structure, and it has emerged in its present form via complex processes of space–time filtering of individuals through a series of geographic and institutional staging points. It is made up for the most part of rising professionals of both sexes, but with a very low representation of minority ethnic and racial groups. Workers in the industry are well educated and trained, and they earn notably high incomes on average. While it is always possible that the survey method used here to gain information about the local labor market may have yielded a very one-sided view of its general make-up, more casual data collected in firm interviews corroborate the broad conclusions offered here. It is conceivable that some bias may have entered into the two sample groups in the matter of age, but even in this regard, the degree of distortion is probably not unduly great.

The local labor market that has grown up around the multimedia and digital visual effects industry in Southern California is endowed with rich institutional infrastructures, and workers themselves appear to be extremely involved in job enhancing extra-work activities, including the pursuit of part-time training. Above all, they are joined together in many different criss-crossing networks of association through which they are able to collectivize their individual experiences, know-how, information, contacts, and so on, thus generating organizational frameworks that supplement general processes of worker socialization and job mobility. Such networks have been found in other industries and other regions to be an important basis of worker expertise and innovative activity, no matter whether it be in the case of semiconductor engineers in Silicon Valley (Saxenian, 1994), or international finance workers in the City of London (Thrift, 1994), or visual artists in New York (Montgomery and Robinson, 1993).

In fact, local labor markets typically function not only as simple adjuncts to specialized regional economies, but also as critical sources of the agglomeration economies that keep those economies functioning as dynamic and tightly organized spatial units. When they work well, they ensure that trained and acculturated workers with frequently updated agglomeration-specific know-how and sensibilities are constantly supplied to employment places. The multimedia and digital visual effects industry will almost certainly become one of the driving forces behind the continued growth of urban cultural economies in future years, and Los Angeles – with its highly developed entertainment complex – is already a major center of the industry.

Note

1 Recall that the survey of Californian multimedia firms (carried out in 1995) alluded to in Chapter 9 found the average salary of full-time workers in the industry to be $50,000.

PART 4

LOS ANGELES AND PARIS

The two most recurrently mentioned cities in all of the previous chapters are Los Angeles and Paris. So far, however, my investigative strategy, at least in the empirical sections of the book, has been mainly to concentrate on detailed intra-sectoral issues rather than on more synthetic approaches to the cultural economy as it is manifest in composite structures of place where many different sectors interact. In the following two chapters I deal more resolutely with the question of place (i.e. a localized nexus of sundry but overlapping cultural-products industries in the context of their urban milieu), and Los Angeles and Paris now come much more clearly into focus as world centers of many and diverse cultural industries. These two cities, moreover, contrast markedly with one another in the matter of their economic and cultural order. Los Angeles is a major hub of popular entertainment industries together with a number of associated sectors, and it is almost entirely a recent creation; indeed, while the city's motion picture industry originated in the early years of the twentieth century, much of its cultural-economic development goes no further back than the 1940s and 1950s. Paris, by contrast, is marked by a cultural economy that has its roots in an artistic literary and visual tradition that can be traced back at least to the seventeenth century and that tends to cater to a distinctly more discriminating (but also less numerous) clientele than does the cultural economy of Los Angeles.

The comparisons and contrasts between these two cases that emerge as our story unfolds generate a series of object lessons that shed fresh and sometimes unexpected light on the dynamics of the cultural economy, and that also help us broach the problems of globalization and cultural politics that are the subject of the final chapter of this book. Above all, the outlines of an argument begin to emerge to the effect that if the cultural products of Los Angeles are today relatively dominant on world markets whereas those of Paris are relatively restricted, it is nevertheless possible to envisage a possible rectification of this situation in the future. More generally, there are important reasons for supposing that cultural production in capitalism in the twenty-first century may be rather more polycentric, in geographic terms, than it was in the twentieth.

11

LOS ANGELES: THE IMAGE AS COMMODITY

Los Angeles was one of the critical pulses of the economic and cultural condition of twentieth century capitalism, and remains so. Even before the Second World War its aircraft and motion picture industries gave it peculiar visibility and global reach. In the postwar decades, aircraft manufacturing developed into a full-blown aerospace–defense industry, making Southern California the largest high-technology production region in the world (though severe job losses have occurred in this industry since the late 1980s). The motion picture industry also grew rapidly after the Second World War, continually increasing its international influence and spinning off new entertainment industries, especially in television and music recording. In addition, over the last few decades, Los Angeles has witnessed major if not always steady growth in a series of craft-based, design-intensive industries or sectors like apparel, furniture, printing and publishing, and so on. Together with the entertainment industries, the latter sectors can be viewed as constituting much of the core of a regional ensemble of cultural-products industries.

This regional ensemble forms a many-faceted, multisectoral image-producing complex, churning out huge quantities of objects and services that transmit potent social and cultural messages, either as a primary or as a secondary function. The individual sectors that make up the complex, moreover, have strong actual or potential connections with one another in terms of their input–output structures, the kinds of labor pools that they draw upon, and the final markets on which they sell their products. Most importantly for present purposes, the outputs of each sector are heavily laden with cultural content, constituting an interlocking field of meanings with strong developmental and innovative synergies. The power of these synergies is greatly magnified by the circumstance that the cultural-products industries of Los Angeles cater to overlapping markets/audiences that share similar, if increasingly diversified, popular tastes. They are further reinforced by the strong spatial agglomeration that characterizes the locational pattern of producers in these industries. At the same time, the very prosperity of these industries depends at least in part upon their capacity to capitalize on, and to reproduce in ever more imaginative product configurations, the attributes of Los Angeles as a place. In this regard, the clustering within Los Angeles of powerful motion picture and television programming industries projecting distinctive visual and auditory images world-wide is clearly a major externality for all the other cultural-products industries in the region.

The Organization and Location of Cultural Production: A Brief Reassessment

I argued in the introductory chapters of this book that production activities in modern cultural-products industries are frequently – though by no means exclusively – organized on the basis of flexible technologies and labor processes. In contrast to classical mass production, these industries are typically oriented to the creation of either (a) unique and often very complex prototypes or final products (as in motion picture industry or architectural services), or (b) small batches of output for niche markets (as in the clothing industry). Competitive strategy in the cultural-products industries almost always entails constant product differentiation. In these industries, the element of fashion, style, and fad, and the pressures on producers to make their outputs distinctive, accentuate their tendency to flexibility. Hence, many segments of the cultural economy resist high levels of mechanization and the search for internal economies of scale, above all in those sectors where hyper-innovation prevails, and they are typically quite labor-intensive. In some cases (e.g. the motion picture industry) they employ skilled labor in technology- and information-intensive work environments; in other cases (e.g. in much of the clothing industry), firms employ predominantly low-skilled workers in a low-technology work environment. As a consequence, individual establishments in the cultural-products industries are usually small in size, though large firms are not uncommon, especially in distribution activities where relatively capital-intensive and standardized methods do play an important role. The production system as a whole is highly susceptible to vertical disintegration, for the uncertainties and instabilities that flow from the competitive environment in which producers operate tend to accentuate the play of external as opposed to internal economies of scale and scope. For these reasons, as we have seen repeatedly in the previous chapters, cultural-products industries fairly regularly cluster into transactions-intensive agglomerations of specialized firms.

Many of these agglomerations, such as those that are to be found today in Los Angeles, Paris, or the Third Italy, come to acquire well-developed reputations that provide positive spillover effects for all the firms located within them. However, not all cultural-products industrial agglomerations are equally successful in establishing this sort of collective mystique. The flourishing cases can typically be described in terms of at least some combination of the following attributes:

1 Their products are of high quality and diversity, and producers display a capacity for constantly changing design configurations over time.

2 Producers are extremely innovative on all dimensions of their business activities. This feature keeps them ahead of competitors and imitators in other places, and in the most dynamic cases, enables them to shape and anticipate consumer demands rather than follow them.

3 Their products enjoy strong collective reputation effects derived from their places of origin. *Authenticity* is an important ingredient of such effects, in the sense that consumers often put a premium on certain kinds of connections between the products that they buy and the intrinsic qualities of the places where those products are made. This in turn is bound up with consumers' impressions of the real or factitious identities of those same places. We may say, with only slight overstatement, that a Hollywood movie can only be made in Hollywood.

Regional concentrations of cultural-products industries with these attributes (i.e. competitive advantages) often achieve significant power, for a time at least, over extensive markets. The most vibrant cultural-products industrial agglomerations today are all characterized by elements of these prerequisites of success, underlining once again the importance of place as (a) a repository of particular kinds of production capabilities, skills, and know-how, (b) a stock of commercializable cultural associations and images, and (c) a set of localized political and quasi-political institutions providing coordination services and helping to resolve market failures.

Notwithstanding the emphasis here on the notions of agglomeration and place, industrial localities in modern capitalism are far from being self-contained and isolated units; rather, and to an increasing degree, the entire world can be seen as their sphere of market operations, and nowhere is this more the case than in the contemporary cultural economy of Los Angeles. Thus, specialist, often multinational, distribution companies have tended to spring into being at the interface between upstream agglomerated production systems in the cultural-products industries and downstream global markets. The film and music distributors of Hollywood dramatically exemplify the point. These distributors are the external complement of the specialist internal mediating institutions that are almost always to be found in vibrant industrial agglomerations. In this regard, one of the more intriguing puzzles of regional development theory in general concerns the new forms of economic and geographic activity that have arisen in response to the explosion of information in modern industrial systems (see, for example, Hepworth, 1990). Much conventional wisdom sees this explosion as giving rise to a wholesale geographic dispersal of economic activity, but it can be, under suitable conditions, just as much an inducement to intensified agglomeration, above all where it generates new kinds of localized increasing returns effects in the production system combined with reduced transactions costs associated with the distribution of final products (Scott, 1998).

The Craft, Fashion, and Cultural-Products Industries of Los Angeles

Definitions and data

The cultural-products industries of Los Angeles consist of a multiplicity of manufacturing and service activities with varying degrees of overlap. In terms of general functional characteristics, two broad groups of industries can be recognized at the outset. One of these is made up of manufacturing sectors like clothing, furniture, and jewelry, whose labor force is to a significant degree composed of manual workers (though varying numbers of skilled designers and other professionals can be found in each of these industries); the other comprises service sectors, like motion pictures, television program production, the music industry, and advertising, whose labor force tends to be more focused on professional, managerial, and creative workers. In fact, the manufacturing/service distinction that the official Standard Industrial Classification imposes on us when dealing with statistical data for these industries is almost entirely artificial, and the sectors identified are all in different degrees typified by features of both 'manufacturing' and 'service' activities. For our purposes, what they share in common is that (a) their production processes are characterized by strong elements of craft, in the sense that they are dependent on large inputs of multivalent human labor, (b) their markets are subject to rapid changes in consumer tastes and fashions, and (c) their products all play on systems of cultural allusion as an intrinsic part of their commercial appeal.

Data on numbers of employees and establishments in the cultural-products industries of Los Angeles are laid out in Tables 11.1, 11.2, and 11.3, for the years 1962, 1979, and 1996, respectively. There is much at fault with these data, and they need to be scrutinized with great care. In the first place, the definitions of the individual sectors within the Standard Industrial Classification (SIC) change, often radically, from time to time, and intertemporal comparisons are not feasible in many cases. In the second place, as already noted in Chapter 1, any attempt to identify a group of cultural-products sectors on the basis of SIC categories is always going to run up against the problem that few of the official standard industries are devoted exclusively to the making of cultural products. Some attempt to resolve this problem has been made by referring in certain cases to three- and four-digit industrial categories in Tables 11.1, 11.2, and 11.3, but even where these more detailed industrial categories are used the problem cannot be solved with finality on the basis of published statistical sources. In the third place, some important cultural-products industries in (and around) Los Angeles simply cannot be individually identified in the various Standard Industrial Classifications. For example, there is no special designation in any of the classifications, past or present, for recording studios, multimedia production, theme parks, interior decorators and designers, or car design studios; and in classifications that were in use before the present one was adopted in 1987, advertising and architectural services are grouped in with miscellaneous service categories.

Table 11.1   *Selected craft, fashion, and cultural-products industries in Los Angeles County, 1962*

SIC	Industry	Employment	Establishments	Average establishment size (employment)
22	Textile mill products	5,209	178	29.3
23	Apparel and related products	47,869	1,707	28.0
25	Furniture and fixtures	21,902	884	24.8
27	Printing and publishing	36,936	1,619	22.8
31	Leather and leather products	4,609	139	33.2
391	Jewelry and silverware	663	76	8.7
394	Toys and sporting goods	5,379	156	34.5
396	Costume jewelry and notions	860	54	15.9
731	Advertising	6,575	506	13.0
781	Motion-picture production and distribution	26,423	575	46.0
782	Motion-picture service industries	5,012	96	52.2
792	Producers, orchestras, entertainers	4,762	506	9.4
Totals		166,199	6,496	

Source: US Department of Commerce, Bureau of the Census, *County Business Patterns*, 1962

Table 11.2   *Selected craft, fashion, and cultural-products industries in Los Angeles County, 1979*

SIC	Industry	Employment	Establishments	Average establishment size (employment)
22	Textile mill products	11,836	227	53.1
23	Apparel and other textile products	90,489	2,618	34.6
25	Furniture and fixtures	41,663	894	46.6
27	Printing and publishing	50,756	2,114	24.0
31	Leather and leather products	17,500	171	102.3
3652	Phonograph records	4,226	124	34.1
391	Jewelry, silverware, and plated ware	3,086	216	14.3
394	Toys and sporting goods	6,818	169	40.3
396	Costume jewelry and notions	2,122	80	26.5
731	Advertising	7,539	622	12.1
781	Motion-picture production and services	55,293	1,655	33.4
782	Motion-picture distribution and services	7,008	212	33.0
792	Producers, orchestras, entertainers	12,184	1,065	11.4
Totals		310,520	10,163	

Source: US Department of Commerce, Bureau of the Census, *County Business Patterns*, 1979

Table 11.3 *Selected craft, fashion, and cultural-products industries in Los Angeles County, 1996*

SIC	Industry	Employment	Establishments	Average establishment size (employment)
22	Textile mill products	12,825	344	37.3
23	Apparel and other textile products	108,015	4,352	24.8
25	Furniture and fixtures	25,042	773	32.4
27	Printing and publishing	46,264	2,377	19.5
31	Leather and leather products	3,750	111	33.8
3652	Prerecorded records and tapes	1,420	40	35.5
391	Jewelry, silverware, and plated ware	3,253	279	11.7
394	Toys and sporting goods	2,685	123	21.8
396	Costume jewelry and notions	1,899	57	33.3
731	Advertising	11,864	815	14.6
781	Motion-picture production and services	161,794	5,029	32.2
782	Motion-picture distribution and services	8,754	392	22.3
792	Producers, orchestras, entertainers	19,309	3,370	5.7
8712	Architectural services	5,518	698	7.9
	Totals	412,392	18,760	

Source: US Department of Commerce, Bureau of the Census, *County Business Patterns*, 1996

With these reservations in mind, three main observations can be made on the basis of Tables 11.1, 11.2, and 11.3. The first is the extraordinary diversity of the cultural-products industries in Los Angeles; and although apparel, printing and publishing, and motion pictures clearly dominate, the data presented indicate that furniture, toys, advertising, and phonograph records (i.e. record pressing or manufacturing) are also of some significance. The second is the small size of establishments on average, and their evident tendency to become even smaller over time. The third is the vigorous growth of these industries since the 1960s. Indeed, local employment in the cultural-products industries is now considerably greater than it is in high-technology industries. In 1996, employment in the former group of industries in Los Angeles County according to the (imperfect but suggestive) data given in Table 11.3 was 412,392, whereas employment in the latter was just 153,355.

Intra-metropolitan spatial patterns

As we would expect in the case of industries marked by high levels of vertical disintegration and a transactions-intensive mode of operation, almost all of the cultural-products industries in Los Angeles form tightly

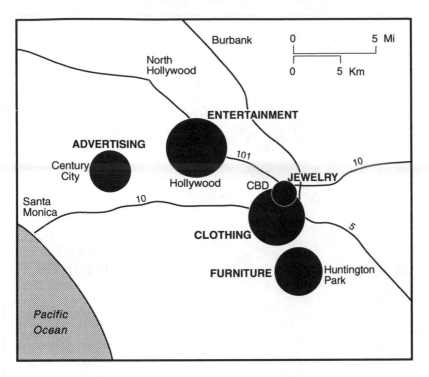

Figure 11.1   *Major craft, fashion, and cultural-products industrial districts in Los Angeles: the map represents a schematic view of what are actually very much more complicated locational patterns; areas of circles are proportional to the logarithm of total employment*

knit and distinctive industrial districts within the confines of the metropolitan area. Figure 11.1 provides a composite view of the locational pattern formed by a selected set of these industries (i.e. clothing, furniture, jewelry, entertainment, and advertising). It should be stressed that the broad geographic outlines of Figure 11.1 are extremely generalized, for while the industrial districts shown are a marked element of the industrial landscape of Los Angeles, they are by no means the only loci of the industries they represent; in all cases there are many production units scattered throughout the metropolitan area, sometimes spilling beyond the confines of Los Angeles County into adjacent counties. The music recording industry, to cite one example, is concentrated in Hollywood though there are also two subclusters of recording studios (one in Burbank, the other in Santa Monica), with a number of dispersed establishments at other locations (Figure 11.2).

Individual cultural-products industrial districts are prone to internal structural and spatial differentiation. This tendency is particularly pronounced in the entertainment industry district which comprises a bewildering variety of subclusters and districts incorporating such specialized

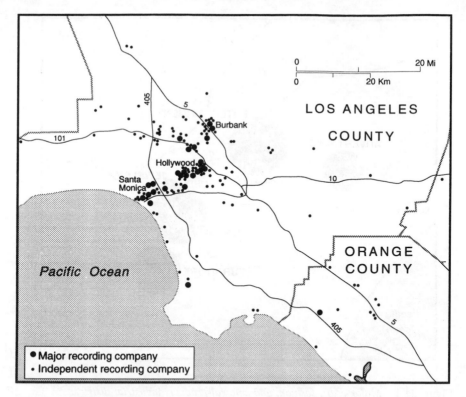

Figure 11.2 *Geographical distribution of major and independent recording companies in the greater Los Angeles region: the map shows the central cluster of firms in Hollywood, with two subsidiary clusters in Burbank and Santa Monica (locations are plotted by address as given in the* Recording Industry Sourcebook, *Los Angeles, 1993)*

sectors as multimedia and visual digital effects, photographic processing, sound recording, television programming, video production, film editing, and many others. These industrial districts, too, exhibit a locational pattern that contrasts conspicuously with the pattern of high-technology industrial districts in the region. In the former case these districts largely coincide with the inner core of the metropolitan region, whereas in the latter the districts (or technopoles) are scattered around the wider periphery of the built-up area of Southern California (Scott, 1993a). One noteworthy exception to the centripetal spatial tendencies of the cultural-products industrial districts in the region is automobile design – of which Southern California is now a major world center with close to two dozen design studios belonging to American, European, and Japanese firms. These studios draw on the twofold advantages of Southern California as a center of skilled technical labor and as a post for observing the latest in car styling fashions – another of the region's peculiar cultural obsessions. The majority of these automobile design studios are located in what appears to

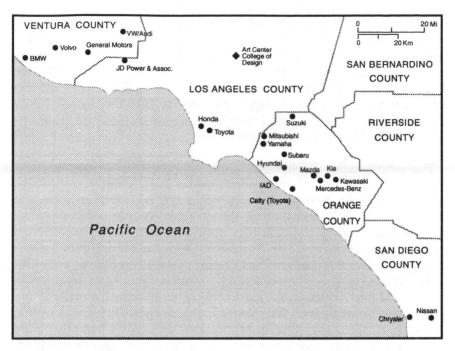

Figure 11.3   *Automobile design studios in Southern California; the Art Center College of Design which has a major automobile design teaching and research program is also shown*

be an incipient agglomeration in Orange County, with a secondary cluster in Ventura County (Figure 11.3). Both of these locales provide upscale suburban environments combined with an abundance of skilled engineering and software workers.

Contrasting sectoral fortunes in Los Angeles' cultural economy

If the region's cultural-products industries are generally quite similar in their locational structure, they often differ sharply from one another in regard to their commercial prospects. One group, represented above all by motion picture production and services, has performed brilliantly, as evidenced by its remarkable threefold employment growth between 1979 and 1996. The other, as represented by the furniture and jewelry industries, has been either stagnant or declining over the same period (see Chapters 4 and 5). The clothing industry falls somewhere between these two extremes, with some segments attaining high levels of success, and others experiencing considerable stress. The former segments revolve mainly around fashion-oriented casual wear and sportswear manufacturers with such familiar labels as Guess?, Bugle Boy, Rampage, and Carole Little; the latter are dominated by non-designer-label, low-cost producers selling to cut-price retailers (Torres, 1995). In fact, the clothing industry as a whole in Los Angeles has done remarkably well over the last couple of decades, and Los Angeles (with 108,015 employees in 1996) has now far surpassed New York (with 55,018 employees in the same year), to become the premier clothing manufacturing center in the United States. A full evaluation of these contrasting patterns of economic performance would require a major effort of analysis that goes far beyond the framework of the present study. However, a preliminary inquiry can be sketched out in a few tentative strokes.

The most successful cultural-products industries in Los Angeles have tended to maintain high levels of skill, worker remuneration, and market appeal, and to have worked out viable, if limited, forms of inter-firm collaboration and coordination in the quest for commercially appealing products. These successful industries are most clearly represented by the entertainment sector (motion pictures, television, and music), but also by a diversity of other business activities like car design, theme parks and allied tourist attractions (from Disneyland to Universal City), advertising, architecture, and interior design. As Jencks (1993) has indicated, a major group of Los Angeles architects is clearly identifiable in figures like Frank Gehry, Frank Israel, John Jerde, Charles Moore, Eric Owen Moss and others, and the work of these architects now constitutes one of the region's significant exports. One is tempted to add to this list of thriving cultural-products industries the admittedly rather whimsical case of cosmetic surgery, for Los Angeles is one of the world's major centers of this activity, and it is in practice all of a piece with the rest of the region's cultural economy. Almost all of these industries and trades have capitalized on a local look and feel – relaxed, informal, colorful, experimental, occasionally fantastic, leisure oriented, democratic, and accessible to mass sensibilities – and much of their success has been a function of their ability to project these qualities in both original and nostalgic forms. The more dynamic of them are also subject to complex inter-industry spillovers of cultural associations and imaginative energy – from set design to interior decoration, from graphic arts to advertising, from architecture to theme parks and vice versa, and especially from movies and television shows to music, clothing, toys, publishing, and so on, sometimes in the form of explicit tie-ins and licensing arrangements. Hollywood production companies now routinely capitalize on these affinities by contracting with large companies to display brand-name products in the films they make (Wasko et al., 1993).

The least successful cultural-products industries are those that have adopted the 'low road' to competitive strategy, as exemplified by jewelry and furniture. These are industries – as I have demonstrated earlier in the present book – that have for the most part failed to exploit their locational advantages within the cultural-products industrial complex of Los Angeles. As they have found themselves under greater and greater competition from low-priced producers around the globe, these industries have tended to respond by unidimensional cost-cutting rather than by trying to move into higher market niches. They have tended to opt for the purely short-run advantages of substituting unskilled low-wage immigrant labor for skilled, higher-wage labor. To be sure, there is a small set of extremely innovative and quality-conscious jewelry and furniture manufacturers in Los Angeles – and these have strong ties to the wider design community in the city – but they represent a distinct minority.

The entertainment industry: mainsprings of success

Of all the more vibrant cultural-products industries in Los Angeles, it is unquestionably the entertainment complex that has pushed the frontiers of organizational synergy, commercial accomplishment, and innovation the furthest outward.

The entertainment business in general is inclined to vertical disintegration, so that the production of films, television shows, musical recordings and multimedia products breaks down into a multitude of detailed tasks carried out by specialized firms and subcontractors (Scott, 1984; Shapiro et al., 1992; Storper and Christopherson, 1987). These specialized producers are brought together in intricate networks of deals, projects, and tie-ins that link them together in ever changing collaborative arrangements and joint ventures. The major film studios, TV networks, and recording companies often occupy a central position in this process by coordinating the financing, production, and distribution of final outputs, but even the majors also subcontract out much of the work of actual production to independent firms. It must be stressed – contrary to the claims of Aksoy and Robins (1992) – that these major companies are probably not so much a threat to or a negation of Hollywood's vertically disintegrated and flexibly specialized production system as they are an extremely positive asset. They have contributed massively to the development and growth of Hollywood over the last few decades by distributing and marketing its products world-wide and by then pumping money back into the local production system. They play this positive role, moreover, despite or even because of the fact that many of them have been absorbed into international media conglomerates. The majors have been enormously effective in commercial terms in projecting Hollywood's cultural products onto global markets. Even though some geographic decentralization of the motion picture industry to other regions has occurred (Christopherson and Storper, 1986) it still remains one of the most rapidly growing sectors in Los Angeles, and its intrinsic connection to Southern California seems assured for the foreseeable future.

At the same time, a number of important organizations help to keep the entertainment industry economically and culturally powerful. It draws considerable strength from the professional associations that coordinate much of its political and public relations activities. Three of the most important of these are located in Los Angeles, namely, the Academy of Motion Picture Arts and Sciences, the National Academy of Recording

Arts and Sciences, and the National Academy of Television Arts and Sciences. These organizations are responsible for the annual Academy Awards, Grammy Awards, and Emmy Awards, respectively. Two other organizations, the Motion Picture Association of America (with important office facilities in Los Angeles) and the Recording Industry Association of America, represent the industry in Washington, DC, where they lobby the federal government and foreign diplomatic delegations on behalf of their members.

The vitality of the entertainment complex is further reinforced by the publication and circulation of many newspapers and magazines such as *Billboard, Casting Call, Drama-Logue Casting News, The Hollywood Reporter*, and *Variety* in the local community. These publications are widely read, and they provide a wealth of useful information on new production and financial opportunities, job openings, and emerging technologies, as well as news about local, national, and international entertainment business activities.

The existence of powerful professional guilds and labor unions also helps the industry by protecting the interests and sustaining the commitment of workers in an extremely unpredictable employment environment. Some of the more noteworthy of these are the Writers' Guild of America, the Screen Actors' Guild, the Directors' Guild, the American Federation of Musicians, the American Federation of Television and Radio Artists, and the International Alliance of Theatrical and Stage Employees. The unions and guilds help to govern the complex relations between management and labor, and in numerous ways preserve orderly local labor markets (for details see Christopherson and Storper, 1989, and Paul and Kleingartner, 1994). Perhaps their most positive effect has been to impede large sections of the entertainment industry from implementing the kinds of cheap labor strategies that the jewelry and furniture industries have pursued, thereby contributing to the maintenance of entertainment industry skills and product quality.

Lastly, large numbers of universities, colleges, and schools throughout Southern California ensure a steady supply of skilled labor to the industry. Among these are the School of Arts and Architecture and the School of Theater, Film, and Television at UCLA, the School of Cinema–Television at the University of Southern California, the Otis College of Art and Design, the California Institute of the Arts in Valencia, and the Los Angeles County High School for the Arts.

Reprise

The cultural economy of Los Angeles represents in general one of the largest and most dynamic aggregates of cultural-products industries anywhere in the world. Above all, it draws enormous strength from its many-sided organizational-institutional base as well as from its location in a city that has earned a reputation as a place in which – and ever more forcefully

– much of the contemporary culture of global capitalism is forged and in which the instruments of its propagation have been brought to a high pitch of perfection.

Toward a Twenty-First Century Production Complex

Even though the cultural-products industries of Los Angeles are on the whole remarkably successful, their occasional failures and deficiencies are troubling. These industries face fierce competition at the global scale as other places, from Tokyo to New York to London, have cut into some of their most lucrative markets. The historical geography of capitalism is replete with cases of prosperous regions that managed for a time to become dominating foci of a certain kind of economic activity, only to subside into crisis as they failed to maintain their leading edge. It is therefore of critical importance for local policy-makers to face up to the current problems that confront the cultural-products industries today, as well as those that may arise in the future. Two interrelated questions call for attention. The first is what, if anything, can policy-makers do to ensure that successful sectors maintain and augment those capabilities that have hitherto kept them in the forefront of national and world markets? The second is, are there any courses of action that policy-makers can pursue that might encourage those sectors where cost-cutting strategies have been single-mindedly implemented to shift to another trajectory involving competition on the basis of product quality rather than purely on the basis of cost?

Some preliminary answers to these two questions can be found in the theoretical and substantive considerations laid down in earlier chapters of this book. I shall elaborate on these answers here by further comments on the bottom-up approach directed to improving total stocks of agglomeration economies and hence to stimulating the entrepreneurial and creative capacities of all local firms. The approach is one that acknowledges the possibility of, and seeks to facilitate many kinds of, unexpected and unpredictable outcomes (new firm formation, technological and organizational improvements, innovative product developments, and so on) as agglomerative forces accelerate through time.

Five main lines of attack may be considered. These run parallel to, and add detail to, the policy discussion on the Los Angeles furniture industry as presented in Chapter 5.

First, the competitive success of cultural-products industries is intensely dependent on excellence in technology and design. Today, many of these industries are undergoing rapid transformation with the application of computer hardware and software systems to virtually every aspect of their operations. Multimedia technologies, in particular, hold out great promise for the further expansion of the entertainment and information sectors in Los Angeles. Individual firms, of course, can do much to help themselves in these respects, though they often underinvest in basic research needs because it is always difficult for any given firm to secure exclusive appropriation (i.e. to prevent leakage) of any new knowledge that its private research activities might generate. As a result, public investment in technology and design centers providing agglomeration-specific services may be required in order to boost local productivity and innovativeness. An important problem in this connection is how to construct the organizational interface between such centers and private firms so as to optimize the flow of useful information in both directions.

Second, and similarly, educational services and worker training needs are commonly subject to severe problems of underprovision and market failure (Sabel, 1995). Skilled labor is essential to the long-run viability of the cultural-products industries, for without it, high quality of outputs is impossible to attain. Accordingly, collective provision of adequate instructional institutions to serve the local industry is an essential ingredient of success. As indicated earlier, an impressive array of educational services in support of the cultural-products industries is already in place in the Los Angeles area; but much remains to be accomplished, especially in upgrading labor skills in craft manufacturing sectors like clothing, furniture, and jewelry.

Third, market competition is one of the conditions under which industrial efficiency is secured. However, when competition impedes producers from pooling certain kinds of resources and endowments (e.g. technologies, skills, information), to the detriment of competitive advantage, then ameliorative intervention is appropriate. Certain forms of collective action and institution-building can mitigate the worst effects of cut-throat competition by helping to build degrees of trust, to overcome barriers to cooperation, and to forge effective conventions of business practice. The entertainment industry, with its pervasive culture of contractual collaboration around specific projects, has made some headway on resolving these kinds of issues, but the 'low-road' industries of Southern California remain largely untouched.

Fourth, industrial agglomerations typically contain large numbers of small specialist producers. Such producers, indeed, are invariably an essential underpinning of agglomeration economies. Precisely because they are small, these producers often face problems in raising capital, gathering business information, providing critical services for themselves (e.g. accounting, payroll preparation, labor recruitment), and so on. Both private and public organizations can play a significant role in responding to these problems by pooling the demands of many small firms and efficiently serving them on a collective basis. One example of this phenomenon is the Pacific Design Center in West Hollywood. The inauguration of periodic high-prestige design and fashion fairs would also do much to help large and small producers throughout the region to build national and international recognition of their products.

Fifth, in view of the dense interdependencies that run through any agglomeration, an organizational structure that coordinates local economic development strategies and that pushes for consensus on these strategies among important local constituencies is highly desirable. Many regions in different parts of the world have put into place systems of local economic coordination (e.g. regional economic councils or development consortia) and there is much that a comparable system might accomplish in regard to the cultural-products industries of Los Angeles. To take just one example, the deteriorating neighborhoods and social climate of Hollywood are clearly harmful to the area's function as the heartland of Southern California's cultural-products industrial complex (including its function as a major center of tourism). Only forceful political action can reverse this trend and break the free-rider syndrome that impedes private developers and property owners from addressing the pervasive problem of blight.

These main points represent generalized policy concerns that in one way or another are relevant in any modern industrial agglomeration, no matter what its economic base (e.g. cultural-products industry, high-technology industry, financial services, etc.). They also suggest some possible lines of attack on three overarching challenges that are highly specific to the cultural-products industries of Los Angeles today. The first of these is to reorient at least significant portions of those industries, like furniture, jewelry, and parts of the clothing industry, that have headed down the low road of development. The second is to encourage the formation of more tightly knit interactive arrangements between different segments of the cultural-products industries in order to enhance the innovative potentials of the region, as well as to ensure that successes in one sector can be leveraged into commercial advantages for the others (like the commercial spinoffs from such major Hollywood films as *Malcolm X*, *Dick Tracy*, *Batman*, *Jurassic Park*, or *Star Wars* into the clothing, toy, music, and publishing industries). The third, and perhaps most important, challenge is to protect those critical qualities of Los Angeles as a place-bound system of cultural associations that beget potent and commercializable images, sounds, and styles, and that give the outputs of its industries a unique cachet. This challenge involves the shoring up of those monopoly powers of place that Los Angeles already possesses in abundance, but that are always prone to rapid erosion under stress. Despite its many social problems, Los Angeles is one of those unique cities that is instantly recognizable as having a distinctive cultural allure or mystique. It is an allure composed of a relatively stable background of sunshine, surf, and palm-tree-lined boulevards (with the occasional, but thrilling, hint of lugubrious presences), complemented by an ever changing foreground of media personalities, movie stars, pop singers, fads and fashions (in everything from cars to clothing to retail store design), and lifestyle experiments. This allure, moreover, is constantly being recreated in the films, television programs, musical recordings, and other cultural products that flow out of the region to the rest of the world. It is one of the city's decisive economic assets, and is the basis on which its various cultural-products sectors will almost certainly continue to function as one of the most vibrant regional economies of the twenty-first century.

An assumption frequently made by local economic development practitioners is that high-technology industry represents the one best pathway
to regional prosperity. As the present investigation has shown, however,
cultural-products industries can also be a powerful vehicle of job creation
and growth. Paradoxically (in view of its long and massive engagement
with the aerospace–defense business) Los Angeles may find that its destiny
ultimately is more closely bound up with cultural products than it is with
high technology. I would add the cautionary note that any failure on the
part of the industry to lead rather than to follow consumer tastes leaves the
door open to its competitors and imitators to surpass it on global markets.
This is not necessarily a plea for the industry to become something other
than the instrument of demotic, post-bourgeois culture that it has always
been (I shall have more to say on this sort of issue in the final chapter),
though it *is* meant to be a reminder that the endemic economic temptation
that profit-maximizing firms face to slash labor costs, to routinize production, to standardize outputs, and systematically to fall back on old
formulas is in the end a recipe for disaster. Any flagging in the industry's
capacity for creativity and originality will be met by sharply intensified
competitive pressures from other regions that are already poised to play a
major role in the international cultural economy of the new century. All of
which underlines once more the urgency for prudent attention by policy-
makers to the problems of the industry and to the incessant threat of
deterioration of its urban base.

City of Dreams

I have sketched out some of the economic dynamics and policy dilemmas
of the craft, fashion, and cultural-products industries of Los Angeles. I
have insisted, above all, on the critical importance of the synergies that lie
at the intersection between agglomeration processes in these industries and
the cultural meaning of place. These synergies are one of the driving forces
behind the rising fortunes of at least significant segments of the cultural-
products industries of Los Angeles, just as they are also the foundation of
the avatar of Los Angeles as the 'City of Dreams'. The industrial-urban
system of Southern California is in permanent flux as a result of the stream
of creative and innovative energies that emerge out of this vortex of
activity; and these energies also serve – so long as they can be perpetuated
– to sustain the region's economy as one of the mainsprings of the culture
of global capitalism.

   That said, the cultural-products industries of Los Angeles face a number
of pressing problems and predicaments, and they will certainly come up
against additional dilemmas in the future. I have tried to derive, therefore, a
set of generalized policy prescriptions for dealing with some of these
difficulties. These prescriptions involve neither centralized economic
planning, nor the kind of entrepreneurial local government action that

was so often advocated as an economic development strategy in the 1980s. Rather, they entail the building of a local institutional milieu that offers attractive developmental conditions by securing certain critical external economies, i.e. those that are apt to be missing or destroyed under conditions of pure market competition (especially the exacerbated forms of competition that have been unleashed in the new global economy). As a corollary, the same prescriptions suggest that local policy-makers need to pay close attention to those fragile processes of cultural creation and reproduction that are the essential basis of the entire system.

12

PARIS: TRADITION AND CHANGE

Economie et culture – même combat
Jack Lang, Mexico City, 27 July 1982

A perceptive nineteenth century observer of social trends, if asked what
city would dominate the cultural economy of the world at the end of the
twentieth century, would almost certainly have replied 'Paris'. A hundred
years and more ago, indeed, Paris had already attained to a position as the
world's most exuberant center of art and fashion, the 'capital of the
nineteenth century' as Walter Benjamin (1989) later called it in a celebrated
phrase. As such, Paris functioned as a great center of cultural creativity
and innovation, constituting an irresistible magnet for artistic talent from
the rest of France as well as from other countries. It also contained major
concentrations of skilled artisans whose workshops turned out an immense
variety of high-quality craft, fashion, and cultural products designed for a
local bourgeoisie that set the tone for sophisticated consumption throughout Europe and North America. Today, many strong traces of this earlier
vibrancy are still in evidence in the cultural economy of Paris, though the
city's reputation as the supreme cultural focus of the modern world has
long since become somewhat tarnished. Our perceptive nineteenth century
observer would have been even more perplexed to learn that such unlikely
places as Los Angeles, Tokyo, or even the Third Italy are now, if anything,
in advance of Paris as hubs of the modern global cultural economy, even
though we would doubtless have had to spend much time and effort in
getting to some agreement about just what the term 'cultural' might mean
in this context.

In this chapter, I present an empirical description of the current state of
the cultural economy of Paris, and more broadly of France as a whole,
together with an investigation of some of the reasons why that earlier
promise alluded to above did not quite turn out as may have been
expected. I shall show that if the cultural economy of Paris faltered somewhat in the twentieth century, and especially in the second half of that
century, it still functions as a major site for many kinds of cultural production from clothing and jewelry on the one hand to cinema and sound
recording on the other, and its future is by no means entirely cloudy.
Above all, its cultural economy remains endowed with rich infrastructures
of specialized production networks, skilled workers, an active framework
of professional and trade associations of all kinds, and other important
assets, not least of which are the traditions and reputations bequeathed to

it from the past. Accordingly, I shall also argue that appropriate doses of just the right kinds of policy stimuli might conceivably breathe new life into the city's cultural economy, helping it to meet intensifying foreign competition more aggressively, and making it once again the dynamic international force that is its historical vocation.

Between Art and Industry

As it happens, the concept of the *cultural economy* has been to a significant degree pioneered and developed by French scholars such as Benghozi and Sagot-Duvauroux (1994), Benhamou (1996), Bourdieu (1971; 1977), Debeauvais et al. (1997), Farchy and Sagot-Duvauroux (1994), Flichy (1991), Girard (1978), Hennion (1981), Huet et al. (1978), Lacroix et al. (1979), Miège et al. (1986), Moulin (1993), and Rouet (1997), among many others. The work of these scholars has ranged over a variety of research topics from the corporate organization of audiovisual industries to the social meanings of cultural commodities, but it has rarely if ever been much concerned with the geographic foundations, as such, of the cultural economy. Here, I shall take it that the cultural economy involves not only the media but also a wide assortment of artisanal industries. In contemporary Paris the cultural economy in its entirety embraces such specific sectors as clothing, fine leather goods, books and magazines, perfumes and cosmetics, furniture, jewelry, film production, musical recording, theater, multimedia, and tourist services, to mention only a few.

As we have seen, the different cultural-products sectors in any particular place often draw competitive advantage and market power from mutual spillover effects, as well as from local public goods that help to consolidate a sense of place (architectural monuments, museums and art galleries, government-supported festivals, and so on). Public goods like these are a notably important element of the fabric of modern Paris. Indeed, there are few places other than Paris where the different elements of the cultural economy, both private and public, fit together into so potent an image-generating complex. Perhaps the only equivalent is represented by Hollywood/Los Angeles, but on an altogether different set of social and psychic registers.

The industrial dynamic of modern France

The French economy in general has long reserved within itself a special place for cultural-products industries. At the end of the nineteenth century, and even down to the 1920s and 1930s, the entire country was marked by a patchwork of specialized industrial districts engaged in the production of goods with strong cultural connotations. Some examples of this phenomenon are silks in Lyon, lace in Calais and Valenciennes, ribbons and trimmings in St Etienne, carpets in Aubusson, hats in Troyes, perfumes in Grasse, china in Limoges, printed images in Epinal, to mention only a few (cf. Courlet and Pecqueur, 1993), together of course with the fine wines and gastronomic products that abound in the traditional *pays* of France. Some of these provincial centers continue at the present time to turn out traditional products, but few are as active economically as they once were, and in many cases their original cultural-products industries have disappeared entirely. Paris no doubt has remained the dynamic core of the cultural economy of France, but even here the record is far from being one of unqualified achievement. The contrast between the rather morose performance of the French cultural economy as a whole and the signal recent success of the many different fashion- and design-intensive industries of, say, the Third Italy offers a sobering lesson in the divergences that can often occur in the developmental trajectories of places that start out with quite similar industrial endowments.

Some of the failings of the French cultural economy need to be accounted for on a detailed sector-by-sector basis, but some of them can to an important degree be understood in the context of the economic development of France as a whole since the Second World War. This is a period in which steadily, and especially over the 1960s and 1970s, the French bureaucracy actively put into place a national system of industrial development and innovation whose logic was based on the imperatives of modernity and scale as opposed, say, to tradition and style. The principal instrument of this 'techno-industrial Colbertism', as Colletis and Levet (1997) call it, was a series of national plans orchestrated by central government agencies to promote large-scale industry and technological advance by means of policy-induced corporate restructuring and mergers, nationalization, and heavy government spending (Gallois, 1983; Morvan, 1983). This approach did indeed give rise to successful results in a number of sectors such as aerospace, high-speed trains, nuclear power, and telecommunications (Ganne, 1997), and for a time the French economy thrived on the remarkable productivity gains that were being generated in its large-scale national champions and their associated sectors. In both government and industry, these transformations were managed by individuals trained in an educational system (with its upper tier of *grandes écoles*) that is celebrated for its unequalled capacity to produce an elite of administrators and technocrats. As Ziegler (1997) points out, however, the same system has been deficient (compared, say, to Germany) in its concern for intermediate and elementary vocational skills, with rather negative consequences for small-firm sectors. Further, the extreme centralization of political decision-making in France left little discretion to lower levels of government in the matter of economic policy and coordination even though administrations at these levels are often best positioned to understand and deal with the detailed needs of local industrial systems. Instead, and in stark contrast to the case of the Third Italy where local government has been a critical catalyst of regional development by means of grass-roots partnerships and initiatives, the notables who are typically at the center of local decision-making in France have always tended to rely upon and take their cues from the mandates of central government (Ganne, 1992). Even when this model of techno-industrial Colbertism came under heavy stress in the crisis years of the middle of the 1970s and after, the reaction of the French state was less to withdraw from its established strategy than to continue to extend its reach by means of heavy subsidization of failing national champions (Cohen, 1989; 1992).

This general climate of top-down economic and policy decision-making was not calculated, as Salais and Storper (1993) have indicated, to promote forms of industrial development sensitive to the subtleties of consumer demand, or to foster aggressive Schumpeterian entrepreneurialism and risk-taking. Policy-makers for the most part made no attempt over the postwar decades to remedy the increasing atrophy of the small-scale traditional craft industries of France with their highly idiosyncratic and seemingly archaic ways of operating, and these industries were not so much actively or intentionally destroyed as they were simply left to their own devices while modernization was pushed forward in other sectors. In practice, this meant that small-scale craft industries were subject to a rising onslaught of cheap imports from less developed parts of the world, especially from East and South East Asia, a problem compounded by the high (direct and indirect) cost of labor in France (Malsot and Passeron, 1996). The atrophy of many of these industries has been further accentuated by rapidly changing consumer tastes, and by the inability or unwillingness of more traditional producers to adapt appropriately. Small firms in artisanal sectors also usually face endemic difficulties in recruiting skilled craftsworkers and in raising new capital – difficulties that were made all the greater by the dirigiste policies of the French state. In addition, the program of 'competitive disinflation' put into effect by the Mitterrand government in the early 1980s resulted in a strong national currency that exacerbated the competitive squeeze on small industry (Taddei and Coriat, 1993). Despite all these difficulties, some of France's cultural-products industries managed over the postwar period to retain something of their customary flair; others only fell deeper into crisis by pursuing sectoral strategies that pushed them yet closer to the point of extinction.

Some alleviation of this general plight was forthcoming over the course of the 1980s and 1990s, as French industrial policy came to recognize something of the commercial and technical needs of small firms. ANVAR (Agence Nationale pour la Valorisation de la Recherche) has played a leading role in this regard, though the agency's programs – as its annual reports reveal – have an overwhelming bias in favor of more technology-driven sectors. Support for selected cultural-products industries has also recently been forthcoming in the context of France's assertion of the need for a 'cultural exception' in world trade (involving, above all, protection of domestic media industries from outside competition), a position that it successfully maintained at the Uruguay Round of GATT. Further encouragement for many of France's cultural industries is provided by the Ministry of Culture through a maze of subsidies and regulations relating to sectors such as the cinema, television, musical performance and recording, publishing, and so on (cf. Farchy and Sagot-Duvauroux, 1994; Kelberg, 1997; Rouet, 1992; Rouet and Dupin, 1991). The Ministry of Culture's programs have focused on preserving, democratizing, and expanding the domain of French culture (Dumazedier, 1988; Urfalino, 1996; 1997), and by and large they have been attended with some success. At the same time, the Ministry's approach has tended to be purely defensive in economic terms, and understandably perhaps, given its mandate, it has not paid much attention to the special tasks of building economic infrastructures for the cultural economy capable of endowing it with more assertive competitive muscle (recall the argument of Chapters 6 and 7).

Over much of the second half of the twentieth century, then, the French national model of economic development was not especially hospitable in regard to most cultural-products industries. Even where policy was directly concerned with these industries, it tended to put the emphasis more on cultural protection than on building a dynamic industrial base capable of increasing not only domestic market share but global share as well. As a result, and despite its early historical start, France squandered – for a time at least – a remarkable opportunity to parlay its rich heritage of traditional assets in the domain of the cultural economy into the kind of growth machine that, for example, has propelled the economic development of Los Angeles forward over recent decades.

Employment, Location and Organization in the Cultural-Products Industries of Paris

Paris has long enjoyed a well-deserved reputation as a haven of intellectual, artistic, and craft activity (cf. Charle, 1998; Clark, 1984; Menger, 1993). This reputation flows not only from centuries of productive effort in philosophy, literature, music, painting, and so on, but also from the city's long history of skilled artisanal labor dedicated to the fabrication of a remarkable array of fancy decorative goods, sometimes at levels of craftsmanship unmatched anywhere else in the world. In the nineteenth century, in particular, Paris was celebrated for its many small craft industries producing so-called *articles de Paris*, including fans, leather goods, umbrellas, canes, artificial flowers, household ornaments, buttons, toys, and so on (Gaillard, 1977). Balzac's comment on Valérie's tastes in decoration in *La Cousine Bette* dramatically exemplify the point:

> In arranging her salon she had put on display those delightful trinkets that are produced in Paris, and that no other city in the world can match . . . enamelled keepsakes decorated with pearls, bowls filled with charming rings, masterpieces of Saxony and Sèvres porcelain mounted with exquisite taste by Florent and Chanor, not to mention statuettes and albums, all those ornaments worth mad sums of money ordered from the craftsman's shop in the first flame of passion or in its final reconciliation.

Employment in these industries in the city in 1860 amounted to 25,748 according to Fierro (1996), but this is almost certainly an undercount given their extensive underside – then as now – of small fugitive workshops and home workers. Occasional traces of these industries can still be found in parts of Paris, but like the craft industries of provincial France, most of them have long since succumbed to the pressures of cheap foreign imports and changing consumer tastes. Even so, some of the cultural-products sectors that flourished in nineteenth century Paris have continued to maintain a strong presence down to the present day. These include clothing (with its prestigious *haute couture* segment established by Worth in the 1850s), leather goods, publishing, furniture, perfume and cosmetics, and jewelry.

At the present time, the main outlines of the cultural economy of Paris are made up of these latter traditional sectors together with a number of distinctly more modern industries, mainly in various branches of the media. Table 12.1 shows employment in a selected cross-section of the cultural economy of Paris in the period from 1992 to 1997 based on four-digit industries as defined by the French industrial classification. The industries shown in the table all have computed location quotients for Paris relative to France as a whole of 2.0 or more[1] (signifying high levels of geographic concentration), except for the two furniture sectors (36.1G and 36.1K), which are included because they form a particularly well-developed industrial district in and around the Faubourg St Antoine in the east of the city. It should be noted that the industries identified in Table 12.1 are a selection only and do not represent the totality of the cultural economy of Paris. Important sectors as defined by the official industrial classification but not mentioned in the table are, to name only a few, clothing industries other than 18.2D and 18.2E, newspaper publishing, advertising, architectural services, and recreational, cultural, and sporting activities other than 92.1A, 92.1C, and 92.1D. If we consider the cultural economy of Paris as a whole, the number of permanent employees is almost certainly at least twice the aggregate number shown in Table 12.1. To these permanent employees we should add the undoubtedly large but unknown number of temporary employees in these sectors.

Of the 16 sectors designated in Table 12.1, 11 show net declines in permanent employment over the period from 1992 to 1997, and 5 show net gains, though only in the women's clothing industry are these gains of any real significance. In total, employment in the sectors shown declined from 104,993 in 1992 to 99,198 in 1997. This, admittedly, was a period of considerable hardship in the French economy as a whole, but the general trend is entirely consistent with a more long-standing pattern of decline in these industries. Unfortunately, direct comparisons with earlier years are not possible due to major changes in the French industrial classification in 1992. Let us, however, consider six main industries with close affinities to those given in Table 12.1, but defined according to the old NAP classification.[2] These industries all showed percentage declines in permanent

Table 12.1   *Permanent employment in selected cultural-products industries, City of Paris, 1992–7*

NAF[1]		1992	1993	1994	1995	1996	1997
18.1Z	Fabrication of leather clothing	649	625	566	518	490	458
18.2D	Fabrication of garments for men and boys (except underwear)	10,941	9,098	7,466	6,180	4,919	4,537
18.2E	Fabrication of garments for women and girls (except underwear)	13,267	14,088	16,106	15,322	15,821	16,580
18.3Z	Fur industry	886	685	626	582	550	513
19.2Z	Fabrication of travel goods and fine leather	4,512	4,863	4,129	3,879	3,701	3,730
22.1A	Book publishing	15,897	14,896	15,820	15,647	14,674	14,463
22.1E	Publishing of magazines and periodicals	24,528	23,911	23,883	23,283	23,308	22,575
22.1G	Sound recording	3,690	3,671	3,709	3,866	3,720	3,881
24.5C	Fabrication of perfumes and cosmetics	18,138	17,798	17,808	17,820	17,159	16,921
36.1G	Fabrication of household furniture	2,514	2,240	2,020	1,854	1,624	1,640
36.1K	Industries related to furniture	1,283	1,171	1,208	1,173	1,170	1,167
36.2C	Jewelry	3,833	3,559	2,787	2,814	2,959	3,003
36.6A	Costume jewelry	2,822	2,398	3,002	2,768	2,359	2,143
92.1A	Production of films for television	358	832	803	883	1,141	1,412
92.1C	Production of films for cinema	700	1,696	2,378	2,404	2,277	2,210
92.1D	Technical services for cinema and television	975	2,927	2,760	2,906	3,743	3,965
Totals		104,993	104,458	105,071	101,899	99,612	99,198

[1] *Nomenclature d'activités françaises*, i.e. French standard industrial classification.

Source: Groupement des ASSEDIC de la Région Parisienne

employment in Paris between 1980 and 1991 as follows: NAP 45.00 (leather), –23.2%; NAP 47.00 (clothing), –27.4%; NAP 49.00 (furniture), –21.2%; NAP 51.00 (printing and publishing), –5.0%; NAP 54.04 (jewelry), –21.7%; NAP 86.02 (film production), –43.3%.[3] If anything, then, the more recent period is one in which the rate of decline appears to have moderated somewhat.

A noteworthy feature that all these sectors share in common is their disposition to form dense specialized industrial districts within the wider fabric of the city. Figure 12.1 offers a schematic map of these districts in Paris, though it must be borne in mind that the map (like its Los Angeles homologue, Figure 11.1) is extremely stylized, and the districts shown are always in practice accompanied by an admixture of dispersed locational activity in the rest of the city. The map immediately brings into focus the twofold distinction in the cultural economy that I alluded to earlier, namely, on the one hand a set of artisanal industries located close to the working class and immigrant neighborhoods to the east and center-east of the city, and on the other a set of media industries located toward the more

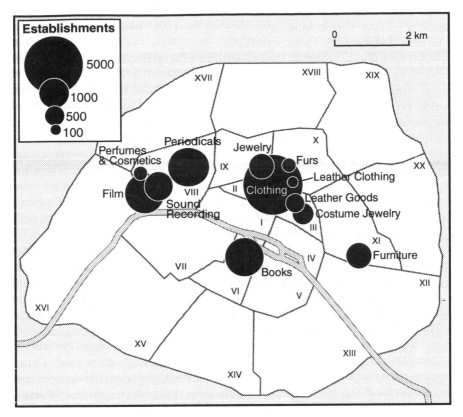

Figure 12.1 *Main industrial districts in the cultural economy of Paris: arrondissements are numbered; circles are proportional to the logarithm of the number of establishments in each sector*

upscale western half of the city. The apparent exception to this generalization is the perfume and cosmetics industry in the west of Paris, but this turns out on closer inspection to be composed of management, administrative, and marketing functions more than it is of actual production activities. Production in the perfume and cosmetics sector is mainly to be found in the booming new 'Cosmetics Valley' that has emerged since the early 1970s in and around Orléans some 110 kilometres to the south of Paris, and where many of the classic French brands of perfume (e.g. Christian Dior, Guerlain, Shiseido, Grès, Paco Rabanne) are now actually made (Plé, 1998).

Data for each of the sectors shown in Figure 12.1 indicate that average establishment size is notably small, rarely in fact rising above 10 permanent employees. In addition, as demonstrated in studies by Couderc (1998), Lacroix et al. (1979), Moulier Boutang (1990), and others, establishments in sectors like clothing, publishing, and film production are caught up in tightly knit networks marked by high levels of flexible subcontracting

offering a diversity of specialized services. Yet its economic performance has on the whole been laggard over the last couple of decades, and even on domestic markets (the case of the cinema being especially critical) it has suffered greatly from foreign competition. A preliminary diagnosis of the predicaments of the Parisian cultural economy has already been set out at earlier stages in this book, but some deeper probing of this matter is now required.

Thriving industrial agglomerations generally possess three major characteristics in addition to those noted in the previous paragraph. These are entrepreneurial risk-taking, innovativeness and adaptability, and effective distribution of final products to the wider world. Some theorists, such as Lorenz (1992), would add mutual trust and inter-firm collaboration to this list. A few French cultural industries score highly on some of these characteristics, but almost all fail on at least one of them, and some on two or three (Colletis and Levet, 1997; Taddei and Coriat, 1993). Probably the most successful of all the sectors scrutinized here is the perfume industry. In this instance, a long tradition of excellence and innovative competence has been combined with the marketing and distribution capacities of major multinationals which over the last few decades have contested global markets with great effectiveness. Women's fashions have also been relatively successful, in part no doubt because of the virtually indelible mystique that adheres to this segment of the cultural economy of Paris (cf. Bourdieu and Delsaut, 1975), and in part because the periodic industry-wide salons have functioned extremely well as an international marketing tool. Against these positive accomplishments in the clothing industry we must set the failed strategy of the *haute couture* segment, which in the postwar decades attempted to deal with international markets mainly by licensing foreign manufacturers to produce under its labels. In the end, this strategy has significantly tarnished the symbolic value of many of these labels (Bergeron, 1998; Grumbach, 1993), and it is in any case a symptom of a traditional diffidence in much of French industry in regard to the cultivation of wider markets. Information gleaned in a number of interviews suggests that this licensing strategy is now being largely abandoned, and top fashion houses and designers in Paris are evidently starting to deal directly with issues of foreign marketing and distribution.

Of all the sectors of the cultural economy that exhibit this syndrome of competitive enervation, the film industry is one of the most conspicuous. This, of course, is a particularly delicate case because it is so clearly subject to strains and stresses emanating from the dual demands of art and commerce. There is no reason in principle, however, why these demands cannot be reconciled in one way or another, or at least why a commercially viable popular cinema cannot be created – without undue sacrifice of quality – alongside the continuing French tradition of *films d'auteur*.[5] We have already seen how the French film industry in practice has been losing ground steadily for decades before the onslaught of American competition. The response to this competition, as discussed at length in Chapters 6 and

7, has been essentially defensive, involving heavy CNC support of domestic production, but at the price of dramatic reductions in levels of entrepreneurial risk and sensitivity to market dynamics. There can be little doubt that without the strong policy intervention of the last few decades, French cinema would have declined even more severely than it has; but what is notably lacking in current policy is a will to create new productive synergies of a type that might promote superior levels of economic performance and market penetration or to shape new and aggressive competitive strategies. Above all, the French film industry is weak in the areas of export promotion, marketing, and distribution.

To varying degree the same sorts of problems are encountered across the gamut of French cultural-products industries (Bergeron, 1998), though signs of some new directions have been making their appearance over the last few years. One aspect of this more hopeful trend is the emergence of a number of large, well-capitalized firms in symbiotic relationship with relatively small and specialized subsidiaries in different cultural-products sectors. These firms have shown an increasing capacity to master the intricacies of large-scale international distribution networks and to exploit the marketing advantages created by their multisectoral presence. Another aspect is represented by changes in the overall industrial policy environment with its apparently rising concern for sectors other than those dominated by large-scale industry. Although few dramatically new lines of policy development have emerged as yet, there is a definite shift in the direction of a policy mix that caters more effectively to the needs of small firms, and to the tasks of shoring up their competitive capacities, while simultaneously developing programs that build imaginatively on their configuration as regionally based clusters (Ganne, 1997). This is a domain in which creative policy partnerships between the Ministry of Industry and the Ministry of Culture would be likely to pay handsome dividends (cf. Rigaud, 1996).

In fact, as the discussion in this chapter makes evident, the cultural-products industries of Paris, despite much current backing and filling, are still in possession of a number of trump cards. They continue to operate on a significant scale as agglomerated networks of producers; they are supported by local labor markets comprising a diversity of finely honed skills; and they are endowed with institutional infrastructures which, if they are not always as effective as they might be, represent for the most part a positive culture of corporatist interaction and coordination whose full capacities might be unleashed with appropriate reform. These industries possess, as well, an unequalled accumulated symbolic capital, both sector-specific and place-specific, providing further momentum to the incipient commercial remobilization that seems to have been gathering momentum of late years. Above all, perhaps, all of these industries share in a common aura of symbolic meanings and consumer appeal, and there are enormous latent synergies and economies of scale to be obtained by an appropriately orchestrated program of joint global marketing of their products.

Conclusion

The preliminary nature of the findings discussed here needs to be stressed, and more detailed sectoral studies as well as much more conceptual development of the pertinent issues urgently need to be carried out. Notwithstanding the limitations of the present account, it has indicated how cultural-products industries in one major city are constructed as intricate fabrics of social, economic, and geographic relationships, and it helps to bring further into relief the significance of cultural-products industries in large cities generally as we enter the twenty-first century. Like it or not, our culture is increasingly going to be served up in the commodity form. In this process, Paris may well come to play an important and rapidly expanding part, for it has all the necessary economic and political resources with which to assert and reassert its role as a world center of creativity within the new cultural economy. Notwithstanding the excesses of commercial entertainment at its worst, or the tirades of Fumaroli (1992) about the 'technocratic philistinism' of the French state's ventures in the domain of culture, there is every reason to believe on the basis of past experience that this role will be conspicuous for its flair and style. It is just possible that Paris may emerge as an alternative pole of commodified culture in the new global economy, and that it will seek to redefine its status as a cultural exception not in terms of defensive gestures, but as an aggressive exporter of distinctive cultural products to the rest of the world.

Notes

1 The location quotients are calculated on the basis of number of establishments, since this study is focused on industrial systems as networks of producers as much as it is on patterns of raw employment.

2 NAP (*nomenclature d'activités et de produits*) is the terminology used in the older French industrial classification to designate a standard industrial category.

3 Calculations are based on data contained in the records of the Groupement des ASSEDIC de la Région Parisienne.

4 Firms belonging to the Comité Colbert represent a variety of sectors including crystal, leather, porcelain, hotels and restaurants, jewelry, fashion, perfume, and champagne and wine.

5 In fact, from Chaplin through the French cinema of poetic realism in the 1930s and 1940s to Woody Allen today, much that is best in the cinema has always worked on multiple levels of audience appeal.

PART 5

CODA

The chapter that now follows brings the discussion to a close by laying out some elements of a political economy of the cultural commodity. The increasing convergence of the cultural and the economic orders in modern capitalism is reaffirmed, and the predicament-laden nature of this situation is stressed. The local and the global dimensions of the cultural economy are also reviewed, with special attention being paid to the increasingly important role of large multinational corporations in mediating between the different spatial scales over which the modern cultural economy operates. The chapter concludes with a series of remarks on cultural politics, not only in terms of the aggressive incursions of the cultures fabricated in a few privileged places into other places all over the world, but also, and in the end perhaps even more importantly, in terms of the tension-filled and unequal balance between progressive and regressive tendencies in the modern cultural economy.

13

TOWARD A POLITICAL ECONOMY OF THE CULTURAL COMMODITY

I have sought to sketch out an economic geography of cultural production in modern capitalism, and to show how the images that ever more forcefully define our cultural environment emerge out of concrete production systems and their geographic milieux. I have argued that the production of culture today is irrevocably bound up with the logic of commodification. No matter whether we are referring to culture as it is embodied in the styling of common utilitarian objects (like cars or clothes), or in mass entertainment products (like popular music or theme parks), or in aesthetically contrived products for specialized tastes (like theatrical performances or avant-garde architecture), both the cultural and the economic orders in modern society are rapidly coming to be coterminous with one another (Anderson, 1998). In other words, the floods of images and messages that now impinge daily on our existence are for the most part generated like any other goods and services within the complex sectoral structures of capitalist production; and this proposition leads on to another, equally important, namely, that culture-producing sectors are now moving to the very forefront of capitalist development and growth. These trends will surely intensify as new information technologies make it possible to produce, distribute, and consume cultural products (notably media products) on hitherto unprecedented scales of quantity and variety.

The net result of all this appears to be what some commentators have diagnosed as a postmodern cultural condition, in which, among other things, the conventional barriers between high culture and low culture are steadily being eroded away. Jameson effectively captures the social meaning of this condition in these dramatic terms:

> what characterizes postmodernity in the cultural area is the supersession of everything outside of commercial culture, its absorption of all forms of art high and low, along with image production itself. The image is the commodity today, and that is why it is vain to expect a negation of the logic of commodity production from it, that is why, finally, all beauty is meretricious. (1998: 135)

Whether we agree or not with all the theoretical baggage that comes along with Jameson's use of the term 'postmodernity', his identification of the genesis of the image at the core of capitalist production points straight to a number of urgent tasks of theoretical inquiry. One of these is Jameson's own pursuit of the cultural logic of contemporary capitalism. Another is the investigation of the economic structure and geographic manifestations of cultural production, as stressed in the present book. At the intersection of these two, so to speak, lies a third as yet little understood area of research focused on what we might call the political economy of the cultural commodity, i.e. on the concrete political and social interests that are entwined within the cultural economy and their condensation in the image.

* * *

At the outset, and by way of a quick summary of the argument so far, recall how large segments of the cultural economy today are constituted in the form of dense networks of specialized but complementary producers clustered together in industrial districts whose roots extend deeply into the fabric of some of the world's major cities.

In these districts, much of the actual work of conception and production of cultural products is carried out by small artisanal and neo-artisanal firms, that is, by firms whose basic labor processes range from handicraft skills (such as sewing or jewel setting) to high-order conceptual activities combined with modern digital technologies (as perhaps most dramatically exemplified by firms in the multimedia industry). Large firms also play important roles in these districts in various functional domains from financing to distribution, and I will have more to say about this in the following section. Agglomerations of cultural-products industries, moreover, are necessarily complemented by pools of labor residing in adjoining areas, and each pool is subject to processes of internal social differentiation based in part on the occupational division of labor prevailing in production. Local labor market processes then help to match the varied demands for labor in the production system with local and (via interregional migration streams) more distant sources of supply. These agglomerations and the urban environments within which they occur are the sites of powerful creative and innovative effects secreted within the networks that constitute their primary social form. Further, each agglomerated body of firms and its adjoining local labor markets comprises a wellspring of cultural memories and resources created in previous rounds of work, and these typically feed back into production activities as catalysts of new images or as recycled/reinterpreted allusions to earlier cultural accomplishments.

The localized complexes of production, work, and image generation that come into being in this manner compete increasingly with one another on global markets. This competition is greatly intensified by the increasing efficacy of the transfer (and marketing) functions through which their outputs are dispersed across geographic space. In most cases, transfer is accomplished either by conventional modes of transportation or by electronic means such as cable or satellite broadcasting. In the specific case of tourist resorts (which are specialized cultural production centers like any other), consumers must travel to the point of production in order to partake of the immobile stock-in-trade. The penetration of local and national markets for cultural products by distant producers is leading on the one hand to many shifts in the entire global landscape of cultural consumption, and on the other hand to much reorganization of the geography of production. One expression of this phenomenon is the resurgence of specialized cultural-products agglomerations at many different sites in various countries, often with tentacles that ramify around the globe.

These agglomerations are engines of local economic development and sources of socially and ideologically transformative effects that radiate outward on massive scales. All of these circumstances raise serious policy concerns at every level of government.

* * *

As noted, the local–global relationships that characterize the cultural economy today are frequently – but not necessarily always – mediated by large firms, many of them being represented in practice by powerful and highly capitalized multinational corporations. Such firms assume a wide assortment of functional forms. Some are directly involved in everyday cultural production activities within particular agglomerations; others play a major role in the financing and coordination of extensive projects involving many different independent firms (as in the case of film-making); yet others have important stakes in marketing and product distribution. Many, if not most, are integrated in varying degree across all of these operations. By means of their multiple activities in production, financing, coordination, and distribution, multinationals often make important contributions to the continued functioning and competitiveness of given agglomerations. Although incursions of multinationals may on occasions disturb the delicate economic ecology of long-standing industrial districts, at least where the latter are socially fragile in comparison to the business muscle of the former, they also play quite positive roles in helping to maintain the prosperity and vitality of individual districts (see Chapter 11). The subsidiaries of multinationals are in any case almost always directly dependent on the long-run economic survival of the agglomerations in which they locate, for the evident reason that they are usually there in the first place in order to tap into local agglomeration economies. Where this is the case they clearly have a vested interest in working in ways that help to secure rather than to destroy the bases of local industrial performance.

Multinational corporations with interests in the cultural economy are typically organized as labyrinths of subsidiaries, affiliates, and joint venture activities (cf. Figures 6.1 and 8.1), often spread out over a variety of sectors in many different parts of the globe. Table 13.1 provides a list of all corporations in the world with sales in excess of $7 billion a year that also have a significant presence in different sectors of cultural production. The primary SIC (Standard Industrial Classification) of each corporation is indicated in the table, though this information is in practice sometimes deceptive given that many of the firms listed are conglomerates with

Table 13.1 *Major international corporations with interests in cultural production*

Company name	Head office location (country)	Primary Standard Industrial Classification		Most recent annual sales ($ billion)
Sony Corp.	Japan	Household audio and video equipment	3651	50.7
Deutsche Telekom AG	Germany	Telephone communication	4810	37.6
Suez Lyonnaise des Eaux	France	Refuse systems	4953	31.7
Disney Co.	USA	Amusement parks	7996	23.0
Daewoo Corp.	S. Korea	Electrical goods	5060	18.8
Bouygues SA	France	Heavy construction not elsewhere classified	1629	15.1
Time-Warner Inc.	USA	Periodicals: publishing or publishing and printing	2721	13.3
Viacom Inc.	USA	Motion picture and video production	7812	13.2
Bertelsmann AG	Germany	Record and prerecorded tape stores	5735	12.7
News Corp Ltd	Australia	Motion picture and video production	7812	11.7
L'Oréal SA	France	Toilet preparations	2844	11.5
Telstra Corp.	Australia	Telephone communication	4810	10.4
Seagram Co.	Canada	Wines, brandy, and brandy spirits	2084	8.7
Havas SA	France	Motion picture and video production	7812	8.6
Thomson Corp.	Canada	Periodicals: publishing or publishing and printing	2721	8.5
Christian Dior SA	France	Luggage	3161	8.2
LVMH SA	France	Toilet preparations	2844	8.0
MCI Worldcom Inc.	USA	Telephone communications, except radio	4813	7.4

Sources: various directories and company reports

extensive holdings of subsidiaries in both cultural-products and non-cultural-products sectors. Consider, for example, the three largest firms presented in the table. Sony is engaged in the production of a wide range of electronic consumer products as well as films and musical recordings, the latter via its ownership of Columbia Tristar Pictures and the Columbia Records Group. Deutsche Telekom is primarily a telecommunications firm (the largest in Europe), but it has important subsidiaries in cable television services and in software and multimedia production. Suez Lyonnaise des Eaux has a primary interest in water distribution systems and basic infrastructure development, and from there it has branched out into cable and satellite broadcasting systems and associated entertainment products.

The actual activities of large multinationals in the cultural-products arena involve various combinations of film and TV program production, music and video recording, magazine and book publishing, advertising, theme parks, sports teams, cosmetics and perfumes, clothing, and so on (cf. Alger, 1998). A major feature of all the firms identified in Table 13.1 is the diversity of their individual holdings, not only in cultural-products sectors, but in other sectors as well. Strong relations of symbiosis seem to run through their core holdings in and around the cultural-products area. Such relations are evident in firms that combine productive assets in consumer electronics, communications systems, media, and entertainment, all of which are sectors with many exploitable economies of scope at their mutual points of interface.

A perhaps unanticipated feature of the multinational corporations identified in Table 13.1 is that they originate from many different countries. The world's biggest multinational corporations with cultural-products interests, as defined here, have their headquarters offices in as diverse a set of countries as Japan, the USA, Germany, France, South Korea, Australia, and Canada. The dependent branch plants and affiliates of these corporations are scattered over an enormous geographic area, though more often than not their specific locations coincide, as we have frequently noted, with dense agglomerations constituted by multifaceted local production networks. Few individual establishments (however powerful the multinational corporation to which they may belong) in and of themselves can master all of the organizational complexities and creative verve that constitute the bedrock of commodified cultural production, especially where market instabilities prevail. To be maximally effective, they generally need to insert themselves into regional cultural-economic systems where they can establish close linkages and working relations with a variety of other firms, and tap into the specialized skills and aptitudes of the local labor force.

* * *

The rising importance of large multinational corporations in the modern cultural economy is both a cause and a symptom of the steady globalization of markets for cultural products, even if production remains anchored in definite places. This state of affairs is often seen as being virtually synonymous with American cultural imperialism, and this is certainly a view that we must take seriously given the dominance of American cultural products (notably films, television programs, and popular music) on world markets throughout much of the postwar period. It is a view, however, that needs to be qualified in light of the industrial/ locational logics that have been adumbrated in previous chapters of this book. It is assuredly the case that American multinationals pioneered the global marketing of cultural products, and they have as a rule been far more aggressive and successful than the multinationals of other countries in selling to foreign consumers, even in instances where these consumers belong to societies whose culture is not even remotely similar to that of the United States. However, there is no reason in principle why the current dominance of American multinationals in global cultural-products markets should continue indefinitely into the future, and there are potent reasons in practice to think that a more spatially variegated structure of cultural production might well come into being in the not-too-distant future.

We have already examined one small piece of evidence in favor of this point as represented by the diversity of the national origins of the firms listed in Table 13.1. More important are the implications of the argument made *passim* in the present volume to the effect that commodified cultural production systems regularly assume the form of place-bound agglomerations. As things now stand, New York and Los Angeles appear to be well in the forefront of commercialized cultural production for world markets, especially in regard to the key sectors of film, television, and popular music. Concomitantly, a number of cultural-products agglomerations outside the United States have suffered and still suffer from the depredations of American competition (recall the account of the film industry of Paris presented in Chapters 6 and 7). Many, however, are at a stage of development where they are either now mounting effective challenges to American cultural products (even media products) on world markets or poised at a stage where they are becoming ready to do so. For the most part, too, these agglomerations are situated within large city-regions, which, by virtue of their size, density, and heterogeneity are almost always endowed with large bundles of the miscellaneous ingredients necessary for effective cultural production and innovation. Cities like London, Paris, Milan, or Tokyo are in this category, and are no doubt capable of assuming roles on the world stage as centers of cultural production equally as important as New York or Los Angeles. Other centers like Toronto, Montreal, Barcelona, Amsterdam, Seoul, Hong Kong, Rio de Janeiro, and so on, are also foci of important cultural production activities, and are now at a point in their development where they may well rapidly come to compete effectively with the top-ranked cities. Provided that the right mix of entrepreneurial know-how, creative energy, and public policy can be brought to bear on the relevant developmental issues, there is little reason why these cities cannot parlay their existing and latent cultural-products sectors into major global industries. Even quite small cities, especially in

Europe, are now aggressively seeking to play the cultural economy card as a way of promoting local business and job growth. They are doing this by building new cultural facilities and promoting local cultural events, thereby increasing employment directly (via the creation of new jobs) and indirectly (by making the local area more attractive to investors from outside) (Frith, 1991; Kearns and Philo, 1993; Wynne, 1992).

In any case, the dominating presence of American films, television shows, or popular music on world markets (not to mention products like Coca Cola or McDonald's hamburgers) does not occur because they possess some irresistible inner mystery that non-American firms find impossible to replicate. It is, rather, an outcome of the commercial know-how and energetic world-wide marketing strategies of American corporations. These corporations learned at an early stage (stretching back even to the period before the Second World War) how to reach out to large numbers of potential consumers in both domestic and foreign markets, and how, above all, to maintain the appeal of their products in those markets by means of vast investments in commercial propaganda. The advertising budget for a major Hollywood film nowadays is often equal to its direct cost of production. In the contemporary era of globalization, barriers to the circulation of cultural commodities are less matters of absolute geographic or social impenetrability than an effect of deficient financial resources or business acumen. Even language, following the discussion in Chapter 7, is probably less of an impediment to the flow of cultural commodities across social and political boundaries than might at first be thought, as the success of American films among general, non-English-speaking audiences itself suggests. As the requisite marketing knowledge and capabilities become more widely diffused, the cultural-products industries of other countries are finding that they, too, can have significant impacts on global markets. Accordingly, and despite the early lead of American producers and distributors of many kinds of cultural products, international networks involving counter-flows and cross-flows of such items as British pop music, Italian fashions, French cosmetics and perfumes, Scandinavian design, Chinese and Hong Kong films, Japanese gastronomic products, and so on, are proliferating on all sides. These flows are a reflection of the commercial vigor of cultural-products sectors and agglomerations all over the world, and a portent of a future in which they play an ever expanding role in the global economy. To be sure, certain agglomerations – especially in cases where development is boosted by robust increasing returns effects – may well come to occupy monopolistic positions in global markets for their specific kinds of products. However, rising market demand combined with shifting consumer preferences and limits on intra-agglomeration product-differentiation capabilities (due to the specific historic and geographic characteristics of the creative field as discussed in Chapter 3), will more probably result in multiple agglo-merations producing different genres or styles of the same basic product (e.g. musical recordings or fashion clothing).

A possible counter-argument to these remarks about the latent diversity of the cultural economy in the twenty-first century might be advanced on the grounds that if cultural-products industries are flourishing in a number of countries (certainly, in most of the economically developed ones), they nevertheless seem to be on an evolutionary trajectory that is taking them to a point of common convergence in terms of basic product styles and content. The argument might be further extended by the claim that this point of convergence is represented by practices and norms already firmly established by American producers of commodified culture. However, the theory of urban and regional economic development laid out in Chapter 2 suggests that divergence rather than convergence in output configurations is inclined to occur when multiple and competing centers of cultural production come into existence. This follows not only from the fact that different centers are usually marked by quite dissimilar traditions and conditions of production, but also, and more forcefully, from the theoretical proposition that the long-run economic vitality of any center is apt to be dependent on its ability to offer real alternatives to products originating in competing centers. In particular, any agglomeration whose outputs are essentially imitations of those of a more firmly entrenched production locale will usually be unable to compete on equal terms because of the latter's superior command of increasing returns and reputation effects, meaning that it can almost always offer the best standard of quality (which includes the factor of authenticity) in relation to price for that category of output. That is one of the reasons why American or British fashions in the 1950s, for example, were of minor significance as long as they were essentially copies of those of Paris; or why Nashville-style popular music recordings made by non-American groups face intrinsically limited markets; or why the French film industry would be likely to atrophy altogether should it attempt to imitate Hollywood-style production values on any significant scale. We must, of course, acknowledge that our basic point of reference here is to cultural products that emerge from capitalist economic structures and that the essential meaning and imagery of these products are likely to be expressive in various ways of these social origins. But this is something rather different from 'Americanization' in the strict sense of the term.

The prognostication, then, is for a global but polycentric and multifaceted system of cultural production – straddled by large multinational corporations – to make its appearance over the course of the twenty-first century. No doubt many kinds of American cultural products will continue to hold sway on markets throughout the world for some time to come, though the view that the spread of a standardized global culture fabricated in New York and Los Angeles is now unstoppable would seem to be overstated in light of the empirical and theoretical evidence suggesting that definite counter-trends are under way and will most probably intensify with the passage of time.

* * *

Notwithstanding the latter comment, the symbology that is embedded in cultural products is always problematical for those on the receiving end, no matter whether we are dealing with transfers of these products from one society to another or from one stratum or segment to another within a given society. It is all the more problematical because culture in every form is intrinsically and intimately bound up with issues of selfhood and social representation. Hence, all traffic in culture, equal or unequal, necessarily raises delicate political questions. From this perspective, the position of the US Department of Commerce as expressed at the Uruguay Round of GATT in favor of free trade in cultural products betrays a fundamental failure to grasp the full complexity of the issues at hand.

Questions of this sort are posed insistently as rising levels of trade in cultural products lead to widening circles of cultural collision, above all as cultural products originating in major centers of world capitalism come into contact with societies that find them alien or threatening. These collisions conjure up extremely varied responses in receiving societies, and probably in no case more so than when American media products are involved. In some instances, systematic opposition to these products is the order of the day; in others, selective import barriers and other restraints on trade have been imposed; in yet others, the inflow is relatively free, but with active cultural hybridization tending frequently to occur at the point of consumption. In few societies have massive inward movements of cultural products from outside been welcomed as an unmitigated blessing. Producers for their part display an almost disconcerting genius for responding to stresses and strains on the demand side with reconfigured outputs. This is manifest above all in the alacrity with which product imageries and messages are redesigned as market resistances are encountered, even to the point of accommodating political dissent and marginality and then reflecting them back again in the guise of sellable products. Feminists, environmentalists, gays, and ethnic minorities, to mention only a few, have all seen their attitudes and slogans absorbed into the design of cultural commodities and then recirculated – often in recuperated form – over extended markets.

Somewhere within this problematical nexus of consumption/production relations there is a fine line between what we might loosely call progressive and regressive tendencies in the cultural economy of capitalism. It is at this line, finally, that the political dilemmas of commodified culture condense out in their most acute form. Despite the reservations that I expressed earlier in Chapters 1 and 3 about the alarmist views of the Frankfurt School, it is emphatically the case that many of the outputs of the cultural economy are carriers of socially and psychologically enervating effects. Moreover, one of the most perplexing features organically built into the logic of contemporary cultural production is that it is agnostic – anyway up to a point – about cultural values and predilections as such, just so long as profitability is assured. If there were a killing to be made in broadcasting readings from Milton's *Paradise Lost*, the requisite entrepreneurial energies would no doubt soon enough be mobilized; by the same token, the profitability of cheap daytime soap operas on television has prompted the production of massive amounts of material in this genre over the last few decades. In its very agnosticism, capitalism is capable of producing cultural outputs distinguished by superior design, complex sensibilities, and studied meanings; it is just as capable of churning out debased and mentally numbing products that play to the lowest common denominator of self-delusion or distraction. Notwithstanding the political assaults from all sides to which much of the cultural economy – especially the media – in contemporary America is constantly subject, this latter tendency, rather surprisingly, seems to be the object of only limited and partial concern. In fact, so little do these larger issues of cultural integrity occupy a place in the mainstream of American political agendas and sensibilities that we were presented only a few years ago with the astonishing spectacle of the 'education president' George Bush delivering a major speech on educational reform in no less incongruous a venue than Disney World in Orlando (whose counterpart, Euro Disneyland, has been dubbed by the French a 'cultural Chernobyl').

The current controversy about the social effects of violence in American films and television shows – precisely because it has such a curiously truncated character – rather dramatically exemplifies the point. The strongest voices to be heard in this controversy belong to those who claim that pervasive violence in American society today can be straightforwardly ascribed to portrayals of violence in the media. There is, of course, a certain innocent, if perverse, logic to this argument, which is that visual images lead directly to mimetic behavior. The same argument, however, skims right over another more fundamental issue within which the media–violence connection (if it exists) is at best only an epiphenomenon. I am referring here to the analgesic effect of large doses of the popular media on cultural awareness and critical reflection in general (Stallabras, 1996). In this matter, the films of Walt Disney are implicated as much as those of Wes Craven, CNN as much as the *National Inquirer*. The point at issue here is not so much that specific images induce specific forms of behavior, but that significant elements of the media as a whole create a pervasive culture of triteness and trivialization in which virtually all that they put on display is denatured. Such a culture is in the first place a threat to any vigorous development of personal cognizance or social citizenship, and in the second place a breeding ground for dysfunctional forms of conduct, not out of mimesis, but rather as a function of the abbreviated consciousness that long exposure to it tends to breed. We cannot, of course, lay the full burden of this syndrome at the door of the media – and some parts of the media work strenuously against it – though it probably *is* quite fair to say that the vacuity and fatuousness of large portions of their output help greatly to magnify the effects of whatever it is in American society that begets this tendency.

Portrayals of violence are not the only occasion of political attacks upon the media. Many other kinds of organized protest occur against the diffusion (or non-diffusion) of specific sorts of images. The religious right, the family values lobby, feminists, African-Americans, immigrant groups, gays, and many others, have all vociferously lodged specific objections to this or that perceived failure of the media to show things as they would like them to be shown (Trend, 1997). But again, what appears to missing from much of the debate, both on the left and on the right, about the images that emerge from within the modern cultural economy is some more encompassing discussion of the fundamental cultural logic and meaning of the larger system within which those images are produced, and the proclivity of significant segments of that system to cultural debasement as a whole. There is, no doubt, much explicit concern in this regard among a small cultural elite in America, but this group for the most part represents an essentially conservative and backward looking element whose programs often look suspiciously like a search for reinstatement of the mystified forms of social distinction that Bourdieu (1979) has so powerfully analyzed. Also, strong opposition to the American media is embodied in the cultural policies of countries like Canada, France, China, or South Korea, and even though in certain cases such policies are motivated by a genuinely disinterested distaste for the more half-witted products of these media, they are also just as much inspired by cultural and economic nationalism.

This discussion boils down to the proposition that the media and the cultural economy at large are implicated in very complex ways in the essentially political question of how we come to construct our individualities and how we arrive at one form or another of self-realization and social being. In this sense, Adorno, Horkheimer, and other members of the Frankfurt School were on the right track in their critique of commodified culture, even if their essentially bourgeois, Middle European prejudices led them into the exaggerated notion that full-blown cultural massification was imminent. Indeed, and as a counterpoint to the discussion in the previous paragraphs, we must acknowledge not only that not all commodified culture is an instrument of infantilism and conformity, but also that consumers often exhibit a marked degree of resistance to the more immoderate absurdities of the media. Contemporary theorists such as Frith (1996), Garnham (1987), or Jameson (1992) have developed a considerably more nuanced view of the cultural economy than was to be found among the critics of mass culture in the early postwar decades, and they have pointed to the existence of a far greater degree of criticality and self-consciousness on the part of the individual consumer than was allowed for in much earlier cultural theorizing. Other observers of cultural trends have commented insistently on the ways in which the meanings of cultural products originating in one society but consumed in another are almost always subject to some degree of reinterpretation and transformation (Appadurai, 1996; Featherstone, 1996; Jackson, 1999). Postmodern theory has even made it possible to conceive of something like a genuine aesthetic of commodified culture and its reflections in more personalized arts such as writing, painting, or photography. Indeed the whole argument that commercial imperatives and cultural integrity are necessarily and indelibly in conflict with one another is now widely seen as a romantic notion, itself based on a historically specific concept of the artist as the inspired, instinctive 'genius'. The political point at issue, then, is not, *à la* Frankfurt School, how to block the further spread of commercial culture – this is no longer an option – but how to promote its positive sides and to curtail its negative. It goes without saying that any meaningful approach to this issue must itself be part of a wider political debate about the very meanings of 'positive' and 'negative' themselves in this context.

* * *

I have drawn attention in this chapter to a number of economic and social predicaments that lie at the heart of the modern cultural economy. I have suggested in particular – though admittedly without the detail that a more compelling discussion would demand – that the cultural economy is a contradictory site of progressive and regressive messages and images. Just as, on the economic front, capitalism is a fountainhead of prosperity but also a source of economic deprivation, so also does it function on the cultural front as a means of regeneration but also as an instrument of penury. The negative side of the latter polarity points in the direction of a number of critical political tasks in contemporary society. I hasten to add in this context that cultural control or censorship, even when their intention is benevolent, are apt in the long run to be ineffective and counterproductive. The production of culture in contemporary society has anyway become far too closely interwoven with the very fabric of capitalism itself for the blunt exercise of administrative authority – except in the most extreme cases – to be politically feasible or workable. If struggles over gross economic inequities have long been at the center of political contestation in capitalism, we still have far to go and much to learn in regard to effective mobilization around this other, more elusive, but deeply significant struggle. In the continued battle against the irrationalities of capitalism, cultural concerns – by which I mean the clash between culture as an instrument of self-realization (whatever specific social forms it may take) and culture as a form of stupefaction – are now more than ever at stake.

Whatever the changing fortunes of this battle, there is every likelihood that more and more of the cultural goods and services we consume will be produced in the commodity form for a considerable stretch of historical time to come. That indeed is one of the principal reasons why the question of the cultural economy is of such burning interest. Given that the cultural economy also now seems to be well on the way to becoming a commanding element of capitalism as a whole, the interest of the question is pushed to a yet more extreme level of urgency. Culture theorists of different stripes have provided us with many useful and important insights into the meanings of commodified images as they enter into the sphere of consumption, but our knowledge of the supply side of the cultural economy and of its effects on the symbolic content of outputs is comparatively defective. I have tried in all of the above to provide some small redress of this imbalance while also showing how the cultural economy is intrinsically bound up with a number of important and puzzling issues of spatial organization. Not the least of these is the tendency for the emerging global cultural economy to condense out on the landscape in the form of a scattered patchwork of urban and regional production systems constituting the basic nerve centers of contemporary aesthetic and semiotic production.

REFERENCES

Acheson, J.M. (1982) 'Limitations on firm size in a Tarascon pueblo', *Human Organization*, 41, 323–9.

Adorno, T.W. (1991) *The Culture Industry: Selected Essays on Mass Culture*, London: Routledge.

Adriani, C. (1993) 'Pour le cinéma français et le cinéma en France', *La Pensée*, no. 296, 95–107.

Aksoy, A. and K. Robins (1992) 'Hollywood for the 21st century: global competition for critical mass in image markets', *Cambridge Journal of Economics*, 16, 1–22.

Albertson, N. (1988) 'Postmodernism, post-Fordism, and critical social theory', *Environment and Planning D: Society and Space*, 6, 339–65.

Alexander, P.J. (1994) 'Entry barriers, release behavior, and multi-product firms in the music recording industry', *Review of Industrial Organization*, 9, 85–98.

Alexander, P.J. (1996) 'Entropy and popular culture: product diversity in the popular music recording industry', *American Sociological Review*, 61, 171–4.

Alger, D. (1998) *Megamedia*, Lanham: Rowman and Littlefield.

Amin, A. and N. Thrift (1992) 'Neo-Marshallian nodes in global networks', *International Journal of Urban and Regional Research*, 16, 571–87.

Amorim, M.A. (1994) 'Lessons on demand', *Technology Review*, January, 30–6.

Anderson, P. (1998) *The Origins of Postmodernity*, London: Verso.

Appadurai, A. (1990) 'Disjuncture and difference in the global cultural economy', *Theory, Culture & Society*, 7, 295–310.

Appadurai, A. (1996) *Modernity at Large: Cultural Dimensions of Globalization*, Minneapolis: University of Minnesota Press.

Arroyo, L.L. (1979) 'Industrial unionism and the Los Angeles furniture industry, 1918–1954', unpublished PhD dissertation, Department of History, University of California, Los Angeles.

Arthur, W.B. (1990) 'Silicon Valley locational clusters: when do increasing returns imply monopoly?', *Mathematical Social Sciences*, 19, 235–51.

Baker, A.J. (1991) 'A model of competition and monopoly in the record industry', *Journal of Cultural Economics*, 15, 29–54.

Balio, T. (1997) 'Les films français et le marché du cinéma d'art et d'essai aux Etats-Unis, 1948–1995', pp. 195–210 in P.J. Benghozi and C. Delage (eds) *Une Histoire Economique du Cinéma Français (1895–1995)*, Paris: L'Harmattan.

Banham, R. (1960) *Theory and Design in the First Machine Age*, London: The Architectural Press.

Barbu, T. (1992) 'Evolution du marchi des studios des prises de vues', *Bulletin Trimestriel du Groupe Crédit National*, no. 68, 44–65.

Barnes, B. (1974) *Scientific Knowledge and Sociological Theory*, London: Routledge and Kegan Paul.

Barnes, B., D. Bloor, and J. Henry (1996) *Scientific Knowledge: A Sociological Analysis*, London: Athlone.

Barnett, R.J. and J. Cavanagh (1994) *Global Dreams: Imperial Corporations and the New World Order*, New York: Simon and Schuster.

Baskerville, D. (1985) *Music Business Handbook and Career Guide*, Los Angeles: The Sherwood Company.

Bassett, K. (1993) 'Urban cultural strategies and urban regeneration: a case study and critique', *Environment and Planning A*, 5, 1773–88.

Baudrillard, J. (1968) *Le Système des Objets: La Consommation des Signes*, Paris: Editions Gallimard.

Becattini, G. (ed.) (1987) *Mercato e Forze Locali: Il Distretto Industriale*, Bologna: Il Mulino.

Becattini, G. (1992a) 'Le district marshallien: une notion socio-économique', pp. 35–55 in G. Benko and A. Lipietz (eds) *Les Régions qui Gagnent. Districts et Réseaux: les Nouveaux Paradigmes de la Géographie Economique*, Paris: Presses Universitaires de France.

Becattini, G. (1992b) 'Les systèmes de petites entreprises: un cas paradigmatique de développement endogène', pp. 57–80 in G. Benko and A. Lipietz (eds) *Les Régions qui Gagnent. Districts et Réseaux: les Nouveaux Paradigmes de la Géographie Economique*, Paris: Presses Universitaires de France.

Becker, H.S. (1974) 'Art as collective action', *American Sociological Review*, 39, 767–76.

Becker, H.S. (1976) 'Art worlds and social types', *American Behavioral Scientist*, 19, 703–18.

Becker, H.S. (1982) *Art Worlds*, Berkeley and Los Angeles: University of California Press.

Béghin, F. (1997) 'Mode: menaces sur la suprématie française', *Capital*, no. 74, 74–8.

Belinfante, A. and R.L. Johnson (1983) 'An economic analysis of the US recorded music industry', pp. 132–42 in W.S. Hendon and J.L. Shanahan (eds) *Economics of Cultural Decisions*, Cambridge, MA: Abt Books.

Benghozi, P.J. (1989) *Le Cinéma: Entre l'Art et l'Argent*, Paris: Editions l'Harmattan.

Benghozi, P.J. and C. Nénert (1995) 'Création de valeur artistique ou économique: du festival International du Film de Cannes au marché du film', *Recherche et Applications en Marketing*, 10, no. 4, 65–76.

Benghozi, P.J. and D. Sagot-Duvauroux (1994) 'Les économies de la culture', *Réseaux*, no. 68, 107–30.

Benhamou, F. (1996) *L'Economie de la Culture*, Paris: Editions La Découverte.

Benjamin, W. (1973) *Illuminations*, London: Fontana.

Benjamin, W. (1989) *Paris, Capitale du 19ᵉ Siècle: Le Livre des Passages*, Paris: Cerf.

Bergeron, L. (1998) *Les Industries du Luxe en France*, Paris: Editions Odile Jacob.

Best, M.H. (1989) 'Sector strategies and industrial policy: the furniture industry and the Greater London Enterprise Board', pp. 191–222 in P. Hirst and J. Zeitlin (eds) *Reversing Industrial Decline? Industrial Structure and Policy in Britain and her Competitors*, Oxford: Berg.

Best, M.H. (1990) *The New Competition: Institutions of Industrial Restructuring*, Cambridge: Polity Press.

Bianchi, P. (1992) 'Levels of policy and the nature of post-Fordist competition', pp. 303–15 in M. Storper and A.J. Scott (eds) *Pathways to Industrialization and Regional Development*, London: Routledge.

Bianchini, F. (1993) 'Remaking European cities: the role of cultural politics', pp. 1–20 in F. Bianchini and M. Parkinson (eds) *Cultural Policy and Urban Regeneration: The West European Experience*, Manchester: Manchester University Press.

Billard, P. (1997) *D'Or et de Palmes: Le Festival de Cannes*, Paris: Découvertes Gallimard.

Bonnell, R. (1978) *Le Cinéma Exploité*, Paris: Seuil.

Bonnell, R. (1996) *La Vingt-Cinquième Image: Une Economie de l'Audiovisuel*, 2nd edn, Paris: Gallimard.

Bordwell, D., J. Staiger and K. Thompson (1985) *The Classical Hollywood Cinema: Film Style and Modes of Production to 1960*, New York: Columbia University Press.

Bourdieu, P. (1971) 'Le marché des biens symboliques', *L'Année Sociologique*, 22, 49–126.

Bourdieu, P. (1977) 'La production de la croyance: contribution à une économie des biens symboliques', *Actes de la Recherche en Sciences Sociales*, 13, 3–44.

Bourdieu, P. (1979) *La Distinction: Critique Sociale du Jugement*, Paris: Editions de Minuit.

Bourdieu, P. (1980) *Le Sens Pratique*, Paris: Editions de Minuit.

Bourdieu, P. (1983) 'The field of cultural production, or: the economic world reversed', *Poetics*, 12, 311–56.

Bourdieu, P. and Y. Delsaut (1975) 'Le couturier et sa griffe: contribution à une théorie de la magie', *Actes de la Recherche en Science Sociales*, no. 1, 7–36.

Boyer, R. and J.-P. Durand (1993) *L'Après-Fordisme*, Paris: Syros.

Brown, D. (1994) 'Furniture New York: taking more than ideas from Northern Italy', *Firm Connections*, 2, no. 3, 3 and 8.

Burnett, R. (1990) *Concentration and Diversity in the International Phonogram Industry*, Gothenburg Studies in Journalism and Mass Communication no. 1, University of Gothenburg, Sweden.

Burnett, R. (1992) 'The implications of ownership changes on concentration and diversity in the phonogram industry', *Communication Research*, 19, 749–769.

Burnett, R. (1993) 'The popular music industry in transition', *Popular Music and Society*, 17, 87–114.

Cardinal Media Industries, Inc. (1998) *Recording Industry Sourcebook*, 9th edn, Emeryville, CA.

Carney, G.O. (ed.) (1994) *The Sounds of People and Places: A Geography of American Folk and Popular Music*, Lanham, MD: Rowman and Littlefield.

Castarède, J. (1992) *Le Luxe*, Paris: Presses Universitaires de France.

Chalvon-Demersay, S. (1994) *Mille Scénarios: Une Enquête sur l'Imagination en Temps de Crise*, Paris: Editions Métailié.

Chapple, S. and R. Garofolo (1977) *Rock'n'Roll is Here to Pay: The History and Politics of the Music Industry*, Chicago: Nelson-Hall.

Charle, C. (1998) *Paris: Fin de Siècle*, Paris: Editions du Seuil.

Christianen, M. (1995) 'Cycles in symbol production? A new model to explain concentration, diversity and innovation in the music industry', *Popular Music*, 14, 55–93.

Christopherson, S. and M. Storper (1986) 'The city as studio; the world as back lot: the impact of vertical disintegration on the location of the motion-picture industry', *Environment and Planning D: Society and Space*, 4, 305–20.

Christopherson, S. and M. Storper (1989) 'The effects of flexible specialization on industrial politics and the labor market: the motion-picture industry', *Industrial and Labor Relations Review*, 42, 331–47.

Clark, T.J. (1984) *The Painting of Modern Life: Paris in the Art of Manet and his Followers*, New York: Alfred A. Knopf.

Claval, P. (1993) *La Géographie au Temps de la Chute des Murs*, Paris: L'Harmattan.

CNC (1993) *Le Guide du Centre National de la Cinématographie*, Paris: Centre National de la Cinématographie.

CNC (1996) *1946–1996, Cinquantenaire du CNC: 50 Ans de Soutien au Cinéma et à la Création Audiovisuelle*, Paris: Centre National de la Cinématographie.

CNC (1997a) *CNC Info, Bilan 1996*, Paris: Centre National de la Cinématographie.

CNC (1997b) *Les Entreprises de l'Audiovisuel: Cinéma, Télévision, Vidéo, Production de Commande*, Paris: Centre National de la Cinématographie and Service Juridique de Technique de l'Information et de la Communication.

Cohen, E. (1989) *L'Etat Brancardier: Politiques du Déclin Industriel (1974–1984)*, Paris: Calmann-Lévy.

Cohen, E. (1992) *Politique Industrielle ou Politiques de Compétitivité*, Paris: Notes Saint-Simon, no. 45.

Cohen, S.S. and J. Zysman (1987) *Manufacturing Matters: The Myth of the Post-Industrial Economy*, New York: Basic Books.

Coleman, J.S. (1988) 'Social capital in the creation of human capital', *American Journal of Sociology* (supplement), 94, 95–120.

Collaborative Economics (1994) *The Multimedia Cluster in the Bay Area*, San Francisco: Bay Area Economic Forum.

Colletis, G. and J.-J. Levet (1997) *Quelles Politiques pour l'Industrie Française?* Paris: La Documentation Française.

Collomb, J. and L. Patry (1995) *Du Cinématographe au Cinéma, 1895–1995*, Paris: Dixit.

Cooke, P. and K. Morgan (1990) *Industry, Training and Technology Transfer: The Baden-Württemberg System in Perspective*, Cardiff: Regional Industrial Research.

Cooke, P. and K. Morgan (1998) *The Associational Economy: Firms, Regions, and Innovation*, Oxford: Oxford University Press.

Coriat, B. (1990) *L'Atelier et le Robot*, Paris: Christian Bourgeois.

Cornfield, D.B. (1986) 'Declining union membership in the post-World War II era: The United Furniture Workers of America, 1939–1982', *American Journal of Sociology*, 91, 1112–53.

Cornfield, D.B. (1989) *Becoming a Mighty Voice: Conflict and Change in the United Furniture Workers of America*, New York: Russell Sage Foundation.

Cosner, L.A., C. Kadushin and W.W. Powell (1982) *Books: The Culture and Commerce of Publishing*, New York: Basic Books.

Cotton, B. and R. Oliver (1993) *Understanding Hypermedia*, London: Phaidon Press.

Couderc, I. (1998) 'L'edition de livres: etude géographique d'une industrie culturelle en mutation', unpublished master's thesis, UFR de Géographie, University of Paris I.

Coulot, P.J. and R. Téboul (1989) 'Les problèmes du film français à l'exportation', pp. 89–103 in F. Rouet (ed.) *Economie et Culture*, vol. 3, *Industries Culturelles*, Paris: La Documentation Française.

Council on California Competitiveness (1992) *California's Future and Jobs*, Sacramento, CA: Office of the Governor.

Courlet, C. and B. Pecqueur (1993) 'Systèmes productifs localisés et industrialisation', pp. 57–69 in C. Dupuy and J.-P. Gilly (eds) *Industrie et Territoire en France*, Paris: La Documentation Française.

Court, J.F. (1988) *Le Cinéma Français Face à son Avenir* (Rapport au Ministre de la Culture et de la Communication), Paris: La Documentation Française.

Crane, D. (1992) *The Production of Culture: Media and the Urban Arts*, Newbury Park, CA: Sage.

Creton, L. (1994) *Economie du Cinéma: Perspectives Stratégiques*, Paris: Nathan.

Creton, L. (1997) *Cinéma et Marché*, Paris: Armand Colin.

Crewe, L. (1996) 'Material culture: embedded firms, organizational networks and the local economic development of a fashion quarter', *Regional Studies*, 30, 257–72.

Crewe, L. and Z. Forster (1993) 'Markets, design, and local agglomeration: the role of the small independent retailer in the workings of the fashion system', *Environment and Planning D: Society and Space*, 11, 213–29.

Crisp, C. (1993) *The Classic French Cinema, 1930–1960*, Bloomington and Indianapolis: Indiana University Press.

Csikszentmihalyi, M. (1990) 'The domain of creativity', pp. 190–212 in M.A. Runco and R.S. Albert (eds) *Theories of Creativity*, Newbury Park: Sage.

CST (1996) *Plateaux de Prises de Vues, Cinéma et Télévision*, Paris: Commission Supérieure Technique de l'Image et du Son.

David, P.A. (1985) 'Clio and the economics of QWERTY', *American Economic Review*, 75, 332–7.

Davis, M. (1990) *City of Quartz: Excavating the Future in Los Angeles*, London: Verso.

De Baecque, A. and T. Jousse (1996) *Le Retour du Cinéma*, Paris: Hachette.

Dear, M. (1995) 'Beyond the post-Fordist city', *Contention*, 5, 67–76.

Debeauvais, R., C. Vauclare, L. Perk, P.M. Menger, J. Rannou, S. Vari, B. Laplante, F. Piettre, J. Berthelot and S. Voiron-Madi (1997) *Le Spectacle Vivant*, Paris: La Documentation Française.

Denat, J.L. and P. Guingamp (1993) 'Le cinéma commercial français', *Cinémaction*, no. 66, 65–91.

Denisoff, R.S. and J. Bridges (1982) 'Popular music: who are the recording artists?', *Journal of Communication*, 32, 132–42.

Department of Export Promotion (1991) *The Summary of the Gem and Ornaments Industry Case Study* (a report prepared by the Industrial Finance Corporation of Thailand Group and submitted to the Department of Export Promotion, Ministry of Commerce, Bangkok).

Dibie, J.N. (1992) *Les Mécanismes de Financement du Cinéma et de l'Audiovisuel en Europe*, Paris: Dixit.

DiMaggio, P. (1977) 'Market structure, the creative process, and popular culture: toward an organizational reinterpretation of mass-culture theory', *Journal of Popular Culture*, 11, 436–52.

DiMaggio, P. and P.M. Hirsch (1976) 'Production organizations in the arts', *American Behavioral Scientist*, 19, 735–52.

Dollar, D. (1991) 'Public policy to promote industrialization: the experience of the East Asian NICs, and the lessons for Thailand', pp. 1–39 in *Decision and Change in Thailand: Three Studies in Support of the Seventh Plan*, Washington, DC: The World Bank.

Dowds, C.M. (1989) 'Liquidity, entrepreneurship, small enterprise maturation, and the development process: the case of furniture manufacture in the Colonia Libertad, Tijuana, Mexico', unpublished PhD dissertation, Department of Agricultural and Resource Economics, University of California, Berkeley.

Driver, S. and A. Gillespie (1993) 'Structural change in the culture industries: British magazine publishing in the 1980s', *Media, Culture, Society*, 15, 183–201.

Dumazedier, J. (1988) 'Planification et développement culturel: réflexions d'un sociologue sur l'expérience française de André Malraux à Jack Lang (1959–1985)', pp. 33–47 in A. Giraud and S. Didelot (eds) *Economie et Culture*, vol. 2, *Culture en Devenir et Volonté Publique*, Paris: La Documentation Française.

Farchy, J. (1992) *Le Cinéma Déchaîné: Mutation d'une Industrie*, Paris: Presses du Centre National de la Recherche Scientifique.

Farchy, J. and D. Sagot-Duvauroux (1994) *Economie des Politiques Culturelles*, Paris: Presses Universitaires de France.

Faulkner, R.R. and A.B. Anderson (1987) 'Short-term projects and emergent careers: evidence from Hollywood', *American Journal of Sociology*, 92, 879–909.

Featherstone, M. (1995) *Undoing Culture: Globalization, Postmodernism and Identity*, London: Sage.

Featherstone, M. (1996) 'Localism, globalism, and cultural identity', pp. 46–7 in R. Wilson and W. Dissanayake (eds) *Global/Local: Cultural Production and the Transnational Imaginary*, Durham, NC: Duke University Press.

Fierro, A. (1996) *Histoire et Dictionnaire de Paris*, Paris: Robert Laffont.

Finegan, W.R. (1990) *California Furniture: The Craft and the Artistry*, Chatsworth, CA: Windsor Publications.

Finney, A. (1997) *The State of European Cinema: A New Dose of Reality*, London: Cassell.

Flichy, P. (1991) *Les Industries de l'Imaginaire: Pour une Analyse Economique des Médias*, 2nd edn, Grenoble: Presses Universitaires de Grenoble.

Friedmann, D. (1993) 'Getting industry to stick: enhancing high value-added production in California', pp. 135–77 in A.J. Scott (ed.) *Policy Options for Southern California*, University of California, Los Angeles: Lewis Center for Regional Policy Studies, Working Paper no. 4.

Friedmann, D. (1994) *The New Economy Project: Final Report*, Los Angeles: The New Vision Business Council of Southern California.

Frith, S. (1991) 'Knowing one's place: the culture of cultural industries', *Cultural Studies from Birmingham*, no. 1, 135–55.

Frith, S. (1992) 'The industrialization of popular music', pp. 49–74 in J. Lull (ed.) *Popular Music and Communication*, Newbury Park, CA: Sage.

Frith, S. (1996) *Performing Rites: On the Value of Popular Music*, Cambridge, MA: Harvard University Press.

Fröbel, F., J. Heinrichs and O. Kreye (1980) *The New International Division of Labour*, Cambridge: Cambridge University Press.

Frodon, J.M. (1995) *L'Age Moderne du Cinéma Français: de la Nouvelle Vague à Nos Jours*, Paris: Flammarion.

Fumaroli, M. (1992) *L'Etat Culturel: Une Religion Moderne*, Paris: Editions de Fallois.

Gaillard, J. (1977) *Paris, La Ville*, Paris: Editions Honori Champion.

Gallois, L. (1983) 'La politique industrielle en France', *Revue d'Economie Industrielle*, no. 23, 1–6.

Ganne, B. (1992) 'Industrial development and local industrial systems in post-War France', pp. 216–29 in M. Storper and A.J. Scott (eds) *Pathways to Industrialization and Regional Development*, London: Routledge.

Ganne, B. (1997) 'Politiques publiques industrielles et systèmes d'aide aux entreprises en France depuis 25 ans', *Espaces et Sociétés*, no. 88/89, 259–96.

GAO (1991) *Some US Wood Furniture Firms Relocated from Los Angeles to Mexico*, Washington, DC: General Accounting Office, National Security and International Affairs Division.

Garnham, N. (1987) 'Concepts of culture: public policy and the cultural industries', *Cultural Studies*, 1, 23–37.

Garnham, N. (1990) *Capitalism and Communication: Global Culture and the Economics of Information*, London: Sage.

Gauthier, G. (1993) 'Retour aux Sources', *Cinémaction*, no. 66, 12–17.

Gertler, M. (1992) 'Flexibility revisited: districts, nation-states, and the forces of production', *Transactions of the Institute of British Geographers*, 17, 259–78.

Giedion, S. (1948) *Mechanization Takes Command*, New York: Oxford University Press.

Girard, A. (1978) 'Industries culturelles', *Futuribles*, no. 17, 597–605.

GLC (1985) *London Industrial Strategy: Summary*, London: Greater London Council.

Granovetter, M. (1985) 'Economic action and social structure: the problem of embeddedness', *American Journal of Sociology*, 91, 481–510.

Gronow, P. (1983) 'The record industry: the growth of a mass medium', *Popular Music*, 3, 53–75.

Grumbach, D. (1993) *Histoires de la Mode*, Paris: Seuil.

Guenzi, F. and M. Marelli (1965) *L'Industria del Mobile nella Brianza Comasca*, Como: Camera di Commercio, Industri e Agricoltura.

Hall, P. (1962) *The Industries of London since 1861*, London: Hutchinson University Library.

Hall, P. (1998) *Cities in Civilization*, New York: Pantheon.

Hanson, N. (1992) 'Competition, trust, and reciprocity in the development of innovative regional milieux', *Papers in Regional Science*, 71, 95–105.

Harrison, B. (1992) 'Industrial districts: old wine in new bottles?', *Regional Studies*, 26, 469–83.

Harrison, B. (1994) *Lean and Mean: The Changing Landscape of Corporate Power in the Age of Flexibility*, New York: Basic Books.

Harvey, D. (1989) *The Condition of Postmodernity*, Oxford: Blackwell.

Hennion, A. (1981) *Les Professionels du Disque: Une Sociologie des Variétés*, Paris: Editions A.M. Métailié.

Hennion, A. (1983) 'The production of success: an anti-musicology of the pop song', *Popular Music*, 3, 159–93.

Hennion, A. (1989) 'An intermediary between production and consumption: the producer of popular music', *Science, Technology and Human Values*, 14, 400–23.

Hepworth, M.E. (1990) *Geography of the Information Economy*, New York: Guilford Press.

Herman, S.M. (1994) 'The Los Angeles household furniture industry: an alternative view based on an industrial district analysis', unpublished master's thesis, Urban Planning Program, Graduate School of Architecture and Urban Planning, University of California, Los Angeles.

Herrigel, G. (1993) 'Large firms, small firms, and the governance of flexible specialization: the case of Baden-Württemberg and socialized risk', pp. 15–35 in B. Kogut (ed.) *Country Competitiveness: Technology and the Organizing of Work*, New York: Oxford University Press.

Hesmondhalgh, D. (1996) 'Flexibility, post-fordism and the music industries', *Media, Culture and Society*, 18, 469–88.

Hirsch, P.M. (1969) *The Structure of the Popular Music Industry*, Institute for Social Research, University of Michigan, Ann Arbor, MI.

Hirsch, P.M. (1972) 'Processing fads and fashions: an organization-set analysis of cultural industry systems', *American Journal of Sociology*, 77, 639–59.

Hirschman, A. (1958) *The Strategy of Economic Development*, New Haven, CT: Yale University Press.

Hise, L. (1992) 'The role of environmental regulations in industrial location: furniture manufacturing in Southern California', unpublished master's thesis, Urban Planning Program, Graduate School of Architecture and Urban Planning, University of California, Los Angeles.

Holmes, G. (1992) 'Bangkok's changing jewelry image', *Jewelers' Circular–Keystone*, June, 132–6.

Horkheimer, M. and T.W. Adorno (1972) *Dialectic of Enlightenment*, New York: Herder and Herder.

Huet, A., J. Ion, A. Lefèbvre, B. Miège and R. Peron (1978) *Capitalisme et Industries Culturelles*, Grenoble: Presses Universitaires de Grenoble.

Isard, W. (1960) *Methods of Regional Analysis*, Cambridge, MA: The MIT Press.

Jäckel, A. (1996) 'European co-production strategies: the case of Britain and France', pp. 85–97 in A. Moran (ed.) *Film Policy: International, National, and Regional Perspectives*, London: Routledge.

Jackson, P. (1999) 'Commodity cultures: the traffic in things', *Transactions of the Institute of British Geographers*, 24, 95–108.

Jacobs, J. (1969) *The Economy of Cities*, New York: Random House.

Jameson, F. (1992) *Postmodernism, or, the Cultural Logic of Late Capitalism*, Durham, NC: Duke University Press.

Jameson, F. (1998) *The Cultural Turn: Selected Writings on the Postmodern, 1983–1998*, London: Verso.

Jeancolas, J.P. (1995) *Histoire du Cinéma Français*, Paris: Nathan.

Jencks, C. (1993) *Heteropolis: Los Angeles, the Riots, and the Strange Beauty of Hetero-Architecture*, London: Academy Editions.

Jessop, B. (1992) 'Fordism and post-Fordism: a critical reformulation', pp. 46–69 in M. Storper and A.J. Scott (eds) *Pathways to Industrialization and Regional Development*, London: Routledge.

Kaldor, N. (1970) 'The case for regional policies', *Scottish Journal of Political Economy*, 17, 337–47.

Kealy, E.R. (1979) 'From craft to art: the case of sound mixers and popular music', *Sociology of Work and Occupations*, 6, 3–29.

Kearns, G. and C. Philo (eds) (1993) *Selling Places: The City as Cultural Capital, Past and Present*, Oxford: Pergamon Press.

Keating, M. (1998) *The New Regionalism: Territorial Restructuring and Political Change in Western Europe*, Cheltenham: Edward Elgar.

Kelberg, D. (1997) *La Chanson Française et les Pouvoirs Publiques*, 2 vols, Aix-en-Provence: Presses Universitaires d'Aix-Marseille.

Knox, P. L. (1995) 'World cities and the organization of global space', pp. 232–47 in R.J. Johnston, P.J. Taylor and M.J. Watts (eds) *Geographies of Global Change: Remapping the World in the Late Twentieth Century*, Oxford: Blackwell.

Kristensen, P.H. (1992) 'Industrial districts in West Jutland, Denmark', pp. 122–73 in F. Pyke and W. Sengenberger (eds) *Industrial Districts and Local Economic Regeneration*, Geneva: International Institute for Labor Studies.

Krugman, P. (1990) *Rethinking International Trade*, Cambridge, MA: The MIT Press.

Krugman, P. (1991) *Geography and Trade*, Leuven: Leuven University Press.

Lacroix, C., M. Petit and F. Rouet (1979) *Les Industries Culturelles*, Paris: La Documentation Française.

Landry, C. and F. Bianchini (1995) *The Creative City*, London: Demos.

Lash, S. and J. Urry (1994) *Economies of Signs and Space*, London: Sage.

Latour, B. and S. Woolgar (1979) *Laboratory Life: The Social Construction of Scientific Facts*, Beverly Hills, CA: Sage.

Lazar, J. (1995) 'Entre rêve et réalité', *Le Débat*, no. 86, 108–24.

Lebel, C., A. Casalonga and C. Ménage (1990) *La Distribution des Produits de Luxe*, Paris: LGDJ.

Leborgne, D. and A. Lipietz (1992) 'Conceptual fallacies and open questions on post-Fordism', pp. 332–48 in M. Storper and A.J. Scott (eds) *Pathways to Industrialization and Regional Development*, London: Routledge.

Leontief, W. (1941) *The Structure of the American Economy*, Cambridge, MA: Harvard University Press.

Leyshon, A., D. Matless and G. Revill (1998) 'Introduction: music, space and the production of place', pp. 1–30 in A. Leyshon, D. Matless and G. Revill (eds) *The Place of Music*, New York: Guilford Press.

Lipsey, R.G. (1994) 'Markets, technological change, and economic growth', paper presented to the 10th Annual General Meetings of the Pakistan Society of Development Economics.

Lopes, P.D. (1992) 'Innovation and diversity in the popular music industry, 1969 to 1990', *American Sociological Review*, 57, 56–71.

Lorenz, E.H. (1992) 'Trust, community and cooperation: toward a theory of industrial districts', pp. 195–204 in M. Storper and A.J. Scott (eds) *Pathways to Industrialization and Regional Development*, London: Routledge.

Lovering, J. (1998) 'The global music industry: contradictions in the commodification of the sublime', pp. 31–56 in A. Leyshon, D. Matless and G. Revill (eds) *The Place of Music*, New York: Guilford Press.

Lundvall, B.A. and B. Johnson (1994) 'The learning economy', *Journal of Industrial Studies*, 1, 23–42.

Luong, C. (1996) 'Le jeune cinéma français d'aujourd'hui: une génération sans pères?', *Quaderni*, no. 29, 13–24.

MacDonald, G. (1990) *The Emergence of Global Multi-Media Conglomerates*, Geneva: International Labour Office, Multinational Enterprises Programme, Working Paper no. 70.

MacKinsey & Co. (1990) *L'Industrie de Luxe: Un Atout pour la France*, Paris: Comité Colbert.

Maduro, R. (1975) *Artistic Creativity in a Brahmin Painter Community*, Center for South and Southeast Asia Studies, University of California, Berkeley, Research Monograph no. 14.

Malraux, A. (1946) *Esquisse d'une Psychologie du Cinéma*, Paris: Gallimard.

Malsot, J. and H. Passeron (1996) *Compétitivité et Stratégies Françaises: Entreprises, Secteurs, Régions*, Paris: Economica.

Maltby, R. (1981) 'The political economy of Hollywood: the studio system', pp. 42–58 in P. Davies and B. Neve (eds) *Cinema, Politics and Society in America*, Manchester: Manchester University Press.

Mannheim, K. (1952) *Essays in the Sociology of Knowledge*, Henley-on-Thames: Routledge and Kegan Paul.

Marshall, A. (1920) *Principles of Economics*, London: Macmillan.

Martin, R. (1995) 'The French film industry: a crisis of art and commerce', *Columbia Journal of World Business*, 30, 6–17.

Mead, D.C. (1982) 'Small industries in Egypt: an exploration of the economics of small furniture producers', *International Journal of Middle East Studies*, 14, 159–71.

Menger, P.M. (1983) *Le Paradoxe du Musicien: Le Compositeur, le Mélomane et l'Etat dans la Société Contemporaine*, Paris: Flammarion.

Menger, P.M. (1991) 'Marché du travail artistique et socialisation du risque: le cas des arts du spectacle', *Revue Française de Sociologie*, 32, 61–74.

Menger, P.M. (1993) 'L'hégémonie parisienne: économie et politique de la gravitation artistique', *Annales: Economies, Sociétés, Civilisations*, no. 6, 1565–1600.

Menger, P.M. (1994) 'Appariement, risque et capital humain: l'emploi et la carrière dans les professions artistiques', pp. 219–38 in P.-M. Menger and J.-C. Passeron (eds) *L'Art de la Recherche: Essais en l'Honneur de Raymonde Moulin*, Paris: La Documentation Française.

Michalet, C.A. (1987) *Le Drôle de Drame du Cinéma Mondial: Une Industrie Culturelle Menacée*, Paris: Editions la Découverte.

Miège, B., P. Pajon and J-M. Salaün (1986) *L'Industrialisation de l'Audiovisuel: des Programmes pour les Nouveaux Médias*, Paris: Editions Aubier.

Molotch, H. (1996) 'LA as design product: how art works in a regional economy', pp. 225–75 in A.J. Scott and E.W. Soja (eds) *The City: Los Angeles and Urban Theory at the End of the Twentieth Century*, Berkeley and Los Angeles: University of California Press.

Monopolies and Mergers Commission (1994) *The Supply of Recorded Music: A Report on the Supply in the UK of Prerecorded Compact Discs, Vinyl Discs, and Tapes Containing Music*, London: Her Majesty's Stationery Office.

Montagné-Villette, S. (1990) *Le Sentier: Un Espace Ambigu*, Paris: Masson.

Montgomery, S.S. and M.D. Robinson (1993) 'Visual artists in New York: what's special about person and place'?, *Journal of Cultural Economics*, 17, 17–39.

Moriset, C. (1995) 'L'industrialisation du cinéma, ou l'émergence du triple marché', unpublished doctoral dissertation, Lyon: Université Jean Moulin, Lyon 3.

Morley, D. and K. Robins (1995) *Spaces of Identity: Global Media, Electronic Landscapes, and Cultural Boundaries*, London: Routledge.

Morvan, Y. (1983) 'La politique industrielle française depuis la libération', *Revue d'Economie Industrielle*, no. 23, 19–35.

Moulier Boutang, Y. (1990) *La Confection dans le Quartier du Sentier: Restructuration des Formes d'Emploi et Expansion dans un Secteur en Déclin*, Paris: Ecole Normale Supérieure, Groupe de Recherche et d'Analyse des Migrations Internationales.

Moulin, R. (1983) 'De l'artisan au professional, l'artiste', *Sociologie du Travail*, no. 4, 388–403.

Moulin, R. (1993) *L'Artiste, l'Institution et le Marché*, Paris: Flammarion.

Moulinier, P. (1996) 'L'état et les equipements culturels, (1959–1995)', *Les Annales de la Recherche Urbaine*, no. 70, 140–7.

Mulkay, M.J. (1972) *The Social Process of Innovation: A Study in the Sociology of Science*, London: Macmillan.

Myrdal, G. (1957) *Rich Lands and Poor*, New York: Harper and Row.

Nadvi, K. and H. Schmitz (1994) *Industrial Clusters in Less Developed Countries: Review of Experiences and Research Agenda*, University of Sussex, Institute of Development Studies, Discussion Paper no. 339.

Negus, K. (1996) *Popular Music in Theory: An Introduction*, Hanover and London: Wesleyan University Press.

Negus, K. (1998) 'Cultural production and the corporation: musical genres and the strategic management of creativity in the US recording industry', *Media, Culture, and Society*, 20, 359–79.

Nelson, R.R. and S.G. Winter (1982) *An Evolutionary Theory of Economic Change*, Cambridge, MA: Belknap Press.

Nicolas, B. (1997) 'Structures d'organisation et paradigmes sectoriels: le cas des studios de cinéma en France et en Royaume Uni (1895–1995)', unpublished doctoral dissertation, Paris: Ecole Polytechnique.

NIST (1992) *A Catalogue of U.S. Manufacturing Networks*, United States Department of Commerce, Technology Administration, National Institute of Standards and Technology, Report no. NIST GCR 92-616.

North, D.C. (1990) *Institutions, Institutional Change and Economic Performance*, Cambridge: Cambridge University Press.

Oliver, J.L. (1966) *The Development and Structure of the Furniture Industry*, Oxford: Pergamon.

Patchell, J. (1993) 'From production systems to learning systems: lessons from Japan', *Environment and Planning, A*, 25, 797–815.

Paul, A. and A. Kleingartner (1994) 'Flexible production and the transformation of industrial relations in the motion-picture and television industry', *Industrial and Labor Relations Review*, 47, 663–78.

Peet, R. (1986) 'The destruction of regional cultures', pp. 150–72 in R.J. Johnston and P.J. Taylor (eds) *A World in Crisis?*, Oxford: Basil Blackwell.

Perroux, F. (1961) *L'Economie du XXe Siècle*, Paris: Presses Universitaires de France.

Peterson, R.A. (1975) 'Single-industry firm to conglomerate synergistics: alternative strategies for selling insurance and country music', pp. 341–58 in J.F. Blumstein and B. Walter (eds) *Growing Metropolis: Aspects of Development in Nashville*, Nashville: Vanderbilt University Press.

Peterson, R.A. (1997) *Creating Country Music: Fabricating Authenticity*, Chicago: University of Chicago Press.

Peterson, R.A. and D.G. Berger (1975) 'Cycles in symbol production: the case of popular music', *American Sociological Review*, 40, 158–73.

Peterson, R.A. and D.G. Berger (1996) 'Measuring industry concentration, diversity, and innovation in popular music', *American Sociological Review*, 61, 175–8.

Peterson, R.A. and P. DiMaggio (1975) 'From region to class, the changing locus of country music: a test of the massification hypothesis', *Social Forces*, 53, 497–506.

Piore, M.J. and C.F. Sabel (1984) *The Second Industrial Divide: Possibilities for Prosperity*, New York: Basic Books.

Plé, C. (1998) 'Le secteur industriel de la parfumerie', *Revue de Géographie de Lyon*, 73, 97–103.

PMR (1997) *Making Digits Dance: Visual Effects and Animation Careers in the Entertainment Industry*, Los Angeles: The PMR Group, Inc.

Pollstar (1998) *Record Company Rosters*, Fresno, CA.

Porter, M. (1990) *The Competitive Advantage of Nations*, New York: The Free Press.

Powell, W.W., K.W. Koput and L. Smith-Doerr (1996) 'Interorganizational collaboration and the locus of innovation: networks of learning in biotechnology', *Administrative Science Quarterly*, 41, 116–45.

Prédal, R. (1993) 'Les réalisateurs', *Cinémaction*, no. 66, 92–6.

Prédal, R. (1996) *50 Ans de Cinéma Français (1945–1995)*, Paris: Nathan.

Pyke, F., G. Becattini and W. Sengenberger (eds) (1990) *Industrial Districts and Inter-Firm Cooperation in Italy*, Geneva: International Institute for Labour Studies.

Rannou, J. (1992) 'Un système de règlementation professionnelle en crise: la carte d'identité professionnelle de la cinématographie', *Formation-Emploi*, no. 39, 19–34.

Rannou, J. and S. Vari (1996) *Les Itinéraires d'Emploi des Cadres, Techniciens, et Ouvriers Intermittents de l'Audiovisuel et des Spectacles*, Paris: Ministère de la Culture, Direction de l'Administration Générale, Département des Etudes et de la Prospective (Observatoire de l'Emploi Culturelle).

Relph, E. (1976) *Place and Placelessness*, London: Pion.

RIAA (1997) *Annual Report*, New York: Recording Industry Association of America.

Rigaud, J. (1996) *Pour une Refondation de la Politique Culturelle*, Paris: La Documentation Française.

Robertson, R. (1992) *Globalization: Social Theory and Global Culture*, London: Sage.

Robins, K. (1995) 'New spaces of global media', pp. 248–62 in R.J. Johnston, P.J. Taylor and M.J. Watts (eds) *Geographies of Global Change: Remapping the World in the Late Twentieth Century*, Oxford: Blackwell.

Romer, P.M. (1986) 'Increasing returns and long-run growth', *Journal of Political Economy*, 94, 1002–37.

Rouet, F. (1992) *Le Livre: Mutations d'une Industrie Culturelle*, Paris: La Documentation Française.

Rouet, F. (1997) 'Industries culturelles et attention publique', *Sciences de la Société*, no. 40, 73–91.

Rouet, F. and X. Dupin (1991) *Le Soutien Public aux Industries Culturelles*, Paris: Ministère de la Culture et de la Communication.

Rowe, D. (1995) *Popular Cultures: Rock Music, Sport and the Politics of Pleasure*, London: Sage.

Russo, M. (1985) 'Technical change and the industrial district: the role of inter-firm relations in the growth and transformation of ceramic tile production in Italy', *Research Policy*, 14, 329–43.

Ryan, B. (1992) *Making Capital from Culture: The Corporate Form of Capitalist Cultural Production*, New York: Walter de Gruyter.

Ryan, J. (1985) *The Production of Culture in the Music Industry: The ASCAP-BMI Controversy*, Lanham, MD: University Press of America.

Ryan, J. and R.A. Peterson (1982) 'The product image: the fate of creativity in country music songwriting', in J.S. Ettema and D.C. Whitney (eds) *Individuals in Mass Media Organizations: Creativity and Constraint*, Beverly Hills, CA: Sage.

Sabel, C.F. (1995) 'Bootstrapping reform: rebuilding firms, the welfare state, and unions', *Politics and Society*, 23, 5–48.

Sack, R.D. (1992) *Place, Modernity, and the Consumer's World*, Baltimore: The Johns Hopkins University Press.

Sadler, D. (1997) 'The global music business as an information industry: reinterpreting economies of culture', *Environment and Planning A*, 29, 1919–36.

Salais, A. and M. Storper (1993) *Les Mondes de Production: Enquête sur l'Identité Économique de la France*, Paris: Editions de l'Ecole des Hautes Etudes en Science Sociales.

Samsel, J. and C. Fort (1995) *The Multimedia Directory*, 3rd edn, Los Angeles: The Carronade Group.

Sanjek, R. (1988) *American Popular Music and its Business*, vol. III, *From 1900 to 1984*, New York and Oxford: Oxford University Press.

Saxenian, A. (1992) 'Divergent patterns of business organization in Silicon Valley', pp. 316–31 in M. Storper and A.J. Scott (eds) *Pathways to Industrialization and Regional Development*, London: Routledge.

Saxenian, A. (1994) *Regional Advantage: Culture and Competition in Silicon Valley and Route 128*, Cambridge, MA: Harvard University Press.

Schmitz, S. (1993) *Small Shoemakers and Fordist Giants: Tale of a Supercluster*, University of Sussex, Institute of Development Studies, Discussion Paper no. 331.

Schorske, K. (1980) *Fin-de-Siècle Vienna: Politics and Culture*, New York: Alfred A. Knopf.

Scott, A.J. (1982) 'Locational patterns and dynamics of industrial activity in the modern metropolis', *Urban Studies*, 19, 111–42.

Scott, A. J. (1984) 'Territorial reproduction and transformation in a local labor market: the animated film workers of Los Angeles', *Environment and Planning D: Society and Space*, 2, 277–307.

Scott, A.J. (1988a) *Metropolis: From the Division of Labor to Urban Form*, Berkeley and Los Angeles: University of California Press.

Scott, A.J. (1988b) *New Industrial Spaces: Flexible Production Organization and Regional Development in North America and Western Europe*, London: Pion.

Scott, A.J. (1992a) 'The spatial organization of a local labor market: employment and residential patterns in a cohort of engineering and scientific workers', *Growth and Change*, 23, 94–115.

Scott, A.J. (1992b) 'Low-wage workers in a high-technology manufacturing complex: the Southern California electronics assembly industry', *Urban Studies*, 29, 1231–46.

Scott, A.J. (1993a) *Technopolis: High-Technology Industry and Regional Development in Southern California*, Berkeley and Los Angeles: University of California Press.

Scott, A.J. (1993b) 'The New Southern Californian Economy: Pathways to Industrial Resurgence', *Economic Development Quarterly*, 7, 296–309.

Scott, A.J. (1995) 'Industrial urbanism in Southern California: post-Fordist civic dilemmas and opportunities', *Contention*, 5, 39–65.

Scott, A.J. (1996) 'Regional motors of the global economy', *Futures*, 28, 391–411.

Scott, A.J. (1998) *Regions and the World Economy: The Coming Shape of Global Production, Competition, and Political Order*, Oxford: Oxford University Press.

Scott, A.J. and D. Rigby (1996) *The Craft Industries of Los Angeles: Prospects for Economic Growth and Development*, Berkeley, CA: California Policy Seminar, CPS Brief, 8, no. 5.

Scott, A.J. and M. Storper (1992) 'Regional development reconsidered', pp. 3–24 in H. Ernste and V. Meier (eds) *Regional Development and Contemporary Industrial Response: Extending Flexible Specialisation*, London: Belhaven.

Segrave, K. (1994) *Payola in the Music Industry: A History, 1880–1991*, Jefferson, NC: McFarland.

Seldon, B.J. and S.H. Bullard (1992) 'Input substitution, economies of scale, and productivity growth in the US upholstered furniture industry', *Applied Economics*, 24, 1017–25.

Shapiro, D., N. Abercrombie, S. Lash and C. Lury (1992) 'Flexible specialisation in the culture industries', pp. 179–94 in H. Ernste and V. Meier (eds) *Regional Development and Contemporary Industrial Response*, London: Belhaven.

Silvestrelli, S. (1985) 'Progresso tecnico e rapporti tra imprese nel settore del mobile in Italia e nelle Marche', *Economia Marche*, no. 1, 3–72.

Smith, A. (1970) *The Wealth of Nations* (1776), Harmondsworth: Penguin Books.

Soares, R. and P. Lerenard (1998) *L'Habillement*, Paris: Ministère de l'Economie, des Finances et de l'Industrie.

Soja, E. (1989) *Postmodern Geographies*, London: Verso.

Soja, E. (1996) *Thirdspace*, Oxford: Blackwell.

Soja, E. and A.J. Scott (1996) 'Introduction to Los Angeles, city and region', pp. 1–21 in A.J. Scott and E. Soja (eds) *The City: Los Angeles and Urban Theory at the End of the Twentieth Century*, Berkeley and Los Angeles: University of California Press.

Stallabras, J. (1996) *Gargantua: Manufactured Mass Culture*, London: Verso.

Steedman, H. and K. Wagner (1987) 'A second look at productivity, machinery, and skills in Britain and Germany', *National Institute Economic Review*, no. 122, 84–95.

Stöhr, W.B. (ed.) (1990) *Global Challenge and Local Response: Initiatives for Economic Regeneration in Contemporary Europe*, London: Mansell.

Storper, M. (1989) 'The transition to flexible specialisation in the US film industry: external economies, the division of labour and the crossing of industrial divides', *Cambridge Journal of Economics*, 13, 273–305.

Storper, M. (1991) *Industrialization, Economic Development, and the Regional Question in the Third World*, London: Pion.

Storper, M. (1992) 'The limits to globalization: technology districts and international trade', *Economic Geography*, 68, 60–93.

Storper, M. (1993) 'Flexible specialisation in Hollywood: a response to Aksoy and Robins', *Cambridge Journal of Economics*, 17, 479–84.

Storper, M. (1996) 'Innovation as collective action: conventions, products, and technologies', *Industrial and Corporate Change*, 5, 761–90.

Storper, M. and S. Christopherson (1987) 'Flexible specialization and regional industrial agglomerations: the case of the US motion-picture industry', *Annals of the Association of American Geographers*, 77, 260–82.

Storper, M. and A.J. Scott (1995) 'The wealth of regions: market forces and policy imperatives in local and global context', *Futures*, 27, 505–26.

Taddei, D. and B. Coriat (1993) *Made in France: l'Industrie Française dans la Compétition Mondiale*, Paris: Le Livre de Poche.

Tasker, Y. (1996) 'Approaches to the new Hollywood', pp. 213–28 in J. Curran, D. Morley and V. Walkerdine (eds) *Cultural Studies and Communication*, London: Arnold.

Thailand Gems and Jewellery Directory, 1991–1992, Bangkok: B. G. & J. Co. Ltd.

Thonon, M., C. Bec, M. Benard, J. Delatte, V. Villègle and J.M. Lepers (1990) *Les Réalisateurs*, unpublished research report, St Denis: University of Paris, VIII.

Thrift, N.J. (1994) 'On the social and cultural determinants of international financial centers', in S. Corbridge, N.J. Thrift and R.L. Martin (eds) *Money, Power and Space*, Oxford: Blackwell.

Throsby, D. (1994) 'The production and consumption of the arts: a view of cultural economics', *Journal of Economic Literature*, 32, 1–29.

Tixier, J.M. (1992) 'Les chemins de la création cinimatographique: une impasse dans le PAF?', *Sciences de la Société*, no. 26, 107–17.

Torres, V. (1995) 'Bold fashion statement: amid aerospace decline, L.A. garment industry emerges as a regional economic force', *Los Angeles Times Business Section*, 12 March, pp. 1 and 6.

Trend, D. (1997) *Cultural Democracy: Politics, Media, New Technology*, Albany, NY: State University of New York Press.

Unifrance (1996) *Les Films Français en Salles à l'Etranger, Bilan 1995*, Paris: Unifrance Film International.

Urfalino, P. (1996) *L'Invention de la Politique Culturelle*, Paris: La Documentation Française.

Urfalino, P. (1997) 'Quelles missions pour le Ministère de la Culture?', *Esprit*, January, 37–59.

Urry, J. (1990) *The Tourist Gaze*, London: Sage.

Urry, J. (1995) *Consuming Places*, London: Sage.

USITC (1987) *A Competitive Assessment of the US Jewelry Industry: Phase II, Precious Jewelry*, Washington, DC: United States International Trade Commission, Publication no. 2013.

Veltz, P. (1997) 'The dynamics of production systems, territories and cities', pp. 78–96 in F. Moulaert and A.J. Scott (eds) *Cities, Enterprises and Society on the Eve of the 21st Century*, London: Pinter.

Virenque, A. (1990) *L'Industrie Cinématographique Française*, Paris: Presses Universitaires de France.

Vogel, H.L. (1986) *Entertainment Industry Economics*, Cambridge: Cambridge University Press.

Von Böhm-Bawerck, E. (1891) *The Positive Theory of Capital*, New York: G.E. Stechert.

Von Hippel, E. (1988) *The Sources of Innovation*, New York: Oxford University Press.

Wallis, R. (1990) 'Internationalisation, localisation, and integration: the changing structure of the music industry and its relevance for smaller countries and cultures', PhD dissertation, Department of Journalism and Mass Communication, University of Gothenburg, Sweden.

Wasko, J., M. Phillips and C. Purdie (1993) 'Hollywood meets Madison Avenue: the commercialization of US films', *Media, Culture and Society*, 15, 271–93.

Webber, M. (1964) 'Culture, territoriality and the elastic mile', *Papers of the Regional Science Association*, 11, 59–69.

White, H.C. and C.A. White (1965) *Canvases and Careers: Institutional Change in the French Painting World*, New York: Wiley.

Williams, R. (1982) *The Sociology of Culture*, New York: Schocken Books.

Wolff, J. (1981) *The Social Production of Art*, New York: St Martin's Press.

Wynne, D. (ed.) (1992) *The Culture Industry*, Aldershot: Avebury.

Young, A. (1928) 'Increasing returns and economic progress', *Economic Journal*, 38, 527–42.

Ziegler, J.N. (1997) *Governing Ideas: Strategies for Innovation in France and Germany*, Ithaca: Cornell University Press.

Zucker, L.G., M.R. Darby and J. Armstrong (1994) *Intellectual Capital and the Firm: The Technology of Geographically Localized Knowledge Spillovers*, Cambridge, MA: National Bureau of Economic Research, Working Paper no. 4946.

Zukin, S. (1991) *Landscapes of Power: From Detroit to Disney World*, Berkeley and Los Angeles: University of California Press.

Zukin, S. (1995) *The Cultures of Cities*, Oxford: Blackwell.

INDEX